The Semiotic Self

Discursive "origin" of the self
p 35

For Christine

The Semiotic Self

Norbert Wiley

The University of Chicago Press

The University of Chicago Press, Chicago 60637
Polity Press in association with Blackwell Publishers

Copyright © Norbert Wiley 1994
All rights reserved. Published 1994
Printed in Great Britain

03 02 01 00 99 98 97 96 95 94   1 2 3 4 5 6
ISBN: (cloth) 0–226–89815–6; (paper) 0–226–89816–4

A CIP catalogue record for this book is available from the Library of
Congress.

This book is printed on acid-free paper.

Contents

List of Figures and Tables

Preface

This is a humanist book about the self. The argument is that there are *sui generis* selves, that they are free and equal, and that they house a variety of rights. I am using the word "self" simply to mean a human being, person, individual, or agent. Somewhat less common words that mean more or less the same thing are ego, actor, and subject. I will not try to define all these words because my theory does not get this fine-grained, nor does it seem useful to do so. The word "self" puts a slightly reflexive or backlooping spin on the concept, although this is merely the way the term is used in ordinary language. It is what we all mean by self.

I hope it is obvious that "self" does not, somehow, imply selfishness. I once mentioned to someone that I was writing a book about the self. The person glared at me and said nowadays there was too much emphasis on the self. I am not writing about the bad (narcissistic, self-centered, selfish, etc) self. But I am not writing about the good (selfless, altruistic) one either. I am simply writing about the generic self, apart from any qualities it might have at any given time or place.

By "semiotic" I am referring to the theory of meaning held by the American pragmatists. Semiotics in general is the theory of signs, both linguistic and extra-linguistic. There are two versions of semiotics: pragmatist (American) and Saussurean (European). The two approaches differ in some basic ways, although there is no scholarly agreement concerning the nature of these differences (and the partisans of both approaches manage to co-exist fairly amicably in the Semiotic Society of America). It is widely agreed, however, that American semiotics is "triadic" (based on the sign, interpretant, and object) and European is "dyadic" (based on the signifier and signified). I am also of the opinion, though there is less agreement on this, that American semiotics recognizes an autonomous self and European semiotics does not.

American semiotics is usually thought to be almost entirely the creation of Charles Sanders Peirce, with minor contributions from William James, John Dewey, and George Herbert Mead. I am arguing that Mead is also a major semiotician, and that his thought can be fruitfully combined with that of Peirce. They both had semiotic theories of the self, defining the self as a "sign," but both theories were fragmentary and incomplete. I argue that the two theories fit together, that each has what the other lacked, and that in synthesis they present a powerful theory of the self.

With this Peirce–Mead model, then, I make several arguments. One is that it gives a badly needed completion or closure to classical American pragmatism. Another is that the semiotic self is both *sui generis* and autonomous, thereby refuting the currently popular self-reductions. And a third is that the semiotic self, with its freedom and equality, is a useful conceptual resource for the theory of democracy.

Contents and Organization

In the first chapter I present the overall argument, with an emphasis on its location in American history. The USA was founded on two major documents that do not fit well together: the Declaration of Independence and the Constitution. The Declaration is radically egalitarian but the Constitution, with its recognition of slavery and its limits on the suffrage, is inegalitarian. The model of the self that underlies the Constitution is a form of "faculty psychology." This theory envisions human nature as a system of faculties or capacities, the relative strength and dignity of which differ among racial and ethnic groups, genders and social classes. This model was adequate to get the Republic started and form the Constitution, but it was highly limited in its implications for the extension and deepening of democracy.

In the 19th century two events stressed faculty psychology to the breaking point: the Civil War and the subsequent emancipation of the slaves; and the arrival of the turn-of-the-century "new immigrants." During this time several new theories of the self were being discussed by American intellectuals. The first was neo-Hegelianism, which had a close connection to philosophical idealism. The second was biological reductionism or social Darwinism, which was extremely inegalitarian and, in my opinion, incompatible with democracy. The third was pragmatism, which mediated the other two, and was by far the most egalitarian of the three.

In the early 20th century the theory of human nature and the self which

PREFACE

underlay the democratic institutions slowly changed to pragmatism. This was a victory for American democracy. Pragmatism and the semiotic self gave a convincing explanation of why all humans are psychologically and morally equal, as well as explaining the sense in which they are autonomous or free. Pragmatism created a powerful theoretical resource for legitimizing and protecting democratic institutions.

At the present time the USA is again under great social stress. Divisions of race, ethnicity, gender, class, and sexual orientation, to mention the most prominent, are placing intense pressure on the democratic institutions. And the "bad economy," which has been around since the early 1970s, is making these divisions worse. Turn-of-the-century pragmatism itself declined in importance during the inter-war period, and at present there is no convincing theory of the self. In a sense we are back to the late 19th century, when the downwardly reductionist social Darwinisms and upwardly reductionist neo-Hegelianism were strong options, although the present versions of these options have new names. Against this background I argue that a revised or neo-pragmatism is the most appropriate theory of the self for the current political situation. This neo-pragmatism is the synthesis of Peirce and Mead, which I explain in the subsequent chapters of the book.

The second chapter defines pragmatism as a whole by comparing it with the other philosophical orientations that it faced: British empiricism and German idealism. After describing the unique traits of pragmatism I show how Peirce and Mead exemplified these traits. This chapter also makes the crucial distinction for defining the semiotic self: structure vs process, container vs contained, or user vs use.

The third chapter turns to the dialogical process which constitutes the self. Here I explain how I integrate Mead's I–me and Peirce's I–you models of the internal conversation. This turns the dialogue into a "trialogue" and shows how the internal conversation flows through the channels of the semiotic triad.

The fourth chapter treats the concept of reflexivity, which is one dimension of the semiotic self. I show how this concept has been used throughout the history of European philosophy and what is distinctive about the pragmatists' usage. I also compare semiotic reflexivity to various other versions in use today.

The fifth chapter takes Durkheim's macro concept of solidarity and lowers it down to the micro level, inserting it into the structure of the self. I show that there has long been a solidaristic theory of the self, although it has not previously been identified or named. I then integrate the two traditions of self, those of reflexivity and solidarity, into the model of the semiotic self. In showing the usefulness of this approach I apply the concept of solidarity to several problems, including the question of how humans could have evolved from the primates.

The sixth chapter begins the anti-reduction argument by introducing the theory of levels. I show that classical American sociology was systematically anti-reductionist. Even though there were theoretical differences among the early sociologists, they were united in their meta-theory. Classical anti-reductionism was also part of the broadly pragmatic effort to save democracy from social Darwinism.

The seventh chapter argues that the semiotic self disallows the upward reductions. I make this argument analytically by showing that these reductions assign the wrong traits to the self. I also make it more concretely by examining and critiquing the upward reductions of Wittgenstein, Lacan, Durkheim, and Derrida.

The eighth chapter turns to the other kinds of reduction, the downward varieties. Here I address the inadequacies of the positivist epistemologies, cybernetics, artificial intelligence, molecular biology, and neurophysiology.

In the ninth, concluding chapter I summarize the major theoretical and political conclusions of the book. I emphasize the sense in which the self is the union of three triads: dialogical, temporal, and semiotic. I also argue the usefulness of the semiotic self for the theory of democracy, particularly at the present time. The USA is currently under great pressure, both from problems of "life chances" (the bad economy) and "life style" (the value and identity issues). The neo-pragmatist theory of the semiotic self is the best model for explaining and negotiating both of these kinds of issue.

Author's Note

I follow the customary way of citing the *Collected Papers of Charles Sanders Peirce* (volumes 1–8); for example, "5.424" refers to paragraph 424 in volume 5 of the *Collected Papers*.

References to the *Writings of Charles S Peirce : A Chronological Edition* (volumes 1–5) follow the form recommended by the editorial staff of the Peirce Edition Project. In this case, "WI:400" refers to volume 1, page 400, of the *Writings*.

Peirce's unpublished manuscripts are identified in terms of the numbers used by Houghton Library at Harvard University; references to these are indicated by the abbreviation MS, followed by the number of the manuscript.

Acknowledgements

I want to thank the following people for reading and commenting on the entire manuscript: Randall Collins, Norman K. Denzin, Anthony Giddens, Donald N. Levine, John J. Lie, and David L. Westby. These generous colleagues were indispensable to my putting together a coherent manuscript.

I got the main idea of the book, for integrating Peirce and Mead, from Vincent Colapietro, to whom I am deeply grateful. Anthony Giddens encouraged me to write *this* book at a time, a few years ago, when I was going in several directions at once. Collins, Denzin, and Westby are old friends as well as long-term colleagues, and they have helped me out in many ways, both personal and intellectual.

I also received valuable suggestions concerning individual chapters and related conference papers from the following people: Eugene Halton, Fred Matthews, Andrew Feffer, Guillermina Jasso, Nancy Chodorow, Stephen Kalberg, Charles W. Smith, Barry Schwartz, G. William Domhoff, Alan Wolfe, Stephen Turner, Lewis Coser, H. S. Thayer, Jonathan Jacobs, Arlie Hochschild, Aaron Cicourel, Stephen Fuchs, Wallace Martin, Michael Lewis, Jane Gallop, Albert Lingis, Michael E. Brown, Harold Garfinkel, Deborah Wright, Arthur Vidich, Thomas M. Conley, Andrew Greeley, James R. Barrett, Judith DeLoache, and Robert G. Wengert.

I was also assisted in a variety of ways by the Sociology Department of the University of Illinois at Urbana. I am especially grateful to Eva Ridenour and Gina Manning for putting my figures and tables into clear, readable form and to Dolores Hill and Monica Shoemaker for showing me how to use the Apple computer.

The staff of Polity Press was extremely competent and a pleasure to work with from beginning to end. Their respect and sensitivity for theory was especially gratifying.

On the home front I must acknowledge the affection and support of my eight children: Frank, Katie, Monica, Paul, Vincent, Barney and the two steppies, Dan and Kate. Above all I am grateful to my dear wife, Christine Chambers, to whom this book is lovingly dedicated.

1

The Politics of Identity in American History

I take the position that there is a universal human nature, characterizing all human beings in the same generic way, at all times and places. Human nature has the distinguishing feature of being rational, symbolic, abstract, semiotic, linguistic, and so on, a point I will clarify as this book proceeds. This feature evolved in our line of primates in a way that is not currently understood (Bickerton, 1990, has what may be the boldest current hypothesis), although phylogenetic evolution is not a major concern of this chapter. I will refer to this uniquely human trait as the reflexive self, the semiotic self or simply as the self.

The notion of identity, etymologically a "sameness," which could be used to refer to generic human nature, is normally used in a more specific way (Giddens, 1991). It usually refers to some long-term, abiding qualities which, despite their importance, are not features of human nature as such. Identities individuate and allow us to recognize individuals, categories, groups and types of individuals. They can be imposed from without, by social processes, or from within, in which case they are often called self-concepts. They may also imply habit in various senses, including Pierre Bourdieu's "habitus" (Bourdieu, 1972/1977, p. 72). Identities, then, are nested within and express the qualities of selves and collections of selves.

The line between (particular) identities and (generic) selves is not easy to draw. History is notorious with peoples who thought their historically specific identities were universal, and who therefore used the name of their tribe as the name of their species. Despite the difficulty of applying this distinction, I will use the terms "self" and "identity" in the way indicated, as distinguished by degree of generality.

Institutions frequently endow individuals with identities, with historically

1

Self as meme, Idem
as an object.
Identity - as Particular Idem
or as Ipse
or No Distinct?

specific traits, that are claimed to be those of universal human nature. This is not only done by states and governments but also by religions, economies, and legal systems.

The recent discussion of the "death of man" and the decentering of the self or subject in European social theory is largely the analysis of historically specific identities, including the kind imposed by institutions. The people who had (or "housed") these identities may have looked upon them as humanity itself, and it is a profound contribution for scholars like Foucault and Derrida to have shown how long-term identities can come and go. Nevertheless to call these goings the "death of man" or the "effacement of the subject" is a category error, not unlike the one the primitives themselves made, for it equates (particular) identities with the (generic) self.

Given these definitions, the politics of identity is the struggle over the qualities attributed, socially and institutionally, to individuals and groupings of individuals. Some may argue that these qualities are the essence of human nature, at least for the groupings to whom they are assigned, and an exhaustive description of the selves in question. In rebuttal others may argue that there are no such things as selves and that the assigned qualities, including the semiotic structures within which they reside, are nothing more than talk or discourse. In my view these claims, both of which erroneously equate identities and selves, are the rhetoric of politics. It is a mistake to say that identities are trans-historical and universal, but it is also a mistake to say that personhood and selves are not. The selves are generic human structures, and the identities, any one of which may or may not be present, are distinct from and inhere in these structures.

The politics of identity in American history is largely a struggle over the definition of politically sensitive categories of people, especially minority groups. This struggle concerns the qualities that will be socially and institutionally applied to these groups, which will define their rights and duties, and which will affect the quality of their lives. American history, characterized by continuous flows of immigration, has had a constant debate over the politics of identity (Curti, 1980). Ethnicity, race, religion, and social class have been staple issues in this debate. In recent years gender and sexual orientation have been added as well, with still other issues possibly in the wings.

In the American past there have been two major theories for explaining the self and its identities: the faculty psychology (Howe, 1987) of the founding fathers and the semiotic theory (Thayer, 1968/1981; Colapietro, 1989) of the classical pragmatists. Neither theory is current and usable for today's politics of identity. The course of theology, philosophy, and science

2

in the 19th century eroded the founding fathers' approach, and the 20th century has had a somewhat similar effect on pragmatism. Today's discussion is largely between those who see the self as a pseudo-problem: those with biological and cybernetic arguments that reduce the self to a lower, ontological level; and those who hold cultural-linguistic positions, for example the post-structuralists, that reduce (or "sublate") the self to a higher level. Both of these positions eliminate selves and their identities, and, because of this displacement, neither group comes to grips with the politics of identity. By arguing that selves do not exist these theorists are really saying that theory cannot contribute to this question. When theory evades or ducks a question it still gets confronted, but in other media, such as politics, law, mass media, religion, and informal social channels. My position in the current discussion of identity is that the pragmatic solution was discarded too soon, that the elements of a usable neo-pragmatism are available, and that this approach can be made superior to the two reductions.

In the following sections of this chapter, I begin with a brief sketch of the founding fathers' faculty psychology, and then go on to review classical pragmatism and the contemporary politics of identity. Finally I show how a revised pragmatism might be used for the current situation.

The Founding Fathers and Faculty Psychology

There is a significant literature on the psychological and social philosophies of the founding fathers (e.g. Wills, 1978, 1981; M. White, 1978, 1987; Diggins, 1984; Boorstin, 1948; Howe, 1987; Matthews, 1990; Schwartz, 1987) but not much comparing these views to those of the pragmatists (Diggins, 1979; Lavine, 1984). Some scholars discuss both the founding fathers and the pragmatists in detail but do not systematically compare the two (D.M. Wolfe, 1957/1970; Flower and Murphey, 1977; Curti, 1980). My purpose is merely to indicate how faculty psychology, or rather "psychologies," explained the politics of identity in the revolutionary and Constitution-building period, and to show why this explanation was no longer usable when the "new immigrants," primarily Catholics and Jews, appeared in the Populist–Progressive era.

The politics of identity in the revolutionary period centered on the human variations that were problematic at the time, primarily "race" (blacks, indians and Europeans), gender, and social class. Religious conflict, which had been a serious colonial problem, was mitigated by the separation of church and state. It did not again become a major problem

3

until late in the 19th century. Homosexuality did not get politicized until late in the 20th century.

The theorists of the revolutionary period, especially Thomas Jefferson, Alexander Hamilton and James Madison, were practical intellectuals, using ideas to build institutions. They were not pure theorists, and their writings are not replete with footnotes and bibliographies. The Declaration of Independence and the Constitution in particular are free-standing documents, the theoretical origins of which must be inferred, and sometimes guessed at, indirectly.

The founders drew eclectically on the English-speaking philosophers of their times: the empiricists Thomas Hobbes, John Locke and David Hume and the Scottish moralists Francis Hutcheson, Adam Smith, Adam Ferguson and Thomas Reid, among others. These philosophers differed from each other, the moralists, for example, being closer to everyday beliefs and common sense. There is also scholarly dispute over which philosophers had the most influence over the Declaration of Independence, the Constitution and the beliefs of individual founding fathers (Howe, 1982).

Nevertheless the founders shared a broad perspective on human nature. In their view human beings were essentially characterized by a set of relatively static and private capacities and powers, some of which distinguished them from the other animals. These were not the innate ideas that the empiricists so opposed, but innate properties or possibilities. The actual list of faculties was not the same for all these thinkers, but it centered on the triad of passions, interests, and reason (Howe, 1987; Hirschman, 1977). In the hierarchy of moral dignity reason was the highest faculty, then the interests (still rational but self-serving), and finally the highly emotional passions. The problem of human nature, however, was that the strength or power of the faculties reversed the moral hierarchy, with passions strongest, then interests and finally reason.

In the Constitution the state was viewed as though it were human nature writ large, i.e. as though it too contained faculties of differing dignity and strength. The system of checks and balances was intended to get the best results from the political "faculties" with the fewest risks.

But the politics of identity, which was another offshoot of the founders' faculty psychology, was not worked out with much precision nor did it continue to be usable as the 19th century progressed.

The founders' interpretations of their own minorities – blacks, indians, women, and the poor – though not uniform or very explicit, were related to the faculty profile attributed to these groupings. In contrast to the propertied white males, in whom reason was thought to be relatively strong, the minorities were viewed as having weaker reason and stronger passions. This might be called the theory of unequal or skewed faculties,

4

although it was not applied in the same way to all minorities. Nevertheless indians and blacks were not offered citizenship, women were not allowed to vote or hold office and property regulations, albeit minor ones, restricted the political rights of white males.

The underlying reasons for or causes of these inferior faculty mixtures were even more obscure in the founders. They did not have the 20th-century distinction between heredity and environment or biology and culture. These categories did not appear until after Darwin expanded the domain of the biological, and the pragmatists and early anthropologists counter-expanded the domain of the cultural. These categories are now taken for granted, but the founders lacked them and had to work with blunter tools.

Jefferson was notoriously ambiguous about the blacks and the indians, mixing hereditarian and environmental ideas in ways that are both unattractive and make little sense today (Boorstin, 1948, pp. 81–98). Of course the founders were power-brokering a compromise between slave and free states, giving them a self-interest in not looking too closely at racism. They were also following the egalitarian Declaration of Independence with the much less egalitarian Constitution, giving them reason to ignore this inconsistency as well. They not only lacked the concepts, but also the good faith to use them unblinkingly.

The founders were also cryptic about social classes. Locke had said classes originate in the state of nature, unequal land ownership having resulted from the invention of money. He thought the poor had less time and energy to develop their rational powers, thereby making them more prone to passions and less fit for democracy (Macpherson, 1962, pp. 221–238). In his "Federalist 10" Madison is reminiscent of Locke when he refers to the "diversity in the faculties of men, from which the rights of property originate" and the "different and unequal faculties of acquiring property" (Madison, 1787/1961, pp. 130–31; Epstein, 1984.) Locke, however, was talking primarily about how unequal faculties are the effect of inequality, and Madison was making them the cause. Why do Madison's humans (actually, white males) have unequal faculties in the first place? Was this a question of heredity (birth) or culture (teaching) or was Madison tacitly drawing on the Calvinist notion of the elect? This last concept would again entail superior faculties in some, but would not fit into the heredity–environment scheme.

Underneath the notion of unequal faculties, then, the fathers had several obscure, now out-of-date explanations. They were not like the racist, social Darwinists of the late 19th century and the early 20th. Nor were they like the more culturological pragmatists and early anthropologists of that same

5

period. They had a third position, which straddled the distinction between biology and culture, using concepts and categories that are now obsolete.

Still, the founders' politics of identity, despite its philosophical roughness, was a "workable" scheme for the times. Of course it was backed up by a great deal of brute force, especially against the blacks and the indians, and this limited its durability. What made it obsolete as the 19th century proceeded, however, is difficult to say, both because of the complexity of the question and the paucity of relevant scholarship.

Most American historians think the central event of that century was the Civil War (McPherson, 1990), although there is little agreement on either its causes or effects. The Civil War in general and the Gettysburg Address in particular certainly deepened the American commitment to equality, but this was not anchored in a new theory of human nature, and it seems an exaggeration to call it a "refounding" (Wills, 1992, p. 40). Nor did this commitment deliver equality for American blacks. The Civil War weakened the founders' theory of human nature but it did not replace it.

Perhaps a stronger, if less bloody, cultural force was the Darwinian revolution. This paradigm elevated the power of the biological, particularly the randomly biological. The extra-biological overtones of faculty psychology, along with its teleological or goal-directed system of faculties made it incongruent with Darwinism.

By the end of the century, when Jim Crow laws had moved race relations back toward slavery and the new immigrants seemed not quite human, the founders' theory of human nature was completely inadequate. The industrialization of the USA and the ethnic and religious peculiarities of the new immigrants completely overloaded the old democratic paradigm. Out of this confusion and political ferment came America's second great theory of democracy, that of classical pragmatism.

The Populist–Progressive Period and Classical Pragmatism

The three major pragmatists were Charles Sanders Peirce, William James, and John Dewey, with George Herbert Mead as the less well-known fourth. In addition there were many other contributing scholars, both within and tangential to the movement (Thayer, 1981). The specific contribution of pragmatism, what might be called its unity, is unclear, both because of the looseness of the movement and because much scholarly work remains to be done on it (Hollinger, 1980). Pragmatism's unity is usually thought to be in its logic, method, or in the corresponding epistemology. This not only makes the unity mushy, but also politically rudderless.

6

Pragmatism, as some kind of vague social engineering, can be, and often has been right-wing and centrist as well as moderately leftist (Feffer, 1993).

I am more interested in pragmatism's theory of self, the family resemblance of which can be drawn from Peirce, Dewey, James, and Mead. This theory, though incomplete, is not mushy at all. The idea of the semiotic self is a technically sophisticated construction, giving anchorage to pragmatism's much looser theories of logic and epistemology. And it gives applied pragmatism a distinctly democratic rudder, orienting it to a populist blend of equality and freedom. In addition the theory of the semiotic self is useful in framing and conceptualizing today's politics of identity.

But the pragmatist theory of self and identity did not directly replace that of the founding fathers. By the middle of the 19th century, well before the appearance of pragmatism, the American transcendentalists were already moving from faculty psychology to a literary form of German idealism (Flower and Murphey, 1977, vol. 1, pp. 397–435). Then Darwinism finished the job. It displaced faculty psychology and created a vacuum in the theory of the self, much like the one that exists today.

Evolution implied a biological reduction of the self, suggesting that variations in human identity were the expression of physical variation in human bodies. In the wide variety of social Darwinist, eugenic, and racist positions in the Populist–Progressive period, the politics of identity was a kind of zoology, and the political implications, particularly for minorities, were decidedly undemocratic.

In the USA the initial response to Darwinism's reductionism was neo-Hegelianism, which went beyond transcendentalism's literary idealism. This was a move to the opposite kind of self-reductionism, to the other side of the boat. The British neo-Hegelian, Edward Caird, referred to these two reductionisms as "levelling down" and "levelling up," his own position implying the latter. As he put it, "We must 'level up' and not 'level down'; we must not only deny that matter can explain spirit, but we must say that even matter itself cannot be fully understood except as an element in the spiritual world." (Caird, 1889/1968, p. 35; quoted approvingly by the early Dewey, 1890/1969, p. 183).

The pragmatists, particularly the Dewey–Mead Chicago wing, began with a religiously motivated reliance on neo-Hegelianism (see Murphey, 1968, for the Harvard wing's religious reliance on Kant). By the turn of the century, both Dewey and Mead had moved into their less dialectical and more secular versions of pragmatism. Eventually, in a reminiscence on this period, Mead took the position that neo-Hegelianism, like social Darwinism, was itself incompatible with democracy (Mead, 1929/1964).

The interesting thing about this period, roughly 1870–1890, is the parallel

7

with today's politics of identity. The conflict between the down-levelling social Darwinists and the up-levelling neo-Hegelians was approximately the same as that between the two current reductions mentioned earlier.

When Dewey and Mead emerged from neo-Hegelianism they developed a position that opposed both reductions, i.e. the classical pragmatist theory of the semiotic self. This position was close to that of Peirce and compatible with that of William James. For the politics of identity it offered a second American theory of human variation, more persuasive than what was left of faculty psychology, and, as it turned out, strong enough to explain and soften the identity stresses of the Populist–Progressive period.

The pragmatist theory of the self was located in an evolutionary framework, i.e. it was intended to explain, or at least begin to explain, how humans evolved, phylogenetically, from the lower primates. In addition it applied an evolutionary analogy to social change. Although pragmatism was compatible with Darwinism, this being part of its superiority to faculty psychology, it was not biologically reductionist as the various social Darwinisms were. Instead the pragmatists interpreted evolutionary theory in such a way that it explained the emergence of human uniqueness and symbolic power, including the capacities for democratic government.

The pragmatist theory of the self never jelled into some specific, definitive statement or set of ideas. Still less did it ever become enunciated by the US government as its official social psychology. Just as with the founding period, the shift to a new theory of the self, with implications for the politics of identity, must be inferred indirectly (for how pragmatist theory entered the legal process see Hamilton and Sutton, 1989; Horwitz, 1992).

To appreciate the impact of pragmatism it should be seen in a systematic triad of philosophy, sociology, and anthropology. While the pragmatists were arguing that human nature is essentially symbolic and semiotic, the early sociologists were showing that social life is based on symbolic interaction, and the anthropologists were showing that this interaction produces culture. Internal semiotic, interpersonal interaction, and the cultural product were intrinsically connected ideas, each being more powerful because of the relations among the three. Of course the concept of culture also sharpened the distinction between heredity and environment, permitting a reasoned argument that human variation was not caused biologically but environmentally, this environment being conceived primarily as semiotic, interactional, and cultural.

The battle between pragmatism and social Darwinism was fought for a long time, at many levels and on many fronts. It not only went on in the three disciplines I mentioned – philosophy, sociology, and anthropology –

it also proceeded in popular magazines, the politics of private organizations, and in public affairs generally. By the time W.I. Thomas and Florian Znaniecki wrote *The Polish Peasant in Europe and America* (1918–1920), in opposition to social Darwinism's "ordering and forbidding" political implications (vol. 1, p. 3), the theoretical triad was completely in place. Biological reductionism as a politics of identity was in retreat, and it would fade out by the end of the 1920s (Wiley, 1986).

In its fight with social Darwinism the pragmatist coalition had an important ally in psychological behaviorism, the position of John Watson. In a way behaviorism was also biologically reductionist, for the difference between humans and the other animals was erased. But it did not explain human variation by innate biological mechanisms, the traits, genes, and instincts of social Darwinism. Instead human variation was a product of learning, a process highly influenced by the environment. Pragmatism's compatibility with behaviorism was quite limited, surrounded by important incompatibilities, and the alliance was at best unstable. Nevertheless the rise of behaviorism in psychology was an important factor in the decline of social Darwinism.

Behaviorism as such never became influential as a model for the democratic actor, i.e. for the politics of identity. Pragmatism and the disciplinary triad took that role. But behaviorism did become quite influential as a model for the economic actor. In other words the "economic man" of classical economics was transformed from utilitarianism to behaviorism. Behaviorism's victory in the economy limited the institutional impact of pragmatism, although the latter did gain hegemony in political life.

In the section below on neo-pragmatism, I discuss the pragmatist theory of the self in some detail. Here, however, I will sketch the differences between pragmatism and faculty psychology, indicating how these differences strengthened pragmatism's role in the turn-of-the-century politics of identity crisis.

(1) *Dialogical* The self of pragmatism was dialogical, both interpersonally and internally (Taylor, 1991, pp. 31–41). The self was initially formed in dialogue with caretakers and this dialogue was constitutive of whatever identities the self would take on. Moreover the inner life of the self, both in content and form, was a continuation of interpersonal dialogue. In contrast the self of faculty psychology was unitary and monological. When it entered into dialogue with others, it did so from a fully formed psychological base.

Later I will show that the dialogical self is also trialogical (and semiotic). This is because all dialogue, both inter- and intra-personal, entails a self–

9

other–self reflexive loop. I will refer to this three-place loop as the "structure," in contrast to the "content," of the semiotic self.

(2) *Social* From dialogicality comes sociality. The pragmatists' self was inherently social and therefore public and political. For faculty psychology the individual and society were at distance, requiring social contracts in politics and markets in economics to unite them. For the pragmatists the individual and the social were interpenetrating. This is because all conscious processes were based on an outside or social perspective. Markets and social contracts merely refined an already existing social solidarity.

(3) *Horizontal* For faculty psychology human nature was a vertical structure, consisting in a hierarchy of faculties. For pragmatism it was a horizontal structure, consisting of temporal phases of the self. For Peirce these phases were called the "I" and the "you." For Mead they were the "I" and the "me." I will look at these temporal phases in more detail later, but for now I want to point out that pragmatism's horizontality suggested a generic uniformity in everyone's rational processes. To describe this uniformity pragmatism demoted the passions of faculty psychology into the less influential category of impulses. In turn, interests and reason were merged in the horizontal semiotic process.

(4) *Egalitarian* The pragmatist theory of the self was distinctly egalitarian. All humans had the same psychological equipment in the same way. Human variation into identity groupings and unique individualities was a matter of differing symbols and their interpretations. The social Darwinists were explaining human identities, particularly ethnicity, biologically, by what they were calling "instincts." The pragmatists explained the same differences non-biologically and semiotically, as a matter of signs, communication, and interpretation. The pragmatists' self was extremely plastic; communication could produce all manner of variations, and the perplexing variations in the new immigrants could be fully explained semiotically, interactionally, and culturally.

(5) *Voluntarist* Concerning the psychological freedom of the person or citizen, the founding fathers were somewhere between Calvinist determinism and Locke–Hume compatibilism, i.e. between hard and soft determinism. The pragmatists, instead, attributed a capacity for self-determination or psychological freedom to the individual, i.e. they believed people could have chosen otherwise. In contrast to the semi-determinism of the founding fathers, this freedom had more deeply libertarian implications for law, civil liberties, and democratic self-government.

(6) *Cultural* Finally the pragmatists' self was part of the great cultural turn of the late 19th century and the early 20th. The anthropologists, particularly Franz Boas and his students, discovered culture macroscopically and from above. The pragmatists discovered it microscopically and from below. The human semiotic/symbolic capacity is the motor of culture. Once humans were theorized as semiotic the psychological preconditions of culture had been found and the cultural level itself could be identified.

Neither British empiricism nor Scotch moralism had the idea of culture, although the latter's "common sense" was a move in that direction. The concept of culture was useful if not indispensable for democracy, for it explained variation in identities in a way that was compatible with an egalitarian form of government.

The founding fathers, to their great credit, created a sturdy if quite imperfect democracy. Unfortunately, like that of the Athenians, their democracy was symbiotic with slavery. Similarly the founders' theory of the self was theoretically undisciplined and allowed of a slave psychology. The pragmatist self, more so than that of the fathers, had an elective affinity with democratic institutions. In addition the pragmatists got rid of slave psychology once and for all, showing how blacks and non-blacks alike have the standard and generic psychological equipment.

These six traits made pragmatism a better democratic instrument than faculty psychology had been. Neither social Darwinism nor neo-Hegelianism could have been a democratic replacement for faculty psychology, the former reducing the self to the body and the latter to the community. In contrast, pragmatism was a workable way of viewing human nature, despite the new stresses of industrialization, immigration, and urbanization, and if there was a "second founding," this was it.

The Politics of Identity Today

The pragmatist coalition, in my opinion, saved American democracy in the early 20th century. This was a case where ideas affected institutions, doing so by way of the social sciences and philosophy, the universities, law, religious liberalization, and some of the Progressive reforms. I think the idea of the (free and equal) semiotic self and the corresponding concept of culture gave equality a much firmer founding in American democracy than it ever had before. And it came just when it was needed, when America was sliding toward an early form of fascism. At the very least, it looks as though citizenship rights and civil liberties would have diminished if social Darwinism had not been checked by pragmatism. But the politics of identity crisis of the turn-of-the-century declined as the immigrants became assimilated, and, perhaps more than coincidentally, pragmatism declined with it. James died in 1910, Peirce in 1914 and Mead in 1931, none leaving any great disciples. Dewey at Columbia lived until 1952, but turned his interest more specifically to education. Except for the logical line of C. I. Lewis, W. V. Quine, and Nelson Goodman, pragmatism trickled off in the 1930s, to be replaced by logical positivism in philosophy. In the decades since pragmatism's decline there have always been disciples of Peirce, Dewey, and Mead, but not many important new developments or ideas. At the present time there are some influential calls for a neo-pragmatism in several disciplines, but not much new theory. The basic ideas of the pragmatist coalition, particularly those of equality and freedom, are still influential in the democratic institutions, but they are "living off their capital."

In the meantime, America's politics of identity situation has become more critical. The Catholics and Jews, who were central to the turn-of-the-century crisis, have been politically incorporated, but the other minorities are now in pronounced dissent. As of recent decades, blacks, hispanics, and women are demanding a fuller participation in democratic life. In addition Asian Americans, new and old, are beginning to form into a powerful minority group. Beyond this there is now a completely new identity problem coming from dissatisfied homosexual Americans, who are also asking for full citizenship.

Exacerbating this crisis is the fact that capitalism's living standards, especially in the USA, reached a plateau in the early 1970s. During the prosperous years after World War II – approximately until the oil shock of 1973 – a workable way of placating minorities was built into the expanding economy, for the growing pie automatically increased everyone's share (Wiley, 1983). Now there is both stalled growth and upward income redistribution, i.e. a static pie of increasingly unequal slices. These economic stresses are worsening the identity tensions.

As I mentioned earlier, the two American theories of the democratic personality – faculty psychology and pragmatism – are not in a position to meet the current challenge. Instead the levelling down and levelling up strategies of biological (Deglar, 1991) and cultural (Rosenau, 1992) reduction are the focus of discussion. But reductionist theories were not useful for the politics of identity in the late 19th century, nor are they any more so today.

In this theoretical vacuum the possibility of a revitalized neo-pragmatism offers an intriguing prospect. I see this as the challenge of completing the pragmatic synthesis in a way that the classical pragmatists never quite did, and of incorporating ideas from other developments in philosophy. In the next section I turn to these possibilities.

12

Neo-pragmatism and the Contemporary Politics of Identity

The key insight of the pragmatists, for the politics of identity, was in seeing human variation as the result of a highly plastic, semiotic process. This process explained identity variation in a way that was compatible with democracy. The theorists sketched the semiotic nature of the self in broad outlines but they did not work it out in detail. The two who contributed the most were Peirce and Mead, James and Dewey having worked primarily in other areas of pragmatism. Neither Mead nor especially Peirce ever completed their theories of the self. In addition, each worked with somewhat different terms and concepts, making it difficult to combine the two sets of insights.

Peirce's theory of the semiotic self, which he never integrated, has been systematized by the Peircean scholar Vincent Colapietro (1989). Colapietro did not actually complete Peirce's theory of the self, but he went a long way toward making it more coherent (Wiley, 1992). His interest was primarily in Peirce, and he did not attempt to combine Peirce and Mead (but see Rochberg-Halton, 1986, pp. 24–40, for some probes in that direction). In a private communication to me, however, Colapietro suggested a tentative way of linking the two theories. This has to do with visualizing the self as a present–past–future, I–me–you semiotic triad.

The major difference between Peirce and Mead, for present purposes, is in the temporal direction of the internal dialogue. Mead has this conversation going temporally backwards, from present to past, or from I to me. Peirce has it going forward, from present to future or from I to "you" (i.e. one's own self in the immediate future). Both versions produce a highly plastic, semiotic self, but at present they are side-by-side and have never been combined. Moreover, they are obviously not both right. If the self is a dialogue between present and future, then it is not a dialogue between present and past, and vice versa.

Colapietro suggests a way of combining the two dialogical theories. He dovetails them by linking them to the sign–object–interpretant structure of the semiotic triad. The details of this synthesis are somewhat technical, but I will gradually work my way back to the ordinary language of the politics of identity.

Peirce's great semiotic insight was in seeing that thought is not in the dyadic form of representation–object, but in the triadic form of sign–object–interpretant. One should keep in mind that Peirce, confusingly, used the word "sign" in two senses: for the overall semiotic triad and, in addition, for one of its three elements. In the triadic scheme the "sign" (in

13

THE POLITICS OF IDENTITY IN AMERICAN HISTORY

the second sense of the word) can be a mere physical vehicle or designator of a concept, e.g. the marks on a page or the sound of a voice, but it is also, more commonly, itself a concept. When the latter, the triad becomes one of thought, object, and interpretation of thought. Peirce's semiotic triad is dynamic and in potentially perpetual motion, involving an indefinite amount of interpretation and reinterpretation. To stretch a metaphor, it is more a (triadic) moving picture than a (dyadic) snapshot.

The sign and the interpretant are in a dialogical relationship, discussing the object, so to speak. In addition the interpretant of one moment often becomes the sign of the next. Peirce anchored his semiotic triad in his metaphysical categories – firstness, secondness, and thirdness – thereby locating semiotics in his overall philosophy, although that is outside the scope of this chapter.

Colapietro's suggestion is that the semiotic process entails both Peirce's I–you and Mead's I–me dialogues. To do this he draws on Peirce's idea that the "self is a sign" (first sense of word), although Peirce never indicated which part of the self is sign (second sense of word), which part object and which part interpretant. Colapietro's suggestion synthesizes three triads: present–past–future, I–me–you, and sign–object–interpretant.

The self on this view is a constant process of self-interpretation, as the present self interprets the past self to the future self. In dialogical terms, the I and the you interpret the me in order to give direction to the you. Semiotically the I–present functions as a sign, the me–past as the object and the you–future as the interpretant. As the self moves down the time-line its semiotic process is constantly transformed, with a past interpretant becoming a present sign and then a future object. The content, i.e. the specific topic of the internal conversation, may be anything, including the stories and narratives with which people interpret themselves, but its semiotic form or structure is one which integrates the three triads mentioned above.

In terms of the politics of identity, to get back to the theme, the I–me–you triad is the overall structure of the self. All selves at all times – subsequent to our evolution from the primates – have an I–me–you, present–past–future structure. And they all think in the corresponding semiotic triad. Exactly what they think, their specific semiotic contents, is a matter of "identities." Similarly the power of the self versus that of the community, a historical variable, is also a matter of identities, ranging from the communality of traditional societies to the heightened individuality of contemporary societies.

Although identities are more general than individual signs, they are less general than the semiotic structure. They are historically specific and "housed" in these structures. Thus I am distinguishing three semiotic levels within the self: individual signs, e.g. thoughts; systematic complexes of signs, e.g. the ethnic, class, gender and sexual identities and self-concepts of this chapter; and the generic capacity for semiosis, anchored in the I–you–me structure.

The strength of Colapietro's suggestion is that it offers a way of visualizing a truly pragmatic theory of the self, i.e. one that unites the disparate strands of the movement and provides a new solution to the problem of pragmatism's unity. More specifically, it unites Peircean and Meadean theory of self at the core, the semiotic (or "selfing") process. Mead's I–me reflexivity and Peirce's I–you interpretive process each becomes part of a more inclusive semiotic process, the I–me–you triadic conversation. This triad is the structure of the self, the universal generic human nature with which I began this chapter and which the reductions are unable to explain.

Viewed in this way, the voluntarist and egalitarian qualities of the self are more solidly anchored. Voluntarism or freedom is built into the semoitic process, which emerges over time. The agent or I of the present interprets the history or me of the past to and with the you of the future. This interpretation does not mirror, nor is it caused by, the past. It creates, and it does so by a kind of cognitive reality construction. It defines and redefines the situation in a somewhat undetermined manner. In this theory, the action itself, which may flow from the interpretation, can be viewed as determined (e.g. by the greater good) or "compatible" with determinism. But the freedom is still there, back a step, in the creative act of interpretation. This is not "free will" in the narrow and traditional sense but "semiotic freedom", which amounts to or (better said) results in the same thing. The clarification of the roles of the I, me and you – present, past, and future – in the semiotic process thus explains pragmatism's theory of voluntarism or freedom.

The notion of the self having an overall semiotic structure, within which it engages in concrete interpretations, is also helpful in grounding pragmatism's egalitarianism. All humans have and are this structure. This is where rationality, and consequently dignity, lies. In addition, freedom and moral power, e.g. Kant's self-inviolability and Durkheim's self-sacredness, is inherent in this structure.

In contrast identities are more superficial. For example, both men and women have the same semiotic structure, the universal human attribute. Then at a more specific, identity level, they have biological differences, along with cultural interpretations of these differences. Then, getting still more specific, there are, within genders, a variety of sexual identities that people can adopt, the various gay and lesbian orientations being among them. The same structure–identity distinction can also be applied, with the

15

same egalitarian implications, to ethnic groups, religious groups, social classes, etc.

It is true that theories of the self have often carried political agendas. If structure and identity are not kept separate, it is easy enough to smuggle traits of the dominating elites into the (alleged) nature of the self. It is understandable that intellectuals who represent minority groups are suspicious of the "self" and drawn to decentering positions. Foucault was a homosexual and Derrida is, by origin, a colonial Jew, for example. These minority connections may well have made the decentering, culturally reductionist position especially attractive to these thinkers (Johnson, 1993).

Nevertheless pragmatism's theory of the self as the foundation and location of human rights does the same job, and, in my opinion, with fewer political risks. In particular, the theory of democracy and legal equality, especially for minorities, becomes less solidly grounded once the level of the self is theoretically annihilated, for then rights have no clear location. In other words, the politics of identity, at the present time, can best be adjudicated with a democratic theory of human nature, such as that offered by neo-pragmatism.

Conclusion

This chapter began with definitions and abstractions, then turned, more concretely, to American political history, and ended with an attempt to apply still more abstractions to contemporary politics. Theory has many offices, but using abstractions to throw light on concrete social problems is one of its most important.

I attempted to contextualize the current politics of identity whirlwind, showing how comparisons, precedents and parallels from the past can help interpret the present. The theoretical models of the self which I distinguished, those of faculty psychology and classical pragmatism, were not written into law or any other government documents. They were implicit, in the air, and part of the common sense of the times.

The same is true for theories of self today. For example, the two reductions that I distinguished (along with their 19th century parallels) are sets of philosophical premises that operate like leaven in public life, even though intellectuals, in their own media, might be quite explicit about them.

The neo-pragmatist contender too, along with the semiotic suggestions I made, is a set of background assumptions, which may or may not influence formal politics. One of its strengths, however, is that, since the

Progressive period, it has been part of the common sense of American public life. The notions that the individual interprets, symbolically communicates, and lives in a culture all now have an implicit "category" status in American thought. The calls for neo-pragmatism are actually calls for a clarification and development of 20th-century American tradition.

In the formal battle of ideas, however, as opposed to the inertia of tradition, neo-pragmatism is not presently a well-developed position, even though a good deal of promising scholarship is going on. There are new pragmatisms in philosophy (Malachowski, 1990; West, 1989), literary criticism (Gunn, 1992; Mitchell, 1985), and law (Brint and Weaver, 1991; Cornell, 1993), as well as in other disciplines. So far, however, these neo-pragmatisms are relatively confined to method and correspondingly limited to the "mushiness" of that approach.

The section on neo-pragmatism, in which I de-emphasized evolution and theorized the semiotic self, is an attempt to say something substantive about this topic. The rest of the book will develop this attempt. This theory of the self is not offered as a solution to the politics of identity crisis. It is not a method or program for public life, but only a theory of the democratic agent. Nevertheless, it is a powerful picture of how the human mind works, and its voluntarist and egalitarian implications may be useful in the current politics of identity.

Let me recapitulate the argument of this chapter. American democracy has worked with two theories of human nature, the faculty psychology of the founding fathers and the semiotic self of the pragmatists. Although the pragmatists themselves never quite completed their theory of the self, this is where the movement's unity lies and this is what gave the USA a "second founding." For the current political challenge, both in the USA and other countries, neo-pragmatism offers a powerful theory of the irreducible democratic agent. In particular the semiotic concept of identity refutes both reductions, for downward reduction (from below) mistakes identities for the body and upward reduction (from above) mistakes them for the self. Finally the semiotic self explains both freedom and equality, giving democracy the foundation it needs in human nature.

2

Peirce and Mead on the Semiotic Self

The last chapter located the theme of the book, the semiotic self, in American intellectual history, and, more specifically, within the current politics of identity debate. To cover that much ground in one chapter I had to use a wide brush, simplifying complexities and omitting important details. This chapter will again examine pragmatism, but less historically, more systematically and at a slower pace.

First I will look at the overall position of classical pragmatism as it contrasts with other philosophies. Then I will turn to the Peirce–Mead synthesis in general. And after that I will begin looking at the major properties of the semiotic self. These are: structure vs content; reflexivity; first vs second order; and solidarity. Only the first of these four will be covered in this chapter.

The Position of Classical Pragmatism

In the last chapter I contrasted pragmatism with faculty psychology and, more implicitly, with German idealism. The six dimensions of the former comparison – dialogical, social, horizontal, egalitarian, voluntarist, and cultural – were oriented toward the theory of the self. That theory, which I am developing in this book, is a major substantive achievement of pragmatism. If the unity of this philosophy is sought in its logic, method or theory of knowledge, the movement is extremely loose, indistinct, and difficult to identify (Hollinger, 1980). But if it is sought in the theory of the self, the unity is based on a more technical claim, specific enough to be testable and prescriptive enough to be politically usable.

Objective Idem.

I have not yet made the contrast with British empiricism, which was included in the last chapter's faculty psychology grouping, because that will turn the discussion to the theory of knowledge, which I have so far wanted to avoid. But now that the idea of the semiotic self has been sketched, pragmatism's theory of knowledge can be more clearly defined. Before turning to empiricism, however, I will make the comparison with German idealism more explicit.

As mentioned earlier, Dewey and Mead began as Hegelians, gradually dropping the dialectic and the absolute self but retaining some of Hegel's flavor and style. Peirce was quite influenced by both Kant and Hegel, and he sometimes referred to himself as an objective or pragmatic idealist. James was the least attracted to idealism, yet he too was influenced by Hegel. All four were influenced by Kant's theory of forms, Hegel's social self and the various ideas of the self's reflexivity running through German idealism. But they gradually realized, Mead (1929/1964) most explicitly, that the Hegelian absolute self was more fit for absolute monarchy than for democracy. In Mead's view, the scaling down of Hegel's over-arching self to the level of the ordinary individual was a democratization of German idealism.

Turning to empiricism, there are not only differences in self theory, as already pointed out, but also in the theory of knowledge (Westby, 1991, pp. 457–60). I will consider three ways in which the pragmatists changed empiricism's epistemology: from retrospective to prospective, from sensation to action and from formal to ordinary language.

Retrospective to Prospective

For empiricism meaning was in the sensations that preceded and led to an idea. For pragmatism meaning was in the effects or consequences of an idea. This was the famous shift from past to future, probably influenced by the same temporal tendency in Darwinian biology. As Abraham Kaplan explains it:

> Classic epistemic empiricism was retrospective: it traced the origin of ideas in sensation, then analyzed meaning in terms of the experiences from which the idea emerged. The pragmatic approach is prospective; what counts is not origins but outcomes, not the connections with experience antecedently given but those which are yet to be instituted (1964, p. 42).

Yet this temporal shift is not necessarily a major departure from empiricism. In fact some scholars have interpreted Peirce's theory of knowledge as only a minor variation on empiricism, moving from antecedents to consequences but retaining the emphasis on observable sensations. Peirce's theory of knowledge was never completely unambiguous through his many years of writing, and the early statement of the "pragmatic maxim" (1878) does seem, at least on one interpretation, compatible with empiricism:

> Consider what effects, that might conceivably have practical bearings, we conceive the object of our conception to have. Then, our conception of these effects is the whole of our conception of the object (5.402).

And in the same article:

> I only desire to point out how impossible it is that we should have an idea in our minds which relates to anything but conceived sensible effects of things. Our idea of anything *is* our idea of its sensible effects; and if we fancy that we have any other we deceive ourselves, and mistake a mere sensation accompanying the thought for a part of the thought itself (5.401).

Some have even interpreted this maxim, with its emphasis on sensation, as an early statement of logical positivism's principle of verifiability. Yet throughout his writings Peirce was constantly tinkering with the maxim, moving it away from sensation and toward habit, semiotics, and the community. As early as 1868 Peirce had developed a version of his semiotics (Alston, 1956, p. 80) which contradicted the empiricist reading of his maxim of 1878. Despite Peirce's occasional early tendencies toward empiricism, the bulk of his epistemological writings were anti-empiricist. The other three pragmatists, although all working within the consequential spirit of Peirce's maxim, were much more clearly anti-empiricist in their notion of "effects."

Sensation to Action

John Watson's behaviorism is an example of a consequentialism, a prospectivism, which is sensorily empiricist. Watson, from whom the pragmatists were careful to differentiate themselves, moved the temporal location of meaning from past to future, but kept the formal, sensory epistemology. But when the pragmatists shifted from retrospective to prospective, they also changed the basis of meaning from sensation to action. Even in Peirce's pragmatic maxim the notion of "practical bearings" sounds more like action than sensation. Peirce himself suggested that the maxim is "scarcely more than a corollary" of Alexander Bain's definition of belief as "that upon which a man is prepared to act" (5.12). Max Fisch further suggested that Peirce's maxim might have been influenced by the predictive theory of law of Oliver Wendell Holmes, Jr., according to which law is "The prophecies of what the courts will do in fact" (Fisch, 1986, p. 7).

The other three major pragmatists were quite clear about meaning being determined by action and not by sensation. The shift from sensation to action, like the one from antecedents to consequences, was in the spirit of Darwin, for action was conceived as an adaptation to the environment, and the meaning of anything was in its evolutionary function.

Formal to Ordinary Language

Finally the epistemological medium or space within which the pragmatists worked was that of ordinary, everyday reality, variously referred to in philosophy as ordinary language, everyday life, the main reality, the natural attitude, common sense, and the everyday world. This category is contrasted with that of formal language, special realities or worlds, and the scientific attitude. Kaplan is again helpful:

> If meanings are to be analyzed in terms of action, they must make reference sooner or later to the ordinary objects and situations which provide the locus for action. . . .
>
> For some decades English-speaking philosophers, especially under the influence of the British schools, have been emphasizing the basic role of "ordinary language." Though the label, I suppose, would be anathema to many, the position taken is in my opinion essentially that of pragmatism. What is insisted on is that language is an instrument, and that to use language is to perform an action. The analysis of meanings must therefore focus on the particular contexts in which the action is performed, and on the purposes which the action as a whole is meant (sic) to achieve (1964, pp. 45–6).

Kaplan's key words are "context," "purpose," and "whole." These words indicate the way ordinary language is cultural and defined from within the community of users. This epistemological space contrasts with the formal space of sensationalism. The empiricist approach to meaning, which anchors it in sensation, would, if pressed, move toward the language of science and

Pura
hermeneutic

its formalized description of sensation. The pragmatist approach, in contrast, moves not toward the meaning of sensations but actions, and these as defined by the ordinary community.

Like the scaling down of the absolute self, the shift to the natural attitude was a kind of philosophical democratization, for reality and meaning were now fully accessible to the ordinary citizen's mind, each person being, in a way, epistemologically sovereign.

This is the opposite of Bertrand Russell's interpretation of pragmatism's epistemology as an invitation to dictatorship. He said:

> The main difference between Dr. Dewey and me is that he judges a belief by its effects, whereas I judge it by its causes where a past occurrence is concerned. . . . The past cannot be affected by what we do, and therefore, if truth is determined by what has happened, it is independent of present or future volitions; it represents, in logical form, the limitations on human power. But if truth, or rather "warranted assertability," depends upon the future, then, in so far as it is in our power to alter the future, it is in our power to alter what should be asserted (Russell, 1945, p. 826).

What Russell misunderstood is that pragmatism's "effects" are culturally coded and in ordinary language. Dictators can have only a modest effect on cultural futures, as Joseph Stalin found out when he tried to change the Russian language. Russell over-estimated the ability to manipulate the future and under-estimated the ability to manipulate the past.

The epistemological differences between pragmatism and British empiricism – to return to futurism, activism, and everyday life – gave a distinct turn to American philosophy, one completely missed by Quine in his comparison of pragmatism and empiricism (Quine, 1981). Moreover the six properties of the semiotic self, discussed in chapter 1, describe the kind of human being who would fit this epistemology. The comparisons I have now made with faculty psychology, German idealism, and British empiricism specify pragmatism's theoretical location. This is a philosophy which gives a semiotic description of the individual, and which is, by that fact, reflexive. The experience and knowledge of this individual are embedded in the socio-cultural order, and the point of view of that individual is inherently "from within" and in the "first person." Some of these concepts I have already analyzed to some extent; others, e.g. reflexivity and point of view, are new and will be discussed later. Nevertheless this profile of pragmatism's traits is crucial to the philosophies of Peirce and Mead, and to their convergence.

IDEM

22

The Peirce–Mead Synthesis

First a word on the backgrounds of Peirce (Brent, 1993) and Mead (Cook, 1993). Peirce (1839–1914) was the first-born of the four pragmatists and Mead (1863–1931) the last. Given the generation gap they differed enormously in terms of life experience alone. Peirce was born early enough to have met Emerson and to have lived through the Civil War as an adult. Mead, instead, was post-Darwinian and a peer of Thomas Watson.

The two men were also quite different in personality. Mead was an impeccably respectable professor at the University of Chicago. Peirce was morally unconventional and, for his times, academically unemployable. Mead was materially comfortable, particularly after he married a woman from a wealthy family. Peirce did not always have regular employment, handled his money badly, and died in poverty. Nevertheless, Peirce was always peacefully, if somewhat idiosyncratically, religious, while Mead appears to have been an anxious, vacillating atheist.

Intellectually they differed in style and emphases. Peirce, who based himself on the formal sciences of logic and mathematics, was the more deductive. Mead, drawing on physiology and psychology, tended to be more inductive. Peirce was also more at home with metaphysical speculation, which Mead tended to avoid. And while all of Mead's key concepts can be more or less transformed into Peircean terms, Mead's ideas were more explicitly and intrinsically social.

I have been emphasizing the differences beween Peirce and Mead to point out the improbability of their convergence. The usual way of pairing the pragmatists is to put Peirce with James and Dewey with Mead. The former pair were age-mates, knew each other, and were Harvard-associated. The latter were also age-mates, also knew each other, and were Chicago-associated. Peirce and Mead do not appear to have known each other, to have used each other's ideas, or perhaps even to have read each other's works. If one were to claim a Peirce–James or Dewey–Mead convergence, this would be in the grain of history, but a Peirce–Mead connection goes against the grain. That makes it both more interesting and more unifying for pragmatism.

Nevertheless there are now quite a few comparisons of Peirce and Mead in the scholarly literature (Morris, 1938; Natanson, 1955; Tibbetts, 1975; Rosenthal, 1969; Lewis, 1972; Rochberg-Halton, 1986, pp. 43–70; M. Singer, 1984, pp. 74–104; Tejera, 1988). These comparisons are in remarkable agreement on the compatibility, and even the convergence, of Peirce and Mead. But the convergences these writers have in mind are similarities in premises and concepts. No one has argued that the two theories can be substantively combined, in such a way that a new theory comes about. But that is what I am arguing. In the previous chapter, building on Colapietro's unpublished ideas, I showed how the two semiotic theories can be integrated. In this and subsequent chapters I will again describe this synthesis, but in a more gradual, step-by-step manner.

The synthesis, it may be recalled, takes off from the seeming discrepancy between Peirce's and Mead's internal conversations, i.e. their theories of how thought works. For Mead it was I to me and present to past. For Peirce it was I to you and present to future. To describe the discrepancy in this way, however, rests on some prior assumptions. I will discuss three major ones.

For one, I am assuming that, for Peirce, thought is always an I–you conversation. He frequently said this, as I will show in chapter 3, and he referred to this conversation as "tuism" (Fisch, 1982, p. xxix). But he also sometimes described thought in ways that seem incompatible with the conversational metaphor. The pragmatic maxim, for example, seems to make the thinker – at least the most effective thinker – into a logic-machine, examining events like a scientist looking for empirical invariants. The notion that thought is dialogical and comparable in any way to a chat between friends or neighbors, is simply too imprecise and loose to fit the (early version of the) pragmatic maxim.

Even the sign–object–interpretant, semiotic definition of thought, which is quite different from the pragmatic maxim approach, is not particularly open to the conversational model. For one thing, neither sign, object, nor interpretant are, for Peirce, persons. The communicating persons – speaker and listener, utterer and interpreter – are tacked onto the two ends of the semiotic triad, making it a pentad. The internal triads themselves are structures of meaning, not agents or persons. The sign does not talk to the interpretant, nor is it at all clear how the interpretant could talk back or respond to the sign. Although the semiotic theory of thought is not as incompatible with the dialogical metaphor as the pragmatic maxim is, it is not particularly open to it either.

I had to take some liberties in making the I–you conversation Peirce's main definition of thought. I softened the pragmatic maxim by locating it within the concepts of futurism, activism, and ordinary language. And I personalized and conversationalized the semiotic triad by equating it with the temporal phases of the self, the sign–interpretant–object becoming the I–you–me. In other words I took Peirce's three, somewhat different definitions of the self – those associated with the pragmatic maxim, the semiotic triad, and the I–you conversation – and showed how the conversational definition could include the other two.

A second assumption and corresponding liberty was in putting the word "I" into Peirce's mouth. When he talked about tuism and how thought is an

but the enjoining conscience

internal conversation he did not explicitly use the word "I." He simply used "self" or the pronoun "he." When the self talks with the upcoming self, he described the conversation as being between the present self and future self or "you." Unlike Mead, Peirce did not formally use the word "I" for the speaker. It was my choice, in the interest of moving Peirce and Mead more closely together, to make Peirce use "I." I could have referred to this agency simply as the speaker, the present, or perhaps the center-pole or center-point. But there are good arguments that Peirce's present self was about the same as Mead's "I."

The mature Peirce did not use the word "I" very often, but earlier he had made it a central concept. The young Peirce had modified and condensed Kant's 12 logical categories into a triad of I, thou, and it. At first these categories were quite close to the linguistic idea of point of view, yielding the first person or I, second person or you (or "thou"), and third person or "it." This idea, not particularly clear to begin with, was constantly transformed by Peirce so that the three points of view eventually became three kinds of reality. Finally Peirce dropped the personal pronouns entirely and shifted to the words "firstness," "secondness," and "thirdness." The three ordinal numbers are still the same as those of point of view, but the meanings have completely changed. Peirce's very early use of "I," then, was that of the first person in the present, much like Mead's I. Eventually Peirce generalized his I into the extra-personal notion of "firstness," but the personal I was still a member of this category, and the notion of firstness does not deny that Peirce's first (i.e. present) person was the "I."

Peirce made another reference to the I, in a way that supports my argument, in an undated, unpublished manuscript (MS 668, pp. 16–17). In the context of discussing Descartes' "cogito" he referred to the I as "the power of voluntary action" and "the idea of an unconstrained cause of some future events." Since this associates the I so intimately with freedom, and since for Mead the present and the I are the locus of freedom, it does not seem unreasonable to refer to Peirce's self of the present as the "I." In any event, for the Peirce–Mead convergence it is not necessary that Peirce's I be exactly the same as Mead's. Mead does not always say quite the same thing when he refers to the I, as I will show in the next chapter. All I need to show here is they both use the I as the semiotic "sign," i.e. as one element of the semiotic triad. With this I can place their shared concept of the I as the intermediary between Mead's me and Peirce's you.

A third assumption is that in the internal conversation only the present self or I can speak. The podium is in the present, and discourse can issue only from this podium. The underlying argument is as follows. Action can go on only in the present, not in the future or past. Since speech is action, speech too can go on only in the present. And since the present of the self is the I, only the I can speak. The me and the you can only listen and be spoken to. If they were to speak, they would have to do so in some way that transformed them into the present, thereby allowing them, indirectly, to use the communicative powers of the I.

These three assumptions – that the internal conversation is Peirce's basic definition of the self, that Peirce's present self is close enough to Mead's I to give it the same name, and that only the I can speak – form the basis of the Peirce–Mead discrepancy, the resolution of which, in turn, leads to the Peirce–Mead synthesis.

In the third chapter I will look more closely at the subleties and ambiguities in the internal conversation. Using such concepts as role-playing, meta levels, time orders and transitional time slots, I will consider the ways in which the I might speak for the you or me. These mechanisms all loosen up the podium rule and permit talk, back and forth, across time. I will also consider whether the I, which does all the talking, might be attempting to address its speech, not to Mead's past or Peirce's future but to the present. It would be talking to a listener that seemed, to the I, to be in the present. In other words the I might regard itself as talking, not to the me or you but to itself. This would not contradict the idea that this communication was actually received by an agency of the self that was in the past (Mead's me) or the future (Peirce's you).

But these subtleties are not needed to explain the Peirce–Mead discrepancy or the I–you–me semiotic trialogue which resolves this discrepancy. They are refinements that assume the Peirce–Mead convergence already in place.

Structure and Content

Having laid out the framework surrounding the Peirce–Mead synthesis, I can now turn again to its substance. As explained in the first chapter, the semiotic interpretation of the I–you–me triad is the core of the synthesis. In this section I will again cover this theme, looking at it in more detail.

The Self as a Structure

I am using the word "structure" to refer to the general relationship among present, future, and past aspects of the self. These temporal phases can be called the I, you, and me, and they can be semiotically mapped as sign, interpretant, and object. This gives the structure of the self three parts, which I will variously refer to as clusters, regions, roles, poles, and

26

agencies: the past–me–object; the present–I–sign; and the future–you–interpretant.

Metaphorically I am viewing this structure as a "container," within which there are "contents." This metaphor is misleadingly spatial, and it does not catch the way in which the semiotic structure and contents interpenetrate. Nevertheless, in somewhat the same loose manner in which a person might say they have something "in mind," I am visualizing the "in" relationship as resembling that between a container and that which it contains. The containment, however, is not physical or spatial but semiotic and meaningful. This containment can be explained by contrasting the abstract semiotic triad with the communication-embedded pentad, or rather "hexad." As Peirce insisted, the pure semiotic triad of sign–interpretant–object is abstract and general (Fisch, 1986, pp. 342–3; M. Singer, 1984, pp. 68–9). It does not include or necessarily imply an addressor–addressee or utterer–interpreter. This additional pair is present only in concrete situations, i.e. when the triadic meaning is actually communicated. In these cases we have the communicator, the semiotic triad by and in which the communication goes on, and the communicatee. This adds up to five places, i.e. a pentad. The outer dyad of this pentad can take various forms. It can be inter-organizational, interpersonal or, in the case I am discussing at present, intra-personal.

This is still not quite complete, however, because there is reason to view the pentad as a hexad. To explain the move from a five-place pentadic to a six-place hexadic scheme the concept of reflexivity is needed. Most communication is linear, between addressor and addressee, but it is also, in part, reflexive, i.e. between the addressor and him- or herself. In other words the semiotic stream of communication not only goes out to the audience or listener, it also goes back, reflexively, to the speaker. The various meanings of the word "reflexivity" and the ways in which this "flexing" process might work will be considered in the fourth chapter. For now it need only need be pointed out that the reflexive undertow of communication is what adds the sixth place. Speaker (1) communicates in semiotic triads (2, 3, and 4) to the listener (5) but in addition the speaker communicates reflexively with him or herself (6).

Figure 2.1 shows, albeit in quite inadequate spatial terms, what the six-place relation looks like. The speaker communicates to the listener, via semiotic triads, in a linear manner. But at the same time the speaker, using the listener as a kind of mirror, communicates back to him or herself. Thus the speaker in the hexad is counted twice, once as communicator and once as reflexive communicatee.

Having now explained the difference between a semiotic triad and a communication-embedded hexad, let me return to the container metaphor.

27

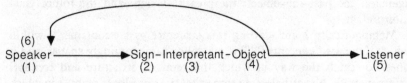

Figure 2.1 The communicative hexad

The hexad "contains" the triad in the same way that the overall structure of the self contains its contents. The containment is functional rather than spatial or physical. It is a triad within a triad, the inner being subordinate to the outer.

Turning to the contents of this structure, what one will see as the nature of these contents will depend on one's theory of the self. I have already mentioned such sub-structures as signs and clusters of signs, the latter being identities and self-concepts. The sub-structures are constructed and maintained by semiotic processes.

More generally the I–you–me triad emerged from the primates, defines our line of primates, contains the other semiotic structures and processes, and is the common denominator, and therefore the democratizer, of all the identity groupings.

The existence of this structure, however, is challenged by both reductionisms, downward (from below) and upward (from above). Only the contents, themselves interpreted differently by each reductionism, would be recognized. Given these challenges, let me again ask whether the concept of structure is really needed, what use it has and whether the contents might not be all there is to the self. In response I will point out three ways in which the concept of structure is useful: it mediates between variants and invariants of democracy; it decenters the Cartesian self without eliminating it; and it unifies Peirce's theory of the semiotic self.

(1) The concept of structure, as pointed out in chapter 1, is what saves the democratic self from political inequality and restrictions on freedom. The reductionisms misunderstand identity variation in such a way that they disallow the psychological requisites of democracy. Biological reduction, which interprets identity differences as rooted in the body, runs the risk of eugenic and racist restrictions on democracy. Cultural and linguistic reduction, at the opposite extreme, interpret identity variations as proof that the self is solely a construct of language and culture, lacking any *sui generis* reality and therefore any rights.

(2) Pragmatism decenters the self without abolishing it. Recent French thinkers have used the idea of decentering the self in many ways (Wiley,

1990, p. 406), but they all tend toward upward reduction. In other words they do not so much decenter the self as eliminate it. "Decentering" suggests that the self is still there, after the decentering process, but more spread out, dispersed or in some way decentralized. If the self is decentered externally, from its environment, as Copernicus did to our planet and Darwin to our biological species, the self becomes less important and its environment more so. If the self is decentered internally, as Freud did with the unconscious and Lacan with the imaginary, there is still a self, albeit more dispersed, after the decentering.

The pragmatists had a form of decentering that combined the external and internal modes. Externally the self was made less isolated by being partially incorporated into the social. Much of this decentering was covered in the previous chapter, in which the six basic differences between pragmatism and faculty psychology are outlined. Internally the pragmatists decentered by dispersing the self among the three agencies: I, you, and me. Descarte's monological, unitary self was spread into three communicating parts.

The I–you–me structure offers an intermediary position between the over-centered Cartesian ego and the effaced or eliminated post-structural one. It is neither unrealistically centered nor unnecessarily reductionistic. It is neither socially isolated nor socially absorbed. Rather it is in a balanced, interpenetrating relation with society. It disperses agency throughout the semiotic triad, but nevertheless recognizes human agency (Colapietro, 1990).

(3) Finally the notion of structure is the missing key to Peirce's semiotics of self. A major problem with Peirce is that his theories do not always hang together very well. He is continuously brilliant and innovative, but in ways that do not always add up. One of his most confusing arguments is in his semiotics of the self. In this semiotics his major assertion is that the human is only a sign or collection of words. But he never mapped the self onto the semiotic triad, i.e. he never explained what part of the self was the sign, what part interpretant and what part object. Nor did it help that he referred to the self as a "glassy essence," without clarifying whether this meant fragility, reflexivity, transparency, (Sartrean) nothingness, or perhaps something else. If the self consisted solely of a word or words, he did not explain how the self is *sui generis* and irreducible to language. If pragmatism is America's greatest contribution to philosophy and Peirce is the greatest pragmatist – both of which I believe to be true – then the problem of Peirce's semiotics of the self is an important piece of unfinished business in America's cultural history.

The Self-Structure as a Sign

Without the concept of the I–you–me structure Peirce's dictum on the verbal self can be interpreted in three ways, none of which holds his theory together very well. These are: that the self is merely its semiotic contents; that the self is just the word "self" and others like it; and, following Josiah Royce, that the self's semiotic structure is not a hexad but only a triad.

If the "self is a sign" formula merely meant that the self is only its semiotic contents, there would be no self, for there would be no entity within which the semiotic flow inhered. The idea of "inhering" makes use of the container metaphor, and Peirce himself used this word in his theory of how the child discovers his or her self. With this theory of self-discovery Peirce transformed Descartes' "cogito ergo sum" (I think, therefore I am) into a "fallor ergo sum" (I err, therefore I am).

> A child hears it said that the stove is hot. But it is not, he says; and, indeed, that central body is not touching it, and only what that touches is hot or cold. But he touches it, and finds the testimony confirmed in a striking way. Thus, he becomes aware of ignorance, and it is necessary to suppose a *self* in which this ignorance can inhere (W2:202).

Since Peirce used "inhere," with its nested or container imagery, one can argue that his semiotic self could not be just its contents. That within which the contents inhere must also, in some manner, be a sign and therefore, on his logic, a self.

A second way in which Peirce's semiotic self can be interpreted is by claiming it is just the word "self" or other words like it (e.g. person, individual, human being, ego, etc.) There would be no actual selves, then; just the names.

This makes no sense within Peirce's thought either. Again, it could not explain his use of the word "inhere." But also the notion that the self is only its own names eliminates the *sui generis* self. Peirce said "I know that I (not merely *the* I) exist" (W2:201). To put it differently, if there were no apples except for the word "apples," there really would be no apples, and we would not get to eat any. Similarly if there were no selves except for the word, we would not get to be selves. But for Peirce the self was unquestionably a *sui generis* entity, characterized by autonomy and self-control (Colapietro, 1989, pp. 99–118).

A third interpretation of Peirce's under-explained semiotic self is the one Royce made. In his later years Royce was influenced by Peirce and constructed a version of Peirce's semiotic self that fit his own religiously tinged idealism. Royce's scheme assumed a distinction between two types of thought: conception, which was traditionally dyadic; and interpretation, which, in the Peircean manner, was triadic. The former were thoughts about things other than the self, or at least other than the deep self. The latter had as their object puzzling features of the self. This is an interesting distinction, but it is not one that Peirce made. For him all thought, including what Royce called conception, was triadic and interpretive. In addition all thought had, at least in an implicit and structural sense, the self as its object.

Nevertheless Royce did make some useful modifications on Peirce, especially in connecting the present with the future and the past. This temporal triadicity is congruent with and supportive of the way I am handling time in the Peirce–Mead synthesis. As Royce put it:

> When a process of conscious reflection goes on, a man may be said to interpret himself to himself. In this case, although but one personality, in the usual sense of the term, is in question, the relation is still really a triadic relation. And, in general, in such a case, the man who is said to be reflecting remembers some former promise or resolve of his own, or perhaps reads an old letter that he once wrote, or an entry into a diary. He then, at some present time, interprets this expression of his past self (1918/1968, p. 287).

And a little later he continues:

> And there are three men present in and taking part in the interior conversation: the man of the past whose promises, notes, records, old letters, are interpreted; the present self who interprets them; and the future self to whom the interpretation is addressed. Through the present self the past is so interpreted that its counsel is conveyed to the future self (pp. 287–8).

Royce's notion of the semiotic self, despite my partial agreement with it, differs from the one I am using in several ways: he referred to the past self as both an object and as a sign, although for me it is only an object; he had the present self presenting, not a sign, but an interpretation – in contrast, his future self did not present an interpretation but just remained in the listener role; finally he had no pentad or hexad, but only a triad. This is because he did not separate structure from contents; for him the two are the same. Royce's interpretation of Peirce's semiotic self is not carefully thought out (J. E. Smith, 1968, p. 28) and not completely true to Peirce's ideas. In addition it is not as open to the semiotic of Mead as my interpretation is. Still, there are several useful features of Royce's Peirce.

I have now shown that Peirce's "self is a sign" dictum cannot mean contents, physical words, or Royce's triad. Then what is left? The only remaining way of interpreting Peirce is to say that the self is, structurally, a sign. This explains Peirce's cryptic idea of the semiotic self and thereby gives unity to his thought. It is also the pivotal concept for ushering in the combination of Peirce and Mead.

Concrete Objects and the Me

Another issue that should be considered here is the relation between concrete semiotic objects and the rather abstract notion of the "me" as a continuous and underlying semiotic object. I have been arguing that the former (concrete) object is contained in and interpenetrates the latter (abstract) object. In other words the inner triad, which contains the concrete object, is systematically connected to the outer triad, which contains the me.

At first glance it would appear that ordinary everyday objects – physical, social, or cultural – are not connected to the deeper regions of the self unless they have highly symbolic meanings. Birthday gifts or other ritual objects, for example, or Royce's letters and diaries may be self-connected in that manner. But an ordinary mundane thought process, such as planning to buy a toaster to toast bread in, seems quite distant from the self and self-interpretation. The toaster as object seems quite far from the me as object. If I am to defend the close relationship I have been claiming between contents and structure, or inner and outer triads, I have to show how ordinary objects, such as toasters, are functionally connected to the overall structure of the self.

This is a complex issue and I will proceed cautiously, but I think it can be shown that an ordinary object is intrinsically connected to the me. I have already been making this argument with ideas from Peirce. I will now show that both James and Mead also had ideas helpful for my argument. After that I will present the concept of "semiotic power," which ties together the ideas of Peirce, James, and Mead, showing how all semiotic processes, however mundane, are dependent on the self's structure. Finally I will show how the "identities" are a special case in the structure–content relationship, functioning as a kind of content in a healthy self but competing with the structure in unhealthy selves.

James and Mead   James had the idea that the things one owned were part of the self:

In its widest possible sense, however, a man's Self is the sum total of all
that he CAN call his, not only his body and his psychic powers, but his
clothes and his house, his wife and children, his ancestors and
friends, his reputation and works, his lands and horses, and yacht and
bank-account. All these things give him the same emotions (1890/
1950, vol. 1, p. 291).

In this passage James, who had an eclectic theory of the self, was drawing
on the "self-feeling" theory, an approach quite distinct from the more
cognitive, semiotic approaches of Peirce and Mead. In the fifth chapter I
will look at self-feeling in relation to the concept of solidarity, but now I am
interested only in the way concrete objects can be part of the self.

For James, virtually anything could be part of the self, since he thought
all possessions could give the "same emotions" as a person's "body and
psychic powers"; feelings like "mine" and "my own" could place anything
in the category of the self. There is a common affect or feeling that
integrates concrete objects, such as the toaster of my example, with the
structure of the self. The inner and outer triads are united by being part of
the same emotional field.

James does not quite say this, but concrete objects that one owns or
would like to own are "for" the self. They are meant to satisfy the desires of
the self. They quickly lead to the self in a means–end fashion or, perhaps
better said, desire vs object of desire. In this connection it is useful to
remember the distinction, implicit in Hegel, between concrete desires and
overall "desire." A form of this distinction is in James Mark Baldwin (1899,
pp. 373–5), and a later version is in Lacan (1966/1977, pp. 292–325), who
may have got the idea from reading Baldwin.

For Baldwin, desires are for the concrete things, material and social, that
we want. In contrast "desire" underlies all the concrete desires and is the
wanting of a complete self. For Hegel, "desire" was the desire for another's
desire (of you), this being a variant of his concept of "recognition."
Baldwin's "desire," then, is an interpretation and domestication of Hegel's.
Accordingly concrete desires are usually, in part, attempts to satisfy
"desire."

These levels of desire never come into harmony or leave the self at peace.
Neither level can ever be completely requited. This is primarily because the
deeper level of desire – at least in most theories of the self – can never be
completely satisfied, i.e. the self can never be fully complete and at rest.
Because of the connection between the levels of desire, little desires can
affect the big one and interpenetrate the structure of the self. For things to
be "for" the self means that they are, in part, for the deepest integrity needs
of the self. James's self-as-property theory, then, is supported by the

33

Hegel–Baldwin–Lacan idea about levels of desire, and the connection between structure and contents is similarly supported.

Turning to Mead, one of his central concepts was "reflexivity," a term I will later translate into triadic, semiotic language. For Mead the overall structure of the self, which he visualized as a dialectic or dyad of I and me, was reflexive. Mead lacked Peirce's notion of the self-as-you, but, as I have shown, Mead's I–me conversation was quite open to that concept. For present purposes I want to point out how the reflexivity that, for Mead, defines and structures the self, is the same reflexivity that is used in concrete thought processes, such as the example of the toaster. The looping or circular pathway of figure 2.1 is the same whether the reflexivity is general or particular, whether a matter of structure or contents.

For Mead, the same reflexive process operates for apprehension of and communication with other people, oneself, and non-personal objects. The infant first learns to be reflexive interpersonally, with the close caretaker or caretakers. Mead called this inter-human reflexivity "role-taking," and it was perhaps his most central concept. Then, drawing on the model and pathway of role-taking, the infant can engage in two other kinds of knowledge and communication: with non-human objects and with the self. I have already shown how intra-personal communication, i.e. communication of the self with the self, is modeled after interpersonal communication, both for Peirce and Mead. The internal conversation is a transformed version of the interpersonal one. But for Mead, the child's observation and manipulation of physical objects also proceeded as though the objects were human beings. The child engaged in reflexive role-taking with these non-human objects, putting gestures if not words into their mouths and anticipating what they were perceived to be about to "say" (Mead, 1938, pp. 426–32).

For Mead then, all reflexivity – whether for the other, self or physical thing – proceeded in the same cognitive pathway or channel. The same recursive path that makes the self a self also channels all self-referencing, whether it is Royce's profound soul-searching or the ordinary thought of everyday deliberation. Like James, but with a cognitive rather than an emotional connective, Mead argues that ordinary objects are closely linked to the self-as-me.

Semiotic power I have now shown that Peirce, James, and Mead all had concepts that linked the me to non-personal objects, i.e. to the it-as-object. The notion of "semiotic power" can connect these concepts and show, dynamically, why all semiotic objects partake in the self, i.e. in the me. "Semiotic power" is my name for the energies that underlie and empower signs. The kinds of sign that Peirce called "symbols" have interpretants that are abstract, general meanings. These meanings may sometimes be connected, e.g. in propositions, in ways that are true, good, or beautiful, or at least seem so. These attributes of meaning – generality, truth, goodness, and beauty – all have what I am calling semiotic power. This notion has the same semiotic function as Levi Strauss's "mana," Lacan's "phallus," or what I will take to be Durkheim's "solidarity." The function is to be the entering wedge into a system of meaning. In addition it is the semiotic resource underlying any concrete meaningful element. In the fifth chapter I will derive semiotic power from my interpretation of solidarity, but it is sufficient her to show how all semiotic acts are dependent on the taproot of semiotic power.

The structure of the self as an I–you–me system, i.e. as a three-point reflexive self-awareness, is the basic source of semiotic power. How our line of primate got this self-awareness is another matter, although I will speculate about it in chapter 5. For now I only want to point out how this three-part self-awareness is the power behind the more concrete acts of self-awareness. The reason we can think about concrete objects, such as the toaster, is that we can think about ourselves. The reflexive structure of the self originates and generates semiotic power in somewhat the same way as the heart pumps blood. All semiotic energy – that of generality, truth, goodness, and beauty – is a more specific form of the energy that flows through the life of the self. Perhaps the word "life" is not a bad metaphor for the power of the structure. Because the self is alive, i.e. because it is a self-aware, I–you–me system, it can engage in the processes of the psychologically living. Without this semiotic life or self-awareness we could not think at all. And the death of the self accordingly is the death of self-awareness.

I am implicitly applying the notion of semiotic power to the more specific ideas I have just reviewed from Peirce, James, and Mead. These ideas connected the particular with the general object, it with me, and inner with outer triads. Running through them is the idea of a shared energy or dynamic. I am referring to this shared dynamic as semiotic power and arguing that this power unites the self. The chapter on solidarity unpacks this argument still more, but here I wish merely to point out the role of semiotic power in funnelling all objects, no matter how concrete and seemingly distant from the self, through the me.

It only remains to explain how identities, which are more comprehensive than particular signs but less so than the overall structure of the self, fit into the structure–content analysis.

The semiotic location of identities The notion of identity has similarities with the pragmatist ideas of habit and attitude, but it is broader and includes them among its parts. Since identities are collections and syntheses of individual signs, their relation to the structure resembles that of individual signs. They are subordinate, contained, dependent, and so on. But in their bulk and their consequences, both material and psychological, they are much more important. If the identities are desired, acceptable, and workable for the person, they can be useful intermediaries between individual semiotic practices and the structure of the self. Indeed they are essential to the healthy self as organizers of personal values, integrators of practice and optimizers of semiotic power. Good identities are the overall self's bridge to the world. But if the identities are uncongenial to the person, psychologically or socially, they can create blockages between contents and structure, distorting the normal flow of semiotic power. The politics of identity is a major producer of uncongenial identities and correspondingly destructive self-concepts, e.g. in the areas of ethnicity, social class, religion, gender, disability, sexual orientation, etc.

There are four properties, which are unique to the overall structure of the self, but which are sometimes thought to characterize one or more of its identities. In other words a part of the self, an identity, may be confused with the whole of the self, the overall structure. The four are: "personal identity," the fundamental reflexive channel: the fundamental source of semiotic power; and the "main reality" of the self.

"*Personal identity*" is the philosopher's term for the continuous relationship a thing has with itself. This is not an identity in the sense in which I have been using the term up to now. It is not a semiotic identity but a sameness or identicality in a thing's stream of existence. In the case of humans it is the continued existence of that person, along with the person's knowledge and recognition of that continued existence. It is your awareness that you are the same you, broadly speaking, that you have always been. The unique features of the self, which may be part of personal identity, can draw on a variety of the self's concepts, but the core of personal identity is in continuous self-awareness or reflexivity. This reflexivity is based on the triadic structure of the self. Personal identity assumes continuous existence of the same, self-aware structure.

If instead a person thinks a particular semiotic identity is the major basis of his or her personal identity – a mistake that Sartre called "bad faith" – that person is incorrectly assigning a property of the structure to one of its parts. That part may be one of the major statuses, e.g. ethnicity, religion, etc.; it could be some other social trait or even a more personalized psychological trait. They all have the potential to usurp the overall self that contains them.

The *fundamental reflexive channel* of the self is in its structure. This is the channel through which we do all our thinking. All semiotic processes are part of this larger I–you–me reflexive process. If some part of the structure, some identity, begins to masquerade as the whole structure, it is possible for this identity to usurp the structure's reflexive function. But it can do so only at the cost of a drastically diminished reflexivity, highly limited in range, inaccurate in what it reveals and distorted by the biases of its localism and historical specificity. The reflexive process will pass through the particular spectacles of that identity, seeing only what the identity wants and needs to see. This identity will be a fake version of the self, hobbled by the ontological insecurity and other incapacities of R. D. Laing's "divided self" (1959) and Winnicott's "false self" (1960).

The *fundamental source of semiotic power*, like reflexivity, is based in the structure of the self. The I–you–me structure has a kind of centrifugal force, which holds it together and gives it solidarity. This intra-personal solidarity permits continuous reflexive self-awareness, but it is also the source of semiotic power. This power flows through the entire semiotic system: structure, identities, individual semiotic practices, etc. If an identity becomes a functional replacement for the structure and takes over its role, it will also have to supply semiotic power to all the semiotic processes. It cannot do this on its own, however, but only if it somehow borrows semiotic power from the structure. In other words the structure must, to some extent, be complicit with the masquerade. It must subordinate itself to the usurping identity and supply semiotic power in such a way that the identity seems to be supplying the whole system on its own.

When Hegel analyzed the master–slave relationship he was usually talking about something interpersonal, between two free-standing human beings. But at times, in a way that was confusing and never clearly explained, he was talking intra-personally, about the relation between parts of the self (Hegel, 1807/1979, pp. 111–19). To translate his intra-personal fight into my terms, the structure must play the role of slave and the identity that of master. Then the structure must "recognize" the identity as though it were the structure, and of course get no such recognition in return. When this happens the self's semiotic power becomes weak and distorted, much as the reflexive capacity gets distorted when it is usurped by an identity. Semiotic range, accuracy, and creativity become much less than the person is capable of achieving.

Finally I am applying the *main reality* idea (James, 1890/1950, vol. 2, pp. 291–3; Schutz, 1973, pp. 207–59) to the self in a way that is analogous to what it means when applied to the universe of experience. In the latter case it is the rock-bottom reality or world, within which the various special realities or worlds are located. These are the worlds of dreams, intoxicants, religious ecstasy, science, sexual intercourse, creativity, ritual, etc. The

37

main world is the one we wake up to in the morning and within which we locate the special worlds. This reality "contains" the special realities, much as the structure of the self contains its contents.

Inside the self the main reality is the structure. This is the source of all semiotic practice and power, and it defines the contents, including the identities. If some identity usurps the structure's overarching role, it makes a pretense of being the main reality of the self. When a special reality lays claim to being the main one, whether inside or outside the self, the "great chain of being" (Lovejoy, 1936) is broken, and the inherently levelled composition of reality is seen in reverse. The container is seen as contained and the contained as container. But a special reality, inside or out, cannot do the organizing job of a main reality. It is ontologically off and on or unstable and will transmit this instability to the overall ontological field of which it is a part. It will surreptitiously depend on the main reality, just as a usurping identity depends on such factors as the solidarity, reflexive capacity, and semiotic power of the self.

In showing how identities fit into the structure–content distinction, I have been emphasizing the bloated, quasi-cancerous identities that take over the self and saying little about the healthy variety. This is because the structure–content distinction is more clearly illuminated by the former case. Also I have not been distinguishing the social from the more narrowly psychological identities. The former include the social identities of the first chapter, in distorted and unconstrained form. The latter are the classic psychological incapacities: Sartre's bad faith, Kohut's narcissism, the object-relations people's false selves, Erik Erikson's premature closure, and perhaps even some readings of Marx's false consciousness. Of course problems with social identities can cause psychological incapacities of this kind, and the reverse may be true as well, but this is too fine-grained for the purposes of this chapter.

Summary

This chapter went further than chapter 1 in characterizing the nature and unity of classical pragmatism. I emphasized its epistemological differences with British empiricism, showing how these differences – futurism, activism, and everyday life – were in good fit with the semiotic self.

Then I turned to the I–you–me self-structure, coming at it from a variety of angles. First I looked at the container metaphor, rooting it in the distinction between a semiotic triad and a hexad. Then I discussed the Peirce–Mead discrepancy in their models of the internal conversation, examining three assumptions of this discrepancy. In the subsequent examination of Peirce's idea that the "self is a sign," three possible interpretations were discarded, showing that my notion of the structure of the self is the only interpretation that makes sense of Peirce. After that I asked whether all thought, however trivial, has to interpenetrate the structure of the self. Ideas from James and Mead as well as from Peirce were used to establish this point, and the notion of semiotic power was presented to tie these ideas together.

Finally I looked at the notion of identity in relation to the structure–content distinction. Here I emphasized identity disturbances, both social and psychological, in which identities dominate the overall structure of the self. These disturbances create monsters that duplicate all the functions of a self but perform these functions in a distorted, self-destructive manner.

3

The Internal Conversation

This chapter is much more processual than those before and after. It will show, not how the self is constituted, but how it works. It functions as a semiotic process, and this process is the internal conversation. This term includes not only "thought" but any and all the modes of interior meaning. Along with verbal conversation these include sensations, emotions, non-linguistic thoughts, habitual practices, and perhaps even such subtleties as "body language," "tone of voice," and so on. There has been some empirical research on the internal conversation, but the concepts have not been standardized, so I will have to make up my own categories, to some extent, as I go along.

There has not been much theory either. Peirce and Mead are among the major theorists, although their ideas have not been extensively developed. In addition their possible synthesis has been held back by the belief that the two are in agreement on all major points. There must be difference before there can be synthesis. If the two do not differ significantly, the one does not add anything to the other and it is not necessary to have both.

The two professional societies devoted to Peirce and Mead, the Charles S. Peirce Society and the Society for the Study of Symbolic Interaction, reflect this one-or-the-other attitude, as is shown in their journals. The *Transactions of the Charles S. Peirce Society* devotes little space to Mead and *Symbolic Interaction* devotes almost no space to Peirce. The membership lists of 1992 (Peirce society, 230 members; Mead society, 344 members) revealed not a single person who was in both societies. Another purpose of this book, then, is to try to stimulate some dialogue between the Peirce and the Mead scholars.

My goal in this chapter is to describe the internal conversation in such a way that it integrates the properties of the semiotic self and captures the convergence of Peirce and Mead. I want to show how the conversation works as an I–me–you triad, encompassing both Peirce's I–you and Mead's I–me and illustrating the nestedness, ordering, and solidarity properties. In the last chapter I worked mostly in the zone of convergence, i.e. instead of spending my time on the actual thought of Peirce and Mead I dealt with still a third thing, their synthesis. That chapter was not primarily about "what they said" but about what a theory of self would look like if the two thinkers were combined. This combination entailed using some of what they said, ignoring some of what they said, and concocting new concepts by putting together some of what they each said.

In this chapter I will pay more attention to the separate thought of the two theorists. After laying out the two models of the conversation I will put them into a synthesis, based on the strong points of each. This synthesis will match the one I have been working with all along, except that it will concern an area of the theory – the process of internal conversation – that I have not said much about so far.

In other words, although I have used a top-down approach up to now, in this chapter I will shift to a bottom-up. I will lay out the raw data, so to speak – the actual views of Peirce and Mead – and, after examining the data, move "up" to the level of convergence. I will do this because the two positions on the internal conversation and the point-by-point comparison are both rich in conceptualization and important in themselves. Despite their limitations, the two theories are simply too good to be skipped over. When I lay them out, compare them, and put them together, the bottom-up approach will give the synthesis a much more solid base.

I will begin by listing some quotations from Mead and Peirce to show the differences between their positions. Then I will discuss Mead's approach in some detail, showing his systematic views on the I–me relationship. After that I will present Peirce's ideas by showing how they differ from Mead's. Then I will move toward a synthesis, combining but also adding to the relatively programmatic ideas of the two theorists. Having formed the synthesis, I will introduce some texts of internal conversations to show how the model can be tested. Finally, I will touch on two research applications – the "internal monologue" of the modern novel and Wittgenstein's arguments against private language – to test the model in another way.

Illustrations of the Two Models

For Mead, "Thinking is simply the reasoning of the individual, the carrying-on of a conversation between what I have termed the 'I' and the 'me' " (1934, p. 335). "The stuff that goes to make up the 'me' whom the 'I' addressed and whom he observes, is the experience which is induced by this action of the 'I.' If the 'I' speaks, the 'me' hears. If the 'I' strikes, the 'me' feels the blow" (1913/1964 p. 143). Or "I talk to my self, and I remember what I said and perhaps the emotional content that went with it. The 'I' of this moment is present in the 'me' of the next moment. There again I cannot turn around quick enough to catch myself. I become a 'me' in so far as remember what I said" (1934, p. 174). And "It is what you were a second ago that is the 'I' of the 'me' " p. 174).

For Peirce, "All thinking is dialogic in form. Your self of one instant appeals to your deeper self for his assent" (6.338). "Thinking always proceeds in the form of a dialogue – a dialogue between different phases of the ego" (4.6). "Mediation is dialogue. 'I says to myself, says I' is a vernacular account of it; and the most minute and tireless study of logic only fortifies this conception" (Colapietro, 1989, p. xiv). "A person is not absolutely an individual. His thoughts are what he is 'saying to himself,' that is, is saying to that other self that is just coming into life in the flow of time" (5.421). And, "all thought is addressed to a second person or to one's future self as to a second person" (Fisch, 1982, p. xxix).

I will not go into the many issues that come up in these two sets of quotations, for all I want at this point is the I–me vs I–you distinction. The quotations are quite clear about Mead's thought process being exemplified in the former and Peirce's in the latter. This difference will be the starting-point for comparing the two versions of the internal conversation. I will begin with Mead, showing the complexities of his distinction between the I and the me. Once Mead's me has been clarified it will be easier to compare it with Peirce's you.

Mead's I–me comments are scattered throughout his writings, although there are two major sources: "The Social Self" (1913/1964) which is devoted entirely to this topic; and at least 30 pages of his *Mind, Self, and Society* (1934), itself based primarily on his class lectures of 1927 and 1930. In contrast Peirce said little about the I–you relationship. He made short, meaty comments here and there, but he never put these comments together or dealt at all systematically with the question. I will combine his scattered comments and also make inferences from what he did say to what he did not.

Mead on the I–me Distinction

In explaining the relationship of the I to the me, Mead makes a variety of contrasts between the two, each of which gives a somewhat different determination or definition to the me. Mead gets ambiguous and murky at times, although when his writings appeared he was so far ahead of everyone else in describing the internal conversation that the basic content was far more important than the blurred edges. For that matter there is so little theory on this topic to this day that his version remains important.

I will distinguish five ways in which Mead contrasted the I and the me. These dimensions contain properties on which the two poles differ. Then I will go back to the same five dimensions, using Peirce and the I–you scheme. The comparison will show the strengths of each position and suggest how the two sets of strengths might be synthesized.

Neither Peirce nor Mead made the sharp you–me distinction that I have been making. Mead stuck with his me and Peirce with his you, neither sensing the power – or, as far as I can see, even the fact – of the other's insight. For this reason Mead sometimes says things about the me that seem to make more sense if applied to the you. And Peirce makes the opposite mistake.

As pointed out earlier, when the I speaks it has two objects: the direct object or you, and the reflexive object or me. Peirce saw only the direct object and the corresponding I–you conversation. Mead saw only the reflexive object and the I–me conversation. After I lay out the two theories and compare them, their synthesis will be a matter of inserting and dovetailing both dyads into the semiotic triad.

The Me as the Past

A major contrast between the I and the me, as Mead sees it, is in temporal location, the I being in the present and the me in the past. His me is composed of all the former "I"s that moved down the time-line, from future to present to past. They moved from Peirce's you to the Mead–Peirce I to Mead's me. Mead's time-line of consciousness was considerably more focused and person-centered than William James's "stream of consciousness." For Mead, this movement was basically that of a self whose future possibilities became present actualities (and inactualities) and then memories.

Mead's me-as-past connected the me, by way of temporality, to the I. While Peirce's you marks the temporal approach and entry into the I, Mead's me marks the exit. There is an intuitive attractiveness to this formulation, for it fits the structure of time and, in addition, facilitates the way Mead tends to merge the me and the "generalized other," to be discussed later. In addition it fits the way I am defining human present–future–past temporality as a semiotic triad.

The Me as the Object

Another of Mead's contrasts is in the subject–object distinction. The I is a subject, and the me is the corresponding object. Mead is not only talking about language and its grammar but also about the ontological structure of the self. The subject–object relation that the I has to the me is not primarily that of a linguistic sentence but of an extra-linguistic reality, characterized by reflexivity or self-reference. It is the distinction between the knower and the known.

The linguistic parallel, however, is clearly that between the two grammatical "cases," the subjective or nominative and the objective or accusative. Later I will contrast the grammatical and ontological qualities of the inner conversation.

Before proceeding to the next I–me contrast, I must point out a connection between the two already mentioned. The me-as-object will always be in the past by the time the action of the I, e.g. the internal conversation, reaches it. It takes a little time for speech to go from the I to the you and then, reflexively, back to the me. On strictly logical grounds, the subject–object relation is extra-temporal, and the me-as-object is correspondingly different from the me-as-past. But Mead did not use logical relations as his data. The world he was trying to explain was real or ontological, and in addition it was coded in ordinary, culturally embedded language. In this world the subject–object relation is as we experience it, i.e. in time.

A related touch of ambiguity for Mead was his use of the term "me" for the objective pole of reflexivity. For the first personal pronoun the English language not only has a term for the accusative case ("me") but also for the reflexive case ("myself"). The reflexive relation that the I has with itself is not well captured by the I–me distinction, for the term "me" is used only when the self is the object of others. "He hit me." "They hit me." But I did not hit me. "I hit myself." So too, "They know me" but "I know myself." The human infant initially refers to itself from the viewpoint of the other as "me," but gradually internalizes this otherness enough to be able to say "myself."

Of course the I–me distinction had been in use long before Mead's time, and he was merely drawing on an established set of terms. But perhaps another reason why Mead said "me" rather than "myself" was that he was tacitly drawing on something that could function like Peirce's you. It need not have been the future self, but it may at least have been a looping device or reflexive pivot. If this were true, Mead would be conceiving the internal conversation as one in which the I speaks to the me via the point of view of

44

the other. This other can be either free-standing and interpersonally distinct or internalized. In the latter case it would have functional similarities with Peirce's you. Mead was certainly aware that inner sociality and reflexive knowledge were from the point of view of some outsider. But since the closest thing he had to an internalized other was the "generalized other," which he coupled to his me, he had no conceptual slot for a concept that functioned like Peirce's you. The confusion between me and myself seems to be an expression of Mead's not having a solid place for otherness in his self.

Cognitive Availability to the I

Already implied in the discussion is a contrast in cognitive availability or accessibility to the I. The I is cognitively unavailable to itself by reason of the reflexive blind spot. In contrast, Mead's me is cognitively available to the I. In other words the same phase of the self cannot be both subject and object at the same time in the same way. That would not only contradict the reflexive semiotic premises of pragmatism, it would also slide off into Hegel's divinized, reflexively fused self.

Toward the end of chapter 4 I will list several broad philosophical positions on the nature of the intra-personal blind spot. Looking at that issue, now, in a more practical manner, there are several ways the self can get around its own blind spot. One is Mead's temporal lag. The rule about the "same time in the same way" is not violated if a small passage of time is acknowledged. Mead's me-as-past allows of an extremely small passage, such that for all practical purposes one would be conscious of the self as present and therefore seeing into the blind spot.

A second practical way in which we can tip-toe around the blind spot is to observe the self from a "meta" level. In chapter 4 I will refer to the second order as "meta," but this is only one meaning of the term. "Meta" in general is an outer standpoint, an observational perch outside an arena or "space," from which the latter can be observed. This standpoint presumably provides some cognitive resource not available within the space or field itself. With this resource the meta should be able to say something new about the field, something not visible from within.

Second order or retrospective thoughts about thoughts do this by revealing things that were unnoticed when the thoughts passed through at the first order. Gödel's meta-arithmetic, a cultural or mathematical kind of meta, revealed semantic properties not visible from the arithmetical level of the first order. And the meta self-awareness that observes the blind spot allows one to look at the self of the present as though one were looking through the eyes of another person. It is the otherness of this notion of meta

45

that permits quasi-penetration of the blind spot. One sees one's present self, not from within but from without, via a position of otherness. This time the rule about "same time in the same way" is circumvented, not by a distinction of "time" but one of "way," for in seeing oneself from a different point of view one is doing so in a different way. I do not think Mead explicitly used this way of getting around the blind spot, but I think he did so in practice or logic-in-use.

Of course a meta strategy, though eliminating the first-order blind spot, merely lifts it to the next higher (meta) level. In certain formal arguments, such as the one Gödel constructed, this upward sliding of the blind spot is extremely important. But in the ordinary language of the everyday world we do not keep ascending meta levels. Rather, if a problem can be solved at the first-order level, even if only by shuffling it to a higher level, it is for all practical purposes solved.

Finally the blind spot can be neutralized by mixing two time schemes – the objective/physical and the subjective/psychological – in the same reflexive act. In other words the observing self can act in the felt present – which is actually a band or swatch of time – while observing itself as though that self were in the knife-edge present. This allows the observing self to surround and encompass the present. In other words the known self is simultaneously in the objective past and in the subjective present. What I will later call Kant's "eavesdropping" notion of self-awareness can be construed in this manner.

These three means of access to the blind spot all fill it in and, in ordinary circumstances, more or less unblind it. They also all three operate in the internal conversation to give us the impression that we have complete access to ourselves. Nevertheless, on strictly analytic grounds and in the absence of the three mechanisms, the blind spot remains completely and permanently blind. Peirce's you, it will be shown, has a quite different relation to the blind spot and to the I.

Freedom vs Determinism in the Two Poles

Another of Mead's contrasts is between the degree of determinism in the I and the me. The I is spontaneous and free, while the me is determined and unfree. Since the me, being in the past, does not act, there is a sense in which it is neither determined nor free but simply extraneous to this issue. The me was free when it, or part of it, was an I. But it had its moment of choice and it then became congealed into the inactive, unchangeable past. In contrast the I is the agent of all action, and, Mead argues, it is always spontaneous or free.

Earlier I interpreted the freedom of the I as a primarily cognitive

46

capacity. The I can choose to define a situation, regardless of habit or precedent, in a new way, thereby making a particular decision inevitable. The me, since it cannot do anything, cannot do this. In addition the definitions and choices that have gone into the me tend to have been repeated and hardened into relatively settled orientations or habits. But the I is the locus of original cognitive definition and therefore freedom of choice.

For the person, i.e. the I, making the decision, the act of choice is for all practical purposes in the blind spot. The cognitive definition was not. That went on over time. But the decision, once it becomes a decision, is confined to the present. The chooser or I is, by virtue of the structure of reflexivity, blind to itself. It cannot observe itself choose, either as neutral spectator or as morally binding watchdog. On this view the I is free, not only because of its underlying cognitive freedom but also because of secrecy. The I is hidden from itself and therefore cannot eliminate its own freedom (try as it may).

When I contrast Peirce's you with Mead's me, the issue of freedom will reappear, for, as we will see, both poles of Peirce's conversational dyad are active and free.

Relation to the Generalized Other

For Mead the me is committed to and merged with the generalized other, the internalized norms of the community or society. This concept is roughly similar to Freud's super-ego or Durkheim's collective consciousness, but it was not well developed by Mead. It would seem to include not only the moral rules, as internalized by the individual, but also the cognitive. The latter in turn would include both the formal rules of language, Saussure's "langue," and those of body language and emotional expression. Mead tended to have an over-socialized individual, whose generalized other was a close replica of the community's rules, themselves pictured as unrealistically consensual. In addition Mead tended to blur the moral and the cognitive, under such imprecise formulas as "response" and "role taking" (Habermas, 1981/1987, p. 23).

The weight of Mead's generalized other, like that of Durkheim's collective consciousness, is toward the moral end, with cognitivity the less emphasized category. Accordingly both thinkers tended to picture deviance or rule-breaking as moral. The rule-breaker was the immoral person, subject to moral and perhaps legal sanctions from without and guilt from within. There is no clear position in either theorist for the cognitive rule-breaker. This form of deviance is not immorality but something quite different. If it is merely a misapplication of a rule, the deviance is ignorance and error. But if it is the outright substitution of new cognitive rules and not just the misapplication of the old ones, the deviance is on the mental health gradient.

The moral rule-breaker suffers the sanctions, internal and external, of the sinner or criminal. The cognitive rule-breaker suffers different sanctions: internally, anxiety and disorganization; externally, depersonalization and possible confinement to a mental hospital.

I am emphasizing the relatively hidden, cognitive aspect of the generalized other because it bears on the I–me contrast. For Mead the me is allied and committed to the generalized other. The I, being spontaneous, is free of it, free to violate the moral rules. But I think it is less free to violate the cognitive rules. These seem deeper and more fundamental than the moral. In John Searle's sense (1969, pp. 33–42), the former are the "constitutive" rules and the latter form one strand of the "regulatory" rules. Mead's me is allied with both sets of rules, despite his having stressed the moral. In other words the I differs from the me in relation to the moral aspect of the generalized other, but less so in relation to the cognitive. Of course in the last analysis the I is cognitively as well as morally free, the former underlying the latter. But this cognitive freedom is one of redefining situations and dissenting from old definitions, not one of disobeying the rules of logic and language. Cognitive freedom works within those rules.

Peirce's you is also pictured as committed to the rules of the community, to one's better and deeper self, as Peirce puts it. However this you differs from the me, both by being in the future and by being the incipient point of action. Therefore its relationship to the generalized other is more complex than that of Mead's me, a point to which I will return.

Having examined five ways in which Mead contrasts the I and the me (temporal location, subject–object position, cognitive accessibility, freedom vs determinism, and relation to the generalized other), I will now contrast Mead's me and Peirce's you, a comparison which will put Mead's theory of thought in a different light. This will also get us closer to testing the Peirce–Mead, I–you–me synthesis, using the bottom-up approach I mentioned earlier.

The Peirce–Mead Contrast

If the two thinkers are compared on the five dimensions, Mead's thought can set the agenda for examining Peirce's. Since Peirce was so laconic and scattered on this topic, the only workable way of organizing a comparison is by using Mead's more articulate categories as the agenda.

Temporal Position

Peirce's you is in the future in a more unambiguous way than Mead's me is in the past. Ontologically, in real time, Mead's me is clearly in the past, but logically, as a member of the subject–object dyad, it has no position in time. In contrast, Peirce's you is not only ontologically but also, by Peirce's definition, logically in the future. This logical difference is possible because, grammatically, the object status of the you is not reflexive, like the me, but direct and "linear."

In this respect Peirce's internal dialogue, in contrast to Mead's, is more clearly isomorphic with interpersonal dialogue, i.e. more like two, free-standing conversationalists. In fact when Peirce said "all thought is addressed to a second person or to one's future self as to a second person" he used "you" in two senses: as the future self and as some other person. This distinction will become important later, when I expand the structure of the conversation to include what Goethe called "guests."

The Subject–Object Contrast

In contrast to Mead's me, Peirce's you is the object of his I in a completely different way. The you is in the second "person," in the grammatical sense, whereas the me (or "myself") is in the first. Both the you and the me can be the object for the I, but not in the same manner. The me, being in the same grammatical person as the I, is necessarily a semantically reflexive object. But the you, being in another, grammatical person, is a non-reflexive object, much as another person might be such an object.

The limits on the objectification of the you are also noticeable on another grammatical dimension. The word "you" can be in two cases in English, serving both as nominative and accusative second person singular (and plural). Unlike the first person, which has distinct terms ("I" and "me") for these cases, the second person stays with the same one. It is simultaneously in both cases, subjective and objective. And it is so both grammatically (in *langue*) and in concrete inner speech (*parole*).

For the I, the you is often in the objective case. But in itself – facing you, so to speak – it is a subject. This is never true for the me or myself; neither can be a subject. And the you can be addressed by the I in either case. If, in an anguished moment, we say to ourselves "When will you stop?," the you is nominative and subjective. But if we command the you and say, "I will stop you!," we have put it into the objective case. Thus the word can be in either case, depending on whether it is being looked at from the I or in itself. And even from the I it can be in either. These multiple roles and oscillations make the you an extremely blurred signifier in the internal conversation.

Another interesting feature of the I–you relationship is that, lacking (intra-subjective) reflexivity, it also lacks the reflexive blind spot of the I–me or I–myself. The I can perceive the you, as can the you the I, without reflexive distance. This means that the you can "see" the I more closely than the I can see itself. This privileged vision, which is available to both the intra- and the interpersonal you, includes a glimpse into the conversational partner's blind spot and freedom, as mentioned earlier.

Cognitive Availability

Since the you is not in a reflexive relation with the I, it has a different kind of cognitive availability than the me has to the I. There is no looping here, no distancing. The you is available in a frontal, linear manner. Moreover, just as the you is available to the I, the I is available to the you.

A helpful metaphor is Schutz's "we experience" (Schutz, 1932/1967, pp. 167–72). Schutz points out that in an immediate, face-to-face relationship the two parties share the temporal present. This is equivalent to saying the relation is I-to-I or subject-to-subject. From Schutz's viewpoint, your own I is not in a blind spot for the other person, even though it is blind to itself. In a sense you get closer to your own I through the other person than you do in your own self-awareness. You see yourself in the other by way of two acts: that person's perception of you and your perception of that person, neither of which entails the blind spot of reflexivity.

The I–you relationship has some of the features of Schutz's "we experience," particularly directness and linearity. The metaphor has limits, however, because the I and the you do not, in a structural as opposed to a conversational sense, share the temporal present (although they almost do, as the you elides, temporally, into the place of the I).

Freedom and Determinism

The you will, in an instant, act. It is moving down the time-line to the present, at which time it will become the I. When it then acts, it will do so with the freedom that characterizes all action. The I–you relation, then, is between two free agents, the former free now, and the latter in a moment.

In contrast the I–me relation is between freedom and determinism, or, more accurately, action and inaction. The I–me relation is not the confrontation of two free agents, but of present and former freedom. The I–you relationship is therefore characterized by a high degree of contingency. Both agents are free, and this mutual freedom multiplies the uncertainty of the outcome. Mead was impressed by the unpredictability of the I, even to ourselves. He thought this was due entirely to the I's ability to disobey the me and the closely related generalized other. Earlier I argued that the I's power to construct cognitive reality, to redefine situations, is the actual mechanism by which the I can break with the me. Now, in the light of Peirce, I am adding the quasi-negotiative relationship between the I and the you as an additional explanation of human freedom, although this negotiation probably influences cognitive definitions.

Relation to the Generalized Other

Peirce clearly meant his you to be in a sympathetic relation to something much like Mead's generalized other. As he says:

> When one reasons, it is that critical self that one is trying to persuade; and all thought whatsoever is a sign, and is mostly in the nature of language. The second thing to remember is that a man's circle of society (however widely or narrowly this phrase may be understood), is a sort of loosely compacted person, in some respects of higher rank than the person in an individual organism (5.421).

Peirce's you clearly has a resemblance to Mead's generalized other, for it is "critical self" and a "loosely compacted person" (Rochberg-Halton, 1986, p. 35). Combining Mead and Peirce, then, would imply that the generalized other is closely related, not only to the me but also to the you. Dividing this rule-bearing function between past and future (me and you) asks less of each and seems more true to life.

In addition, Mead's generalized other is not only the (cognitive and moral) rule-carrier. Although Mead is not sufficiently explicit about this, it is also a reflexing lever or looping device, as the word "other" suggests. It is internalized otherness in the sense of the generic ("generalized") or perhaps average human being. As Mead saw it, this generalized other permits us to have internal reflexivity, for it functions, not only as a regulative principle, but also as a cognitive looking-glass. Peirce's you, which is also a reflexive lever or pathway, takes some of the looping burden off Mead's generalized other.

To summarize, if Peirce and Mead are combined, the functions of the generalized other can be spread – moral regulation, cognitive regulation, reflexive looping, and conversational medium – into both past–me and future–you.

Mead's me and Peirce's you, then, both seem to be the intra-subjective

51

conformists, the more attached to conscience, established rules, and the generalized other. The I, being spontaneous, is the non-conformist and innovator. Yet if we look at the me–you contrast dynamically, there is an important difference. Unlike the me, which had its moment of freedom, the you is approaching and anticipating the moment of decision, which will have to be exercised with spontaneity and freedom.

The second time-frame, the felt or "specious" present, is one source of this anticipation, for in that context the you is already merging with the I. In addition, there will soon be the instant, one might almost say the rite of passage, of entering the present. This will be a moment of becoming, of being you-cum-I. The you, in other words, is anticipating the moment when it will no longer be the "critical self," but the responsible, acting self. This anticipatory freedom distinguishes the you from the me and makes the former's attachment to the generalized other a matter of diminishing commitment.

With Mead's and Peirce's models on the five dimensions thus compared, it seems obvious that Peirce's formulation, however sketchily worked out, solves several of Mead's problems. On each of the five dimensions Peirce's dialogical model has the greater logical simplicity and elegance. In addition, his formulation entails fewer problems in the relations among the dimensions. On the other hand, Mead's model captures unique aspects of the conversation, particularly its reflexivity and blind spots. The two models capture distinct zones or aspects of the conversation, and they fit together quite comfortably, as previously mentioned.

The bottom-up approach of this chapter is producing a Peirce–Mead synthesis much like the top-down version of the first two chapters, although the present approach has more detail. Additional detail and "feel" for the internal conversation can be captured if the various second-order mechanisms, mentioned in chapter 2, are considered.

I have already mentioned the hybridization of the two time orders: subjective and objective. Both the past or me and the future or you can be placed in the slot of the present or I by this time-mixing. The objective future and past can both be placed into the speaker's podium of the present by including them in the subjective or specious present. This is a matter of stretching the magnitude of the felt present from knife-edge to saddle-block and possibly to indefinitely large widths beyond that. It is conceivable that some aspects of a person's felt present, e.g. an unresolved childhood trauma, could even encompass his or her entire lifetime.

The second or meta order offers another set of mechanisms for placing the past or future into the speaking position of the present. An ordinary re-examination of a past thought, placing what had been a first-order experience into the second order, will have the effect of placing a non-present reality into the present. Let us take the example of a past thought we would like to understand more deeply, but which came and went quite rapidly. First the memory has to recapture that thought. Then it has to be re-thought, possibly in a variety of ways, in the temporal position of the present. When this is done, the past or me is, via its being lifted into the second order, occupying the position of the I.

When this happens, it is not the same as the indirect, reflexive addressing of the me. Now the me has been transformed from past to quasi-present and the consequent I–me conversation is direct and linear, as though this (second-order) me were a (first-order) you. Mead's idea that the internal conversation is primarily between the I and the me makes the most sense if this conversation is conceptualized at the second order. In other words the first-order conversation is primarily between the I and the you, a point which Mead's scheme could not explain. But the second-order conversation can be between the I and me, the latter speaking in the role of I and hearing in the role of you. Peirce's scheme is best explained at the first order and Mead's at the second.

It is also possible to permit the you of the future to occupy, at the second order, the position of the present. Of course the you will eventually become the present, in a way that the me never will. Because of this all that need be done is to speed things up a little by expanding the specious present to let the future become the present a bit early. But this can also be done in a second ordering, much as I just described for the me. When this happens it seems to be the I putting words into the mouth of the you, like a ventriloquist, and, in that manner, allowing the you to speak in a second-order present.

Thus the you can occupy the podium and speak in three ways: simply by eventually becoming the I, in the normal passage of time, and saying whatever it has to say, presumably in response to what has been just said to it; by being placed in the specious present; and by having words put into its mouth by the role-playing of the I and uttering these words in a second-order manner.

My purpose in this chapter has been to lay out the separate theories of Mead and Peirce, compare them and then begin to integrate them. But I have also been searching for ways of exploring the internal conversation as such, apart from what Mead and Peirce said about it. The differences between these two thinkers point to the more general "property space" they were trying to say something about. In the next section I will add participants and agencies to the conversation and attempt to integrate this enlarged pool of participants with the five dimensions.

The Larger Structure of the Internal Conversation

Visitors

I will use Goethe's concept of the guest, but change the term to "visitors." When Goethe explained how he came to write *The Sorrows of Young Werther* (1774) as a series of letters, he said (speaking of himself in the first person):

> Accustomed to pass his time most pleasantly in society, he changed even solitary thought into social converse, and this in the following manner: He had the habit, when he was alone, of calling before his mind any person of his acquaintance. This person he entreated to sit down, walked up and down by him, remained standing before him, and discoursed with him on the subject he had in mind. To this the person answered as occasion required, or by the ordinary gestures signified his assent or dissent – in which every man has something peculiar to himself. The speaker then continued to carry out further that which seemed to please the guest, or to qualify and define more closely that of which he disapproved; and, finally, was polite enough to give up his own notion. (1811–32/1974 p. 205).

Let us use Goethe's "guest" as the entry point for conceptualizing any third parties, so to speak, who might become participants in the internal conversation. Peirce referred to this conversational role as "you," in one of his two senses of the word. Mead was also quite aware of the visitor position. As he says:

> It is also to be noted that this response to the social conduct of the self may be in the role of another – we present his arguments in imagination and do it with his intonations and gestures and even perhaps with his facial expression. In this way we play the roles of all our group (1913/1964, p. 146).

The inclusion of visitors into the conversation complicates both Mead's I–me and Peirce's I–you models. Do we now have a three- (or four-)way conversation, or is the I merely swinging from dyad to dyad, or pole to pole? And how does the visitor position fit on the five dimensions previously discussed? I will save these questions for later in this section, and now merely make a closer inspection of the visitor concept.

Goethe's guests were treated with politeness, ceremony, and deference.

54

This can hardly be the only kind of visitor. More generally we could make a distinction between what might be called "temporary" and "permanent" visitors. Goethe's guests were clearly transients to the conversation, carefully introduced and equally carefully dismissed. Mead's others, judging from the preceding quotation, include more important and forceful visitors. Mead's I speaks for his visitors, replete with "intonations and gestures and even perhaps with his facial expression." These visitors may also be temporary, but they are taken seriously, and if the I defers or becomes convinced by one of them, it will be with greater sincerity than in Goethe's drawing-room conversations.

But neither Goethe nor Mead captured the notion of permanent visitors, i.e. people who are continuously present and available to the internal conversation. It seems likely that early-life others, particularly parents, have a privileged position in the conversation. The ideas of "object relations" psychoanalysis (Greenberg and Mitchell, 1983) can be drawn upon here, for this theory attempts to explain the sense in which the self is based on the incorporation of others. The permanent visitors are always available for explicit conversation, and in addition they are foundational to whatever generalized other one may have internalized. They speak both explicitly, as visitors to the internal forum, and implicitly, as sedimented into the regulatory aspects of the self.

The visitors are in a range of roles, from superficial to profound, and when we later look at the visitor position in relation to the five dimensions, this variation will be kept in mind.

The Unconscious

We now have the conscious conversation pretty well populated. The self has three roles: I, me, and you. At times Mead seems to regard the generalized other as a distinct role, but it is so closely connected to the me, for Mead, and to the you, for Peirce, that I will treat it as an extension of those two roles. In addition to the I, me, and you, all non-self or "other" parties are covered by the notion of "visitor."

The classical pragmatists stuck pretty much to the conscious mind, and when Freud's ideas began to reach America, the pragmatists resisted serious confrontation with the notion of the unconscious (although Peirce occasionally used the term).

Nevertheless it would seem incomplete indeed to confine the model to the four conscious roles. Even though the unconscious is, by definition, unavailable to consciousness and therefore to complete analysis, it should be incorporated in some way into the model.

The pragmatists' confinement to consciousness divorced them, not only from the unconscious, but also from border-line, pre- or semi-conscious states. When we are with others, the self is usually in an alert, interpersonally conscious, outwardly oriented stance. When alone, the self may become more inward and "slack." And there are degrees of slackness. The pragmatists' conscious reasoning is the least slack, the state of sleep and dreams the most, and in between are intermediary forms.

Consciously directed "imaginative rehearsals" are much less slack than relaxed daydreams or the yielding to James's stream of consciousness. When Mead applied introspection or the second order to his own internal conversation, he spoke of "asking himself how he could undertake to do this, that, or the other, chiding himself for his shortcoming or pluming himself upon his achievements" (1913/1964, p. 142). The "asking" and the "chiding" sound rather taut, but the "pluming" comes as a much more passive, yielding state. Relaxed daydreams rapidly become much more spontaneous and uncontrolled than the more problem-oriented imaginative rehearsals or the soul-searching chidings.

The pluming type of daydream can easily become the grandiose fantasy, suggesting that unconscious needs and forces have now entered the conversation. In addition, daydreams can elide into frightening paranoid fantasies, so gripping that one must forcibly remove the "suspension of disbelief" from these little dramas. The semi-conscious states, then, are already operating in a zone less structured than the I–me–you–visitor system, drawing the analysis toward some notion of the unconscious.

When we get below the semi-conscious into the unconscious proper, the analysis of the internal conversation clearly needs additional technical concepts. I do not, for example, see why the theory of dreams, imperfect as it is, should not be incorporated into the model, for dreams too are internal conversations, both with visitors and with the self (Domhoff, 1993). Dreams present interesting data for the study of the conversation. People often remember them the next day, particularly the "lucid" kind, in which people are aware they are dreaming while they are dreaming (Gackenbach and LaBerge, 1988). In addition people sometimes talk out loud in their dreams, and researchers have, with tape recorders, captured this "sleep talk" (Arkin, 1981).

I am not going to attempt to fit the unconscious systematically into the model. This would be premature. Lacan has concepts for doing this, e.g. his self vs ego distinction, but these depend on his dubious mirror theory, which I will discuss in chapter 7. Instead, I can only assert that the unconscious belongs in the model and make preliminary attempts to find a position for this agency.

In this discussion the unconscious can be viewed in two ways: as the relatively submerged member and pole of the conscious and semi-conscious; and as a separate conversation, distinct from the conscious one and operating in its own, inner arena. In the unconscious zone, especially in dreams, the unconscious has its own internal conversations, replete with its own separate poles. But in the conscious zone the unconscious seems to operate, not as a multiplicity of interacting persons, but as a single (if multi-faceted) person. This "person" speaks in a unique language, perhaps characterized by something like Lacan's metonomy and metaphor, but it does so in different ways at different points along the consciousness–unconsciousness gradient.

In this discussion of the unconscious I am confining my attention to non-psychotics. Psychotics present additional problems, such as explaining how delusions and hallucinations fit into the internal conversation model, or how multiple personalities relate to the I–you–me–guest scheme. I think the Peirce–Mead model can go a long way toward explaining the peculiarities of the psychotic internal conversation, but to attempt to do this here would take me too far afield and beyond the scope of this book. (See Hurlburt, 1990, for an empirical comparison of normal and schizo-phrenic internal experience).

Profiles of the Six Positions

We now have six positions, participants, poles, agencies, or roles in the conversation: the I, me, you, permanent visitors, temporary visitors, and the unconscious. And from the first section of this chapter we have five dimensions or variables that can be designated for each of the six positions. Throughout the discussion I have been referring to the grammatical variable of "person" as a background resource. But each of the six participants must have a personal status, so I will add this item to the existing five dimensions. This gives a six-by-six layout as represented in table 3.1.

This table is not meant to capture the content of the conversations (which, with its various linguistic, extra-linguistic, and emotional aspects of meaning, is another matter) but its "structure," in however preliminary and exploratory a form. It concerns the syntax of the conversation rather than the semantics, the latter comprising both what can be said and what, in any given conversation, is actually said.

Table 3.1 merely summarizes the discussion of this chapter so far. The first three variables – person, tense, and case – are taken from language, though they are not merely linguistic. These linguistic terms are metaphors for describing a set of non-linguistic "agencies." We tend to describe the self both with and as words, but this does not mean the words are the self, or that the self is only words. (See chapter 2 for my description of the self as

	Me	I	You	(Temporary) Visitors	(Permanent) Visitors	The Unconscious
Person	First	First	Second	Second	Second	Third
Time/tense	Past (and atemporal)	Present	Future	Present	Present	Atemporal
Case	Objective	Subjective	Subjective and object-ive	Subjective and objective	Objective	All
Freedom/ determinism	Unfree	Free	Unfree-cum-free	More free than permanent visitors	Unfree	Determined
Relation to generalized other	Allied	Detached	Diminishing alliance	Less allied than permanent visitors	Allied and constitutive	Free
Cognitive availability to the I	As object	Blind spot	As co-subject	As co-subject	As co-subject but sedimented into generalized other	Veiled by semi-porous language barrier

Table 3.1   Structure of the internal conversation: participants by profiles

a "nested word" or sign, showing the complexity of the self's relation to words.)

The oversimplified idea that the self is nothing more than ordinary words is the post-structural position, spearheaded by Benveniste's and Wittgenstein's purely linguistic "I." I will criticize this view in chapter 7. My position is that the internal conversation is "structured like" rather than being identical with language. The I–you–me elements of this conversation and their interrelations are, within limits, isomorphic with linguistic qualities, but they are nevertheless distinct from these qualities, existing at another ontological level. This is my previously discussed distinction between the structure and content of the self.

Many of the determinations expressed in the 36 boxes of table 3.1 could be disputed. The advantage of the table, however, is that it poses questions – 36, in fact – in an area of research that needs clear questions. The Mead–Peirce comparison underlies this table, but it does not exhaust it. All those thinkers attempted to show was that thought is dialogical in form. They did not attempt the more general task of picturing the overall structure of the dialogue (or trialogue).

The unconscious is more loosely connected to the table than the five conscious positions are. The traits that I assign to the unconscious – that it is in the third person, atemporal, in all cases, determined, unattached to the generalized other, and available only through a semi-porous language barrier – could all be disputed or modified. The inclusion of the unconscious in the table is meant to dramatize the problem of locating that participant in the inner conversation.

Table 3.1, then, is meant as a tool or methodological device for exploring the workings of the internal conversation. In the next section I will discuss the way empirical research might be used to test the model.

Empirical Research on the Model

Content of the Conversation

Before looking at some empirical examples of the internal conversation, let me further distinguish the structure, as described in table 3.1, from the content. Being syntactical, the table is not substantive or content-related. The content itself, or we could say the process, is quite complex. When people explore the content of the inner conversation in the modern, introspective novel they report it in words, although James Joyce began to show the linguistic complexity of these words. Emotion is often a significant component in any conversation, including internal ones. When people audibly externalize their internal conversations – as do young children, people talking in their sleep, psychotics, and ordinary absent-minded folk – there are noticeable emotional components. Perhaps even the notion of non-verbal meaning and body language, treated metaphorically, would be useful for looking at the internal conversation. Vygotsky's analyses of children's egocentric speech, which he took to be the precursor of the inner conversation, are especially insightful on the characteristics of the "code" (Wertsch, 1985, pp.121–8).

Mead's conversation of non-symbolic gestures (1934, p. 63) would seem to apply internally as well as interpersonally. When the internal conversation turns overwhelmingly emotional, for example in a state of intense grief or fear, the conversation of gestures may become animal-like and pre-significant, with the meaning of the gestures available only to the receiving pole of the dialogue, i.e. to one's "you."

Another feature of the content of the conversation is that it varies according to the language of the person in question. Toulmin (1978) points out that the language of the self varies, for instance from English to French to Greek to Japanese, affecting the way the six dimensions might be applied to given individuals. This makes for both syntactic and semantic variation by language, culture, and sub-culture, perhaps including gender. All these questions are being ignored in this chapter, since I am primarily laying out a structure, although to be a sturdy structure it would have to contribute to answering these questions.

Research on the Conversation

Up to now I have laid out Mead's and Peirce's theories of the internal conversation, compared them, combined them, and added some ideas of my own. The result is what might be called the developed Peirce–Mead model. When I now talk about doing research on the conversation, I am talking about the full-scale model, not just its earlier versions.

Let me list the possible sources of data. Earlier I mentioned the cases of people audibly externalizing their internal conversations: little children, ordinary people who talk out loud to themselves, and people speaking during sleep. These data all can and have been captured in texts. There are also the introspective, or retrospective, reports of people on their own internal conversations. This has been a major data source in recent psychological research on "inner experience" (Singer and Kolligian, 1987). Finally there are the internal conversations in literature – dramas, poems, short stories, and novels – about which I will say more at the end of this chapter.

To give an example of how empirical research might proceed and how it tests the model, I will look at six bits of data. The tools for this analysis will be table 3.1 above, the modes of time (specious vs knife-edge), and the brute force of the texts themselves. To a lesser extent I will also draw on two concepts that will be more fully explained in chapters 4 and 5: first vs second order and intra-subjective solidarity.

The first text is from an absent-minded clerk, talking aloud as she went about her job. She said, "I'd better get the DPOs for the new supplies. Oh no! We're not using those any more." There was a touch of anxiety in the monologue, but I will stick to the words. Who is talking to whom, in terms of the six-place list of agencies offered in table 3.1? The first part of the text, the "I'd better get," sounds like the I talking, in standard first-order fashion, to Peirce's you. It is an imperative, telling the future self what to do. Of course it is also speaking, tacitly and reflexively, to itself as me.

But who is talking to whom in the second half of the utterance? Something has changed. It seems as though the you, previously addressed, has moved down the time-line and is now in the place of the I, i.e. the place where speech and action can originate. The former you, now I, is saying something to someone. But to whom? I think it is simultaneously addressing the me and the (new) you. It is answering the agency that was, just a moment ago, the I, and is now the me-as-past. That agency had recommended getting the DPOs (department purchase orders), but the clerk remembered that the DPOs were now an obsolete procedure, and she (her new I) informed the me of that. The second part of the utterance is responding to the first part, and it is thus "talk about talk" or "thought about thought." Accordingly, as I will explain more fully in the next chapter, it is in the second order. The I is addressing the me, or, to say the same thing, the interpretant is responding to the sign, in a second-order manner.

But the I is also talking to the you, the future self, telling it not to bother with the DPOs. This second aspect of the communication is in the first order. Thus in the second part of this text the I is concurrently in both first and second orders. It is how the clerk was able to address both her past-me and her future-you.

Notice that her answering of the me was not the reflexive addressing of the me that the I always does. I have not mentioned that yet. It was a direct, i.e. non-reflexive, communication to the me that had just spoken. Through a second ordering and perhaps also the use of the specious present that me seems to have been addressed as though it were still the I.

Let us turn to a text from Husserl, where he reports an internal conversation to argue against its validity, his phenomenological theory having disallowed the meaningfulness of such conversations.

One of course speaks, in a certain sense, even in soliloquy, and it is certainly possible to think of oneself as speaking, and even as speaking to oneself, as, e.g. when someone says to himself: "You have gone wrong, you can't go on like that" (1891/1970, pp. 279–80).

Confining myself to the last ten words, how does this text, again two-part, fit the model? The first part of the statement – "You have gone wrong" – sounds like the I addressing the me, both as past and as object. This statement is reflexive, not only in the first-order sense in which all inner speech is reflexive to the me. In addition and more pointedly it is reflexive in the second-order sense, for the speaker is placing the past into the place or mode of the present. These wrong acts, which are in the past, are addressed directly. In this way Husserl can address his me as "you."

But in the second part, "You can't go on like that," the speaker seems to have shifted to the first-order you, for now the I is addressing the future self and instructing it to mend its ways. This text resembles the previous one by the clerk, in which the I shifts or syncopates from dyad to dyad, although Husserl's shift reverses that of the clerk. We see here how the I can shift its polar orientation from sentence to sentence, and possibly even in mid-sentence. There may even be time lags and overlaps in these shifts, allowing the I to carry on two conversations at once.

The third example was tape recorded while an experimental subject, a college English student, was sleeping (Arkin, 1981, p. 413).

David – I day David that you – that's you that day – dated – day – dravid – dave dravid about 25 or 30 noked naked day dreams – the second dream tie it all up – you kept bouncing them on – you kept bouncing them on and on as if you had a regular meter.

Most sleep talk is shorter than this text, often a single word, and frequently too imprecise or mumbly to understand. In this case the experimenter, Arthur Arkin, whispered the subject's name ("David") into the subject's ear, and, in his sleep, the subject uttered the words above. Arkin sometimes awakened the subjects to ask what they had been dreaming, but in this case he did not, so all we have is the text.

It sounds as though David is addressing himself in the past, his me-as-past, since he uses the past tense. This would make the interpretation an I–me, second-order conversation, as in the first part of Husserl's utterance. But given the slipperiness of this text, that interpretation seems shaky. We cannot be sure it is David's "I" talking and not his unconscious, or even some blend of the two. Also it is not certain the speaker is addressing David at all.

The interesting thing about the text is rather in the playing on words, especially the subject's own name, and the general incoherence (to the conscious listener, anyway), suggesting the primary process code of the unconscious. This extreme looseness of sleep talk suggests that all internal conversation may have characteristics of looseness that are difficult to spot (e.g. non-verbal dimensions, emotionality, etc.), though not to the extreme it reaches in the unconscious zone.

Next are two bits of "talking out loud" from young children, both of which show the relatively unstructured, labile quality of conversation at this age. The first is from Charles Horton Cooley's three-year-old son, who still had a vivid imaginary companion. As Cooley tells us, "Once when he slipped down on the floor he was heard to say, 'Did you tumble down? No, I did' " (Cooley, 1922/1964, p. 89).

In the second example:

> Thirty-month-old Julia finds herself alone in the kitchen while her mother is on the telephone. A bowl of eggs is on the table. An urge is experienced by Julia to make scrambled eggs. She reaches for the eggs, but now the claims of reality are experienced with equal strength. Her mother would not approve. The resulting conflict within the ego is experienced as "I want" and "No you mustn't" and the case for both sides is presented and a decision arrived at within the moment. When Julia's mother returns to the kitchen, she finds her daughter cheerfully plopping eggs on the linoleum and scolding herself sharply for each plop, "NoNoNo. Mustn't dood it. NoNoNo. Mustn't dood it!" (Fraiberg, 1959, p. 135).

Cooley's son, referred to as "R," and Fraiberg's little Julia are saying things that do not fit, or rather mix up, the categories of table 3.1. An outside observer might say "R" (full name: Rutger Horton Cooley) is addressing his me, the self that just slipped on the floor. Still being in the imaginary playmate stage, however, he initially thinks that the playmate (a "visitor") fell. Then he corrected himself. Presumably the playmate (though "R" had several) will eventually settle into "R's" (Peircean) you.

There are some uncertainties in this Cooley example. Professor Cooley thought, incorrectly, that all people have imaginary companions in their early childhood and that conversation with these visitors eventually becomes the standard internal conversation. For Cooley the imaginary companion experience was an indispensable stage in normal human development. It is now known that most people do not have childhood imaginary companions, so Cooley was wrong (and, so to speak, Mead was right) about the origins of conscious processes. But it is possible that Cooley promoted his son's imaginary companions by suggesting (and rewarding) them. It is also possible that "R" was putting his Dad on! Still, these uncertainties are more refined than we need for the example.

Julia seems to be addressing not her me or you but her I, and doing so in the voice of her mother. Julia is getting her mother, a permanent visitor, mixed up with herself, presumably the part that will become the regulatory me. Eventually the mother will settle into Julia's generalized other, as well as being a permanent and, sometimes, temporary visitor. It is too bad that Fraiberg, or whoever walked in on the egg-plopping incident, did not record the facial expression. Julia may actually have been attempting to look like her mother, as Mead suggested in an earlier quotation about taking the role of the visitor.

Since Julia seems to be addressing her I, she is in her blind spot. Earlier in this chapter I listed several ways in which people might, indirectly, see into their blind spots. Julia suggests a new one. As Schutz said, others can encounter our I directly, though we ourselves cannot. Julia is getting into her blind spot by stepping into her mother's shoes

The final example is from the anthropologist John L. Caughey. A young waitress is reporting ("retrospecting") on her thoughts while walking to work.

"*Only eight minutes, takes five to change. I've got to book* (hurry)." Imagery: A disgustingly filthy locker room. Visions of me running from table to kitchen table. Sounds. Forks and knives scraping plates, customers yelling over each other. "*I have to make money. At least it's not as bad as last summer.*" Memory imagery: A tiny dumpy diner. Visions of me sweating. Sensations of being hot. Visions of thirty marines eating and drinking. Sounds: country music on a blaring juke box. "*Miss, miss.*" "*I'll be right there, just a minute please.*" Sensations of burning my arms in a pizza oven. Visions of dropping glasses. Sounds: Glass breaking, manager yelling, marines cheering. "*Oh God, get me out of here.*" Sensation: Cringe, humiliation. "*I hate waitressing. Can't wait to graduate and get a decent job.*" Visions of a paneled, brightly carpeted office with scenic pictures and healthy plants. Visions of me fifteen pounds thinner in a new skirt suit from Lord and Taylor. A great-looking coworker is pouring us coffee. Sounds of a clock chiming five o'clock. "*Sure, I'd love to go out Friday night*" (Caughey, 1984, p. 135. Italics mine.)

The six bits of this conversation, set off in italic script, are separated by sensory and emotional imagery. The striking feature of this text is the strength of the visitors: the rowdy marines from the previous summer, the yelling manager, and the great-looking imaginary coworker. The waitress

64

is talking to the visitors, and in the case of the marines, they are talking to her. The subject also seems to be alternatively addressing her you and me. Once she addressed "God," although in a purely expressive and metaphorical way. It would be too strong to call God a visitor in this case, but too weak to write him or her off completely. Perhaps God is an emotional visitor. But for people who strongly believe in a personal God, he can be a quite central and permanent visitor. Some people talk dialogically with God, making him not only a passive (eavesdropping) visitor but a speaking participant (Rosenblatt, Meyer, and Karis, 1991). The waitress's reference to God, however, was merely to use him for an emotional catharsis.

In these vignettes I have used both the Peirce and Mead models as well as their combination. I have also referred to the self's properties, particularly nestedness, ordering, and reflexivity, even though the latter two are not formally analyzed until the next chapter. The utterances also have implications for the speakers' inner solidarity. This is another property of the self, which I will not formally consider until chapter 5, although I will now use it informally to look back at the six examples.

The clerk's concern was to follow the rules of her job correctly. Office supplies had previously been ordered on a particular form, called a department purchase order. She had to order new supplies and she began to instruct herself to get and use those forms. Then she remembered the discontinuance of those forms and, still audibly, corrected herself. This pursuit of solidarity was ordinary and obvious. If we contrast solidarity with "cognitive dissonance," using the latter term in the comprehensive way it is used in psychology, the clerk was seeking to avoid dissonance between what she would do and what the office rules required her to do.

More interesting, and presumably also related to her intra-personal solidarity, was why she was talking out loud in front of other people in the first place. Most people who tend to think out loud stop doing so when they know others are within earshot, but the clerk, if anything, got louder and more obvious.

In this case the clerk, through her husband's occupation, had a higher social status than her relatively untrained, clerical job would suggest. She did not take the job seriously and would often distance herself from it in various, observable ways. The job was below her, but she wanted the income anyway. The talking out loud, especially before an audience, intimated her sense of superiority to this job. It softened the edge of her "status inconsistency" and the corresponding cognitive dissonance, giving her the inner solidarity of a more stable social class identification.

The solidaristic implications of Husserl's utterance are hard to assess. There is no way of knowing whether he was revealing something about himself or just picking an example at random. Also the utterance about having "gone wrong" could be either moral or cognitive. In a stinging review, Frege had criticized the "psychologism" of Husserl's early *Philosophy of Arithmetic* (1891), and Husserl was subsequently "silent" for several years. Maybe Husserl was saying that his philosophical orientation had gone wrong. If so, this would be a classic "looking-glass self" embarrassment. According to Cooley, the mortification we feel when we perceive disapproval from others endangers our inner solidarity. But even if the remark was random, having nothing whatever to do with Husserl's autobiography, it is still of interest because of its place in Husserl's theory of consciousness. Husserl thought the self was centered around a unified, i.e. non-dialogical, transcendental ego. The obvious dialogicality in consciousness, which was so important for Peirce and Mead, was a secondary and unimportant phenomenon for Husserl. He immediately followed the text I have been using by saying:

> But in the genuine sense of communication, there is no speech in such cases, nor does one tell oneself anything: one merely conceives of oneself as speaking and communicating. In a monologue words can perform no function of indicating the existence of mental acts, since such indication would there be quite purposeless. For the acts in question are themselves experienced by us at that very moment (1891/1970, p. 280).

In other words Husserl's theory of the self did not permit the divisions that can lead to dissolidarity. His metaphysic of human nature produced such a unified self that the everyday experience of self-reproach and other signs of low solidarity were disallowed.

Husserl's mature phenomenology, in which dialogicality is suppressed and solidarity is therefore not a problem, can also be interpreted as a response to the painful Frege review. This is of course speculation, but if it were true, the suppression of the divisions that require inner solidarity had the effect of protecting Husserl's own need for solidarity.

The texts by Cooley's son and little Julia both indicate confusion about just what it is that constitutes the self. If Cooley's son, little Rutger, actually were, for a moment, uncertain about whether he or his imaginary companion had fallen, he seems to have had some confusion about his personal identity or, put another way, his I. This is a dissolidarity, not in the bond among the parts, but in the nature of the parts. Rutger's confusion is reminiscent of Lacan's "transitivity," an early but now obsolete concept in child development. "The child who strikes another says that he has been struck; the child who sees another fall, cries" (Lacan, 1966/1977, p. 19).

But Rutger was confusing himself, not with another person but with an imaginary companion, and one who seemed to occupy a place inside Rutger's inner space. Thus the dissolidarity seems to be one not of values, mood or inner cohesion, but one of structure and personal identity.

In another way Julia too seems to be having a personal identity problem, if she thinks she is, in some sense, her mother. We could say her superego has not yet been internalized and is still concretely attached to her mother's voice. Later, when she is past what both Vygotsky and Piaget called the stage of egocentric speech, she may continue to "guilt" herself, but do so inaudibly. But one could also wonder whether she has yet discovered the privacy of her own thought processes. In chapter 7 when I reinterpret Lacan's mirror stage I will show how it leads to the discovery of intra-subjective privacy. At the age of three, Julia should already have had the experience of self-recognition in the mirror, but the danger of breaking all these eggs, which her mother was sure to discover, may have weakened her sense of intra-psychic privacy. In any case she seems to be allowing her mother to play the role of her I, while simultaneously making decisions and acting with her own I. As with Rutger, this is a problem in personal identity and a corresponding confusion in the sense of who she was.

David's sleep talk evokes all the dissolidarity there is between the unconscious of his dream and the consciousness of his waking life. In Lacan's language this is the conflict between the (unconscious) "subject" and the (conscious) "ego." David begins with his own name, which had been whispered to him by the experimenter. Then he plays on this name ("day – dated – day – dravid" and on to the crucial switching device, "day dreams") until he finds a way of linking the conscious David to the unconscious "noked naked day dreams." The second of the 25 or 30 dreams did something that his unconscious found highly organizing ("tied it all up"), allowing him to "keep bouncing them on" with "regular meter." David's utterance seems to be building a vertical solidarity between his unconscious and his consciousness, by way of dream content. This contrasts with the horizontal solidarity we are often trying to establish among the temporal phases of the self.

Finally the waitress is trying to calm herself in the face of immediate anxiety: being late for work. She uses the trick of comparing her present waitress job, itself not one she likes, with the one from the previous summer, which she liked even less. And she makes the further contrast between the present job and the one she is imagining for herself after graduation. In each frame – last summer's horrible job, this summer's difficult one, and next year's highly gratifying position – solidarity and dissolidarity with visitors is an important secondary theme.

Since the larger theme is the juggling of present, past, and future, we could simply say she is trying to optimize the relations among I, me and you. This is the classic semiotic task of interpreting the past to and for the future. She is trying to gain immediate solidarity by imagining how pleasant the future will be. The present pressure and rush to work will lead to better things, and if she thinks about those things now, it will be easier to endure the present.

Two Research Applications

I will now show how the Peirce–Mead model of the internal conversation is useful in other intellectual areas, specifically: Wittgenstein's argument against private language and other inner states; and the nature of the internal conversation in literature. Each of these issues is itself the subject of extensive scholarly research and controversy, so my "applications" will hardly be exhaustive, but their purpose is more to show the versatility and strength of the model than to solve theoretical problems.

In the heading to this section I am using the word "research" advisedly, even though the term has usually been used not as a kind of theoretical activity but as its empirical opposite. In recent years the distinction between philosophy and social theory has been breaking down. Philosophers now refer to their work with language previously used exclusively for the sciences: theories, paradigms, hypotheses, anomalies, etc. These terms assume that philosophy is more empirically grounded than previously thought. I will not comment on the validity of this trend, but I do agree with it, and therefore I use the term "research applications" where someone previously might have said "doctrinal implications" or the like.

Turning to my first application, the complex and aphoristic Wittgenstein of the *Philosophical Investigations* (1953) seems to empty the self of all inner states: internal conversation, reflexivity, the second order, the I, and broadly speaking, selfhood. I say "seems" because there are many ambiguities in his arguments and some of his students claimed that his face-to-face teaching and conversation differed from his written word. I also find it difficult to believe a man with such inner conflicts, over his suicidal tendencies and his homosexual inclinations (Monk, 1990, pp. 581–6), could disbelieve in inner states. But the arguments are nevertheless quite influential, whether he actually believed them or not. His general argument is that the seeming autonomy and *sui generis* character of inner states is illusory. These experiences, insofar as they exist at all, are epiphenomenal to interaction and language use ("parole").

There is an initial plausibility to this position, for the reflective self is "an inner copy of social interaction" (Luhmann, 1986, p. 314). It appears as though the infant's reflexivity is first the interpersonal, role-taking variety and only later the intra-subjective reflexivity of the internal conversation. Still, genetic priority is not a causal explanation, much less a valid reductionism.

I think Wittgenstein simply missed the significance of the internal conversation, either despite, or perhaps because of, his intense pre-occupation with his own internal conversation. In addition his thesis of the non-referential I – that there is nothing to which this word can refer, except sometimes to the body – is an unprovable presupposition (Canfield, 1990, p. 53), the opposite presupposition being more congruent with ordinary experience (including Buddhist and Hindu experience, see Perinbanayagam, 1991, p. 24, note 6).

Wittgenstein might have argued, but did not, that the reflexive I is an unacceptable paradox. This would have been another form of the "Indian rope trick" argument (Janik and Toulmin, 1973, p. 189) he used against Russell's logical atomism in the *Tractatus*. Perhaps this was in the back of his mind. But the paradox of the reflexive self is non-vicious, and the resulting blind spot can simply be taken as a given feature of the self.

On the specific issue of private language, Wittgenstein defined "private" as logically private, meaning something that could never be understood by an outsider. Such a language, he argued, could not have a stable semantics, for it would lack "checks," either from other persons or non-personal objects. Language rules could not be followed without checks, and meanings would inevitably drift.

But drift is not peculiar to private language. It is characteristic of public language too. Families sometimes slide into shared psychoses ("folie a la famille"), which results from a paranoid drift in their language use. And various other kinds of group, organization, community, and even entire nations have drifted into similar, mad states. The privacy, stability, and drift of language systems is a matter of degree.

It may be that what Wittgenstein thought of as a totally private language is a contradiction in terms and therefore impossible, but I think the internal conversation is at least "semi-private." Not only are the symbols highly individuated in their contextualization and fusion (see Wertsch, 1985, pp. 124–6, on Vygotsky's "agglutination"). The syntax is particularized too. James Joyce was right when he rendered the internal conversations of his characters as only semi-intelligible, and perhaps the reality would have been even less so. The actual thoughts of the waitress, for example, were probably much more privatized than in the version she gave to Coughey.

But despite this self-styled and unique quality, the inner conversation can still have semantic stability, i.e. the symbols can have boundaried meanings. It is the inner "checks" that Wittgenstein missed. The whole internal conversation is a constant checking process, with participants correcting, adding to, and developing each other's meanings. These may not be as firm as external checks, but they are more firm than no checks at all. In addition the external checks, as in the drifting groups mentioned above, do not always check effectively either.

Of course the inner conversation is connected to the outer, as a play within a play or meanings within meanings. It is neither completely private nor completely public, but somewhere in between.

Turning to the second application, the inner conversation has been discussed in literary criticism quite extensively, perhaps even more so than in social theory and psychology (see Cohn, 1978 and Banfield, 1982 for important recent works). The classics of this discussion are largely Slavic: Mikhail Bakhtin, 1981; Jan Mukarovsky, 1977; V. N. Volosinov, 1973; and Lev Vygostky, 1962. (For the connections among these thinkers see Emerson, 1983; for a Peirce–Bakhtin comparison see Kent, 1989).

Fictional discourse, whether inner or outer, is not natural discourse. It is constructed by an author, and the speech is, in a sense, pretended speech (Searle, 1975/1986). The interposition of the author, and the artificial or cultural status of the discourse, makes the inner speech of fiction logically different from the everyday variety. Much of the critical discussion has, perforce, been concerned with the formal methods used by authors to render the internal dialogue fictionable and convincing. Little systematic attention has been given to the underlying model of the self, although literary critics have drawn variously on Freud, William James, Chomsky, Lacan, and mainstream psychology.

Although there is now talk about a neo-pragmatic approach to literary criticism, and Peircean semiotics is being used in a general way (Sheriff, 1989), the ideas of Peirce and Mead have not been used to analyze literature's internal conversation, even by the critics closest to pragmatism (Kenneth Burke, Hugh Dalziel Duncan, and Wayne Boothe). The term most commonly used in literary criticism to refer to the internal conversation is monologue, not dialogue (e.g. "internal monologue," "dramatic monologue"). This suggests a closer affinity to faculty psychology than to pragmatism. To make the pragmatic connection between fictional and real inner speech, both of author and reader, would require some transformations.

Concerning the author, the dialogue of fiction, both between and within characters, might be visualized as nested within the author's own internal conversation. (1) There is the author's first-level internal conversation, as in the phrase "I must write another book to make the taxes." (2) Then there is the conversation among the people in the book (a sub-conversation in the author's mind). (3) And finally there are the internal conversations within the minds of the characters in the book. "3" is nested in "2," and "2" in "1." In other words literary and natural internal conversations are not two, distinct media. The former is located and contained in the latter, the author's internal conversation being a highly orchestrated and multi-level system of voices. This is not to deny that the discourse of fiction, levels 3 and 2, can be detached from the author's mind and treated as an autonomous reality. But to be born at all it had to first be part of the author's internal semiotic system.

In addition the characters are, as it were, "visitors" in the author's internal conversation. These visitors are different from the temporary and permanent variety in their degree of autonomy. In particular they are allowed to talk, not only with the author, but with each other. There is a greater than usual suspension of disbelief in these visitors. Giving up control and letting them "write themselves" requires an intensification of the ordinary suspension, e.g. well beyond that of Goethe's daydreaming.

Concerning the reader there is a similarly nested semiotic system. (I am drawing now on the insightful paper by Hogan, 1990). At one level the reader is having an ordinary, non-fictional internal conversation. This may concern the decision to read ("Time to knock off work and get back to that novel.") But it will also entail a constant, internal commentary during the reading process (e.g. "Could that be?" "I'll have to show this to my wife." "Is the author talking about herself?") Then the characters will be visitors, their conversations will be nested within the reader's, and any internal conversations the characters may have will be further nested within the visitor level. Of course the processes that connect these levels will be exceedingly complex, both for the author and the reader. For the latter, reader response theory (Tompkins, 1980) is an attempt to get at some of these complexities.

Nevertheless, in broad terms, literature is part of life, by which I mean the discourse of literature is part of the author-reader semiotic system. Therefore the concepts that describe the semiotic self also, with appropriate transformations, describe the semiotics of literature. At specific levels within literature, other psychological models, e.g. the various psychoanalytic approaches, are certainly insightful, but for describing the fundamental status of literature, including its internal conversations, the Peirce–Mead model may be the most useful.

Conclusion

In this chapter I shifted from structure to process, showing the dynamic of the semiotic self. To do this I first clarified the I–you–me model, spending considerable time on the differences between Mead and Peirce. Although the two are alike in overall pragmatic orientation, they differ in how they relate the internal conversation to temporality: Mead sees it as operating in the space between present and past, while Peirce sees it between present and future. I synthesized the two orientations, and, in addition, added visitors and the unconscious.

The analysis of six internal conversational texts was another way of putting the model into a process mode. I found that the model does not dictate solutions, i.e. its application is a matter of interpretation, and it is subject to counter-interpretation. Still, the model holds up; its concepts can explain the semiotic flow. In addition I had to make the model more refined, under the press of empirical test. Each of the six examples presented some brute fact that surprised me and required some innovative way of using the conceptual tools.

Finally I applied the model, not only to texts, but also to two intellectual problems. The first of these was the (alleged) Wittgensteinian model of consciousness, which is relatively impoverished and seemingly behavioristic. Within this model the impossibility of private language was examined. Wittgenstein seemed to think that the words "private" and "language" are contradictory, on the assumption that publicness, interactivity, and inter-subjectivity were inherent to language. My argument is that within the self, i.e. within what is usually considered to be the "private," there is a kind of public square. This square is inhabited by what David Hume called a "community," the members of which are in constant conversation. Within this square the I has the podium, but the I is enough of a chameleon to give all participants the chance to speak. This inner sphere or square, then, has all manner of interaction (Saussure's *parole*), and also has its unique version of inter-subjectivity. This inter-subjectivity is so complex that participants can actually lie to each other (Sartre's bad faith and philosophy's self-deception) and get away with it.

Also the things that these inner participants say to each other are not always neatly verbal. There are not only linguistic thoughts and inter-actions, but also emotions, sensations, non-linguistic thoughts, speech qualities such as "tone of voice," and even something like body language. Modern literature has attempted to render internal conversations into words, or at least into utterances that can be represented by letters of the alphabet. Obviously, several of the items on my list, such as emotions or "body language," cannot be directly represented by words. Literature has given us only a glancing picture of the internal conversation.

I think it is quite possible that the internal conversation can be understood only by the person within whom it is happening. Much of it may be linguistic or otherwise available to linguistic representation. But a significant amount is coded in symbols, so nested within the unique qualities of the person, that no others could ever understand them. I argued that the internal conversation, then, is partly public or publicable, and partly private, i.e. it is a "semi-private" language.

The other application had to do with the logical status of literature's internal conversations. To date, these literary phenomena have not been clearly located within any theory of the self. John Searle tried to locate literary discourse in general, including its internal conversations, within speech act theory. To do this he used an approach like my "nestedness," but he referred to it as being "parasitical" (1975/1986 p. 67). Searle was quite programmatic on this question. In addition he was limited to those aspects of the internal conversation that can be represented as speech acts, i.e. as words, sentences, etc. I think the whole point of the internal conversation, as, say, a "survival" mechanism, is that it is faster, more subtle, and considerably more precise than words.

I used a nested or "boxes within boxes" scheme to relate literature's internal conversations to those of the semiotic self. I did not work out the differences between the reader's and writer's selves although these look significant. My source on this topic (Hogan, 1990) suggests that the overall text may have a unique status for the reader. Hogan argues that the text is a kind of personal identity, different from its parts and possessing visitor status for the reader. Bakhtin's notion of how a novel's title (Gogol's *Dead Souls* was his example) can penetrate organically into a text is the sort of thing Hogan seems to have in mind. Still, a text can be pretty haunting and life-like for an author too, although admittedly its emergent status would be different from what it might be for the reader.

The two applications – Wittgenstein and modern literature – were connected. Literature is nested within the (reader's and writer's) self, and the "language" of the internal conversation is nested within that of the interpersonal conversation. In both cases the thing that is "within" (or a level below) is partly similar to its container and partly unique.

This container–contained relationship is analogous to the one I described in chapter 2, between the overall self and its semiotic stream. In other words the nested relationship between the self's I–you–me structure and its semiotic processes is similar to that between public and semi-private language on the one hand, and the self and its literary productions (or consumptions) on the other, although this is only a partial analogy.

4

Reflexivity

The second chapter referred to the properties of the self, but the only one it looked at closely was the nestedness of structure and content. The third chapter introduced the time schemes, knife-edge vs specious, to analyze the internal conversation. This chapter will examine reflexivity and the distinction between the first and second orders. Solidarity was touched on in the previous chapter, but it will be looked at in detail in the next. The only other major property of self to be considered will be teleology, which will be treated in chapter 8.

These properties interpenetrate, so it is impossible to discuss them in isolation from each other. For that reason I have sometimes had to use these concepts before I have explained them properly. Nevertheless each is a different feature of the semiotic self, revealing a distinct modality of the way this self works.

The Concept of Reflexivity

The etymology of the term "reflexivity" gives a common denominator for the many ways this term is used. The commonality is in the "flex," which designates a looping, back-bending, circling, or recursing. A thing is pictured as though it were moving away from itself, but at some point it reverses direction and moves back toward itself. In figure 2.1, the reflexive aspect of communication was pictured in this looping manner.

Underneath this common denominator there are many meanings of "reflexivity." This is partly because different theories of knowledge produce different versions of whether and how a person can know or otherwise relate to his or her self. In addition there are different kinds of reflexivity at different *sui generis* levels: at the physical and biological levels below the human individual; and at the interactional, organizational, and cultural levels above.

In recent years reflexivity has become a central concept in social theory. The main reflexive problem is the nature of the self, although there are also issues concerning machines, animals, interacting groups, social organizations, and the various spheres of culture. The pragmatists relied heavily on this concept, both for their theory of human nature and their semiotics. To give a careful description of the Peirce–Mead synthesis it will be necessary to look closely at reflexivity. In this section I will begin by looking at this concept in the history of philosophy. This will set up a series of comparisons between the pragmatists and others. Then I will show, in several ways, how this concept and its history fit into the Peirce–Mead synthesis.

Reflexivity in Intellectual History

The concept of reflexivity is implied both in the pragmatists' semiotics and in their epistemological turn to ordinary language. But this concept has a long, if relatively unrecorded, history, and the earlier uses help explain that of the pragmatists.

In Western philosophy reflexivity makes its major appearance with Descartes' "cogito" (Gasche, 1986, p. 13), although the concept was used, in a secondary way, in both classical and medieval philosophy. For Plato's Socrates all thought was a conversation with the self and hence reflexive: "when the mind is thinking it is simply talking to itself, asking questions and answering them, and saying yes or no" (Plato, 368 BC 1961, p. 895, 189e). The Socratic notion of reflexivity is obviously quite close to that of the pragmatists, a point of similarity of which Peirce was well aware (Fisch, 1986, p. 442).

For Aristotle (384–322 BC), thought was not reflexive but abstractive, yet his prime mover or "nous," being perfect, engaged exclusively in reflexive self-contemplation. St Augustine (354–430 AD), in addition to anticipating Descartes' cogito, argued that philosophy was a reflexive return of thought to itself (Kehr, 1916). And St Thomas Aquinas (*c.* 1225–74) found a place for reflexive self-awareness at every point in his complex, multi-stage theory of knowledge (O'Callaghan, 1948). In addition the medieval, trinitarian God, like Aristotle's nous, engaged in purely reflexive self-knowledge.

In the Aristotelian–Scholastic tradition the theory of knowledge was based primarily on abstraction, an intuitive lifting of meaning from particular sensations, and not on the dialogical notion of reflexivity. In the faculty psychology mold, this tradition held that: things have essences; these essences can be known by way of abstraction, all at once; and this knowledge is intuitive and direct. For the pragmatists: things did not have inherent essences, free of cultural definition; we know things little by little and not all at once; and we know, not intuitively or abstractively, but indirectly and semiotically.

Nevertheless the theory of abstraction, which distinguished two intellectual capacities or moments, had a dialogically reflexive component. The active or agent intellect abstracted universal meaning from particulars, but it then communicated this meaning to the passive or possible intellect. The latter, in turn, produced the representation or concept (Pellerey, 1989). The division of labor between these two capacities – one extracting and the other representing meaning – seems dialogical, reflexive and semiotic, similar to the relation between sign and interpretant, although Aquinas viewed it as two stages in the abstractive process.

Despite these earlier uses it was Descartes who first claimed reflexivity as the founding principle of philosophy, initiating a subjective turn that reverberated throughout modern philosophy. For my purposes I am less interested in whether "cogito ergo sum" is true, i.e. whether self-awareness implies the existence of the self, than in the reflexive form of the argument. Descartes' reflexivity, when contrasted with its binary opposite, Hegel's reflexivity, was private, asocial, and quasi-monological in form (Lorraine, 1990, pp. 4–8; Markova, 1982, pp. 6–9). Hegel presented an explicitly social and dialogical notion of self-awareness, in which consciousness of self looped or detoured through the "recognition" granted by the "other" (Hegel, 1807/1979, p. 111). In contrast Descartes' reflexivity rested on absolute doubt, including the privatizing doubt that other people existed.

Another distinctive quality of Descartes' reflexive cogito was its second-order character, a concept to be explained more fully later. In saying "I think, therefore I am," the focus of reflection was not on some first-order object, but on thought itself which made it second order. The reflection concerned another reflective act, namely the doubting process that preceded the cogito. At Descartes' first order level, for example that of the doubts that preceded or the deductions that followed the cogito, thought was purely intuitive and deductive, not reflexive.

Thus the nature of Descartes' subjectivist project required that his reflexivity be both private and second order. These two limitations were not completely transcended until the appearance of Peirce and Mead. Within French thought these limitations hung on longer, most noticeably in the thought of Sartre.

The British empiricists, though disagreeing with Descartes' starting-point and the substantiality of the soul, accepted his private, second-order approach to reflexivity. As Locke put it:

The Mind receiving the *Ideas*, mentioned in the foregoing Chapters, from without, when it turns its view inward upon it self, and observes its own Actions about those *Ideas* it has, takes from thence other *Ideas*, which are as capable to be the Objects of its Contemplation, as any of those it received from foreign things (Locke, 1689/1975, p. 127).

The privacy of Locke's self was one source of the founding fathers' faculty psychology, a position I contrasted with pragmatism in chapter 1. The exclusively second-order view of reflexivity implies a private self, for if your reflexive thought is always about your own thought, you are by that fact isolated from others. But if reflexivity is viewed as first as well as second order, which is the position of pragmatism, then it is easier to conceptualize the self as social.

Hegel would eventually insert the social into reflexivity, preparing the way for the pragmatists, but before him Kant and Fichte made major modifications in this idea. Kant had at least two versions of reflexivity. His major thesis – that we construct the world by giving it the forms of time, space, and the categories of meaning – implies that when we know objects of any kind we are knowing ourselves, for objects get their knowability from what we give to them. This is a highly theoretical and non-experiential notion of reflexivity. Ordinary people are not aware of it, unless they read, understand, and believe Kant's theory of knowledge. Still, with appropriate modifications, Kant's forms lead to the modern idea of culture, the constructed and relative character of which is much more visible to the ordinary, modern human being.

A second Kantian reflexivity is the notion that, running parallel to all our perceptions and knowledge is the awareness that we are experiencing these perceptions and knowledge. As he put it:

It must be possible for the "I think" to accompany all my representations; for otherwise something would be represented in me which could not be thought at all, and that is equivalent to saying that the representation would be impossible, or at least would be nothing to me (Kant, 1787/1965, pp. 152–3, B131–2).

We not only know, we know that we know, however implicit and slight this awareness may be. This self-monitoring is a kind of "eavesdropper" notion, in which the reflexivity or self-knowledge is based on an external "listening in."

Kant thought this implicit self-awareness was necessary for the unity of the self, in his terms its "apperceptive unity" or "transcendental unity of self-consciousness." This was not the diachronic unity, referred to in chapter 2 as "personal identity," but the synchronic unity of totality or wholeness.

The Kantian apperceptive process, by which the self constituted its unity through reflexive self-awareness, was a problem for the post-Kantians. Kant had stated the apperception idea imprecisely and in somewhat varying formulations. It was Fichte who reframed the issue as the "self positing itself," producing a theme which is still discussed to this day. For Fichte, the self got its apperceptive unity not by an implicit self-awareness but by actively creating itself. To some theorists Fichte's argument appears to have the fallacy of logical circularity – that the self exists before it exists – and Fichte revised his formulation several times to avoid what he thought was circularity. Dieter Henrich, in an influential article (1982), argued that not only is Fichte's self-positing self fallacious, but in addition all conceptualizations of a reflexive self are self-contradictory. Other scholars, who quote Henrich's argument approvingly, are Peter Dews (1987, pp. 21–9), Ernst Tugendhat (1979, pp. 49–55) and Jürgen Habermas (1981, pp. 393–5).

Fichte's self-positing self can also be interpreted, despite Fichte's own lack of confidence, as non-circular. Robert Nozick sees it as "self-reference from the inside, which we understand as reference in virtue of a character-istic (or to an entity) created in the very act of referring" (Nozick, 1981, p. 91. See Pippin, 1989, pp. 46–51 and Neuhouser, 1990, pp. 114-16 for arguments which are opposed to Henrich and compatible with Nozick).

One reason why the Fichte version of reflexivity is important is that several contemporary theorists, interpreting Fichte as circular, have decided that the very notion of a self is a contradictory one. Recent German social theory, for example, has been structured by a long-running debate between Niklas Luhmann and Jürgen Habermas, the former taking the self "down" to the mechanistic, cybernetic level and the latter "up" to that of interaction and interpersonal communication. Neither finds the concept of the self valid and non-circular at its own level.

Hegel, who was dissatisfied with Fichte's and others' modifications of Kant, was the first to introduce a social loop into reflexivity, solving, in my opinion, any problems of circularity that Fichte may have had. For Hegel, reflexivity is not directly self-to-self, but indirect, via the other. Self-awareness, and therefore Kant's unity of apperception problem, is based on the recognition received from another. This recognition, in effect, creates the self, i.e. the self does not originally come into existence by positing itself in a private solitary manner. It is posited by another – the infant's close caretaker or caretakers – and thereby obtains the Fichtean capacity to posit itself. In other words self-recognition, which internalizes the recognition received from the caretaker, is the same as self-positing. Nozick is right insofar as he goes, but he does not see how "self- reference from the inside" is derived from recognition from the outside.

When Hegel discussed the recognition process, he did not keep the two levels – interaction and self – adequately distinct, as I mentioned earlier, and his argument is therefore unclear at times. It makes sense only if it begins with the other granting recognition to the self, and then moves to the internalization of this other in such a way that the self, via the internalized other, can grant recognition to itself. Hazards lie in both fields of recognition and in the connection between the two. This notion of recognition and the flow from the inter- to the intra-personal is rather close to the thought of Mead, but neither Mead nor Peirce fully used these Hegelian conceptual resources.

Hegel's analysis of recognition and reflexivity, and the master–slave scheme in which it is embedded, has had an enormous impact on recent social theory, particularly in France (Butler, 1987, pp. 61–100) and in feminist circles generally. But despite the improvement on Fichte, Hegel was dissatisfied with this formulation. It avoided circularity, but for him it still did not provide enough self-unity. In particular his socially reflexive scheme was located in the subject–object framework and therefore entailed an unavoidable blind spot.

The reflecting pole, in this framework, can know only the reflectee and never itself. The problem of the blind spot was not only a problem for Hegel; it runs through the entire discussion of reflexivity to this day, some seeing it as an unacceptable paradox and others as an unavoidable but acceptable given. In the Peirce–Mead semiotic scheme the I can know itself only through the interpretation of the you, and as the me. Even though there are indirect ways of evading the blind spot, it is built into the triadicity. But for Hegel, this was an excessive limitation on self-unity, particularly as this idea might apply to an absolute or God-like notion of the self.

Accordingly Hegel regarded reflexivity, even with its social–dialogical underpinnings, as a defective picture of human consciousness. To remedy this he invented the idea of speculation or "absolute reflection," in which the two reflexive poles were fused and the blind spot transcended (Harris, 1983, pp. 14–22). This completely self-transparent and unblinded reflexivity was the kind that the Christian theologians had attributed to the trinitarian God, a model which may have influenced Hegel's thought (Wall, 1973).

Hegel's pure reflexive fusion, however – influential as it was with his successors – does not seem useful for the contemporary theory of the self, except as a limiting concept. It is too false to ordinary experience. We do experience rare moments of quasi-fusion – Mead found these in religious mysticism, creativity, and communal rituals (Mead, 1934, pp. 273–281) – but most of the time we experience inner division and the absence of fusion.

By the time the pragmatists appeared, the discussion of reflexivity had gone through some 2,000 years, and Hegelian intonations were still very much in the air. To a great extent pragmatism's reflexivity was a de-absolutizing of Hegel, i.e. an acceptance of his social–dialogical reflexivity but a rejection of his solution to the blind spot. As I mentioned earlier this was a democratizing of Hegel.

The last thinker in this genealogy of reflexivity was Adam Smith, author of *The Theory of Moral Sentiments* (1759). Smith used the looking glass metaphor in discussing how we adapt to the views we think others have of us. He also spoke of the duality of the self, within the framework of which we examine our moral qualities (pp. 112–13). In the self-reflecting process he recognized and accepted the blind spot: "But that the judge should, in every respect, be the same with the person judged of is as impossible as that the cause should, in every respect, be the same with the effect" (p. 113). Smith was probably the source for Cooley's looking-glass self (Cooley, 1922/1964, p. 184). Cooley in turn was in close contact with the four University of Michigan people who went to Chicago to form Chicago pragmatism: James Tufts in 1892 and John Dewey, George Herbert Mead, and James Angell in 1894. Smith's formulation had already provided the means for democratizing Hegel, making it easier for the pragmatists to construct an American version of reflective philosophy. Among the Scottish moralists, who had so influenced the American founding fathers, Smith was the one who appears to have been the most useful to the pragmatists.

Reflexivity and Semiotics

The way pragmatism's "reflexivity" fits into the history of this concept can be summarized as follows: It is more social than the version of Descartes or that of the British empiricists but less social than that of the German idealists, the individual being less absorbed by society. In addition pragmatism's reflexivity can operate at both the first- and second-order levels, as I will show in the next section.

The Peirce–Mead reflexivity is inherent in their semiotics, in several ways. First, the triadic schemes, both the inner and the outer, indicate the reflexive pathway. Since I am interpreting these philosophers to have a triad within a triad, they must also have a reflexive act within a reflexive act, the two being related as contents to structure. The outer triad of I–you–me is a reflexive arc, definitive of the self's structure. In addition the agencies of this structure communicate in and with individual signs, themselves also composed of semiotic triads. These inner triads are reflexive within a similarly reflexive outer structure. In chapter 2 I argued that every semiotic object, no matter how mundane, is tied to the me-as-object. It is the same with reflexivity. The overall structure is reflexive. The contents are tied to the overall structure. Therefore the contents have to be reflexive.

Less deductively, Peirce and Mead also thought that all human communication or semiotic was reflexive simply in the way it operated. In particular for both of them, all thought, no matter how fleeting or mundane, was the self talking to itself. As mentioned earlier, Mead's talk was I–me and Peirce's, I–you, creating disagreement on the nature of the reflexive pathway; but on the broader genus of reflexivity they were in agreement.

There is a third, somewhat more complicated, way in which ordinary semiotic communication was reflexive for the two pragmatists. This has to do with the three parts of the inner triad and how they relate to each other.

Peirce's sign–interpretant–object and the corresponding definitions are fairly clear, even though he sometimes treated these three terms ambiguously. Mead was less standardized in his terminology, but his most common statement of the inner triad was in terms of "gestures," a concept that allowed him to combine animal and human communication. One can get the flavor of Mead's triad from the following quotation:

> The logical structure of meaning, we have seen, is to be found in the threefold relationship of gesture to adjustive response and to the resultant of the given social act. Response on the part of the second organism to the gesture of the first is the interpretation – and brings out the meaning – of that gesture, as indicating the resultant of the social act which it initiates, and in which both organisms are thus involved. This threefold or triadic relation between gesture, adjustive response, and resultant of the social act which the gesture initiates is the basis of meaning; for the existence of meaning depends upon the fact that the adjustive response of the second organism is directed toward the resultant of the given social act as initiated and indicated by the gesture of the first organism (1934, p. 80).

For Mead the three parts of the inner triad were: the gesture of the first organism; the responding gesture of the second organism; and the "resultant" of the social act. The two gestures can be roughly equated with

Peirce's sign and interpretant, although Mead's language has a more behavioral tone. The third element, the "resultant of the social act," however, is too ill defined, in this and other texts, to be automatically equated with Peirce's object.

Mead's resultant can be interpreted in at least four ways. Sometimes it is the (Peircean) object of the two gestures, which Mead calls the "denotation" (1922/1964, p. 246). Sometimes it is the concept corresponding to the object, which he calls the "connotation" (p. 246). A third meaning, suggested at one point in the foregoing quotation, is merely the combination or synthesis of the two gestures. And a fourth could be whatever subsequent conversation or social action might transpire between the two organisms.

For example, if I ask my son to get me a beer and he gets me one, my asking is the gesture of the first organism and his getting is the gesture of the second. From this the resultant can be: the object, i.e. the can of beer or possibly my thirst for it; the concept of the beer, or possibly of the fetching process; the synthesis of my asking and his getting; or any subsequent conversation or social action, such as my sharing the beer, between my son and me.

Some scholars have argued that Mead's various statements of his semiotic triad, including the ambiguous "resultant," all cohere, and that his triad is essentially the same as Peirce's (Rosenthal, 1969; Lewis and Smith, 1980, p. 141). To do this you have to interpret Mead's resultant as Peirce's object, making Mead's term more precisely defined than it is. But for purposes of the Peirce–Mead synthesis it does not matter if the two thinkers disagree somewhat on the inner semiotic triad, for I am using Peirce's terminology in the synthesis in any case. If Mead's third semiotic element is not quite the same as Peirce's I can ignore that.

Despite the complexities of the two inner triads and the ambiguity of Mead's resultant, it is still possible to see the reflexivity inherent in both semiotics. The relation between the second and first elements, in both cases, seems clearly reflexive. Peirce's interpretant modifies and comments on the sign; its meaning depends on and is reflexive to that of the sign. It is talking to, or rather back to, the sign. The same is true for Mead's two gestures. The adjustive or responding gesture of the second organism in Mead's dyad is commenting on the initiating gesture in some way, often in a less narrowly behavioral or instrumental manner than Mead seems to think. This gesture talks back to the originating gesture.

In the synthetic model, as opposed to the two separate theories, reflexivity is even more sharply etched. Both Peirce and Mead were triadic in their theories of that which is communicated, but in their notions of the communicators, my structure, they were dyadic and dialogical. I added the third leg to each, giving Peirce the "me" he needed to complete his structural triad and Mead the "you" he needed to complete his. The synthesis is quite different from its two components, although one could say that both Peirce and Mead implied, or at least asked for, their missing thirds. In any case the synthesis is inherently reflexive in structure, operations, and contents. The I–you–me structure means that the I communicates directly with the you and indirectly or reflexively with the me. Triadicity implies the two communication circuits, the direct linear one (I to you) and the indirect, reflexive one (I to me). Reflexivity, then, is an essential and invariable ingredient of the semiotic, in addition to being the underlying source of semiotic power. When I talk about reflexivity I am also talking about semiotic, and vice versa. The semiotic self is therefore the same as the reflexive, or dialogical, self.

Beyond the forms of reflexivity I have already described, the inner triads are also reflexive in being embedded in the worlds of ordinary language, the natural attitude, and the culture. These media, to draw on Durkheim, are in the "collective consciousness," and like all forms of consciousness, they are reflexive (Luhmann, 1982, p. 7).

Since I have now shown how the pragmatists are reflexive in several ways, it should be clear that this concept pervades their semiotics. In this respect they are very much in fashion, for the concept of reflexivity is now widely used in philosophy and social theory.

First and Second Orders

First-order signs, meanings, or reflexive acts are about ordinary objects. In contrast, those of the second order are about other signs, meanings, or reflexive acts. This is similar to David Hilbert's distinction between mathematics and metamathematics (Kline, 1980, pp. 250–51), but it is more general. It is also similar to the distinction in Scholastic philosophy between first and second intentions, the former being thoughts about objects and the latter being thoughts about thoughts (Schmidt, 1966, pp. 122–9). For the pragmatists all thought is reflexive, but sometimes the reflexive process is applied to itself. When this happens we have a kind of double, stacked, or bi-leveled reflexivity, for now the thought process, itself always reflexive, is coiled back onto itself.

Take, for example, the practicing social theorist, informally ruminating about an intellectual problem, e.g. Max Weber lying on the couch smoking a cigar (Marianne Weber, 1926/1975, p. 187). This person's thought process is relatively undirected, spontaneous, and stream-like, although, as in all thought, it is reflexive. Suddenly a new idea appears in the person's reveries, and the theorist's mind becomes poised and attentive. This person then does a careful replay or retrospection of these thoughts, trying to grasp the emerging idea more firmly and perhaps also trying to remember exactly how this new idea was brought into consciousness. At this point the theorist has shifted from first- to second-order reflexivity, for the object of reflection is now an earlier reflection, and the thought is "thought about thought." The new vantage point is "meta" to the original cognitive activity, the new intentionality is of the Scholastic's "secondary" variety, and, again in Scholastic language, the object of thought is a "being of the mind" ("ens rationis").

Mead, for whom reflexivity was a major concept, never developed a terminology for this distinction, nor did any of the other pragmatists. In fact Mead (and many others) sometimes used the term "reflexivity" exclusively for the second-order variety. Nevertheless in his logic-in-use if not in his reconstructed logic (Kaplan, 1964, pp. 3–11) Mead made this distinction. Another subtlety of this distinction is that in ordinary human experience, first- and second-order meanings glide into each other so imperceptibly, with so many border-line cases, it is easy to get the two confused and not easy to find the line of demarcation.

Nevertheless the distinction is real, useful, and obvious upon analysis. Not only does this distinction clarify the modes of reflexivity, it also bears on the modes of solidarity, as I will show in the next chapter. Internal solidarity seems especially important and at risk for second-order reflexivity. This is illustrated, to take an extreme case, by the fact that psychotics tend to be more delusive at the second order than at the first.

It is possible to lay a third order (or meta-meta level) onto the second, or for that matter an infinite number of additional orders, but the returns usually diminish drastically after the second. In principle you can escalate levels indefinitely but in practice the cognitive advantages are all at the second level, except in highly specialized cases.

The distinction between the orders can be applied at any *sui generis* (as opposed to meta) level – self, interaction, social organization, or culture – but it is most easily explained in relation to the first two. In this discussion the notions of meaning, communication, semiotic, and reflexivity are all connected, and the distinction in orders applies to them all. But for my purposes I will stay with Mead and his emphasis on reflexivity.

I have already used Mead's notion of reflexivity in several ways, but I have not formally examined it. I will now do so, showing the various ways in which he used this concept. After I have done this it will be clearer how the distinction between the two orders bears on the modes of reflexivity.

For Mead "The self has the characteristic that it is an object to itself, and that characteristic distinguishes it from other objects and from the body"

(1934, p. 136). His reflexivity is the quality of being simultaneously subject and object. When he discussed interpersonal communication he again drew on the concept of reflexivity, but in this case he refers to it as "role-taking." Role-taking is the process whereby humans engage in meaningful or significant communication, in contrast, as Mead saw it, to the non-significant communication of the other animals.

It seems clear that the reflexivity or self-referencing of the self and the role-taking of significant interaction are isomorphically similar processes, even though Mead did not get around to pointing that out explicitly. In either case an entity is both subject and object. In the case of the self and intra-subjective processes this is done through self-awareness, self-consciousness, and the semiotic triad. In the case of interpersonal or intersubjective communication, this is done by way of a detour through the mind of the other, the partner in communication. In interactive communication the communicator is both subject and object, though in contrast to the intra-subjective case, the loop is even more mediated and indirect. Nevertheless both inter- and intra-personal meaning have the same structural form of looping, flexing, back-bending, returning to origin, recoiling, dialecticizing, etc., i.e. they both follow the circuit of reflexivity.

In addition the two levels of reflexivity illuminate each other. Intra-personal reflexivity can be imagined as a collapsing or internalization of the interpersonal process, and interpersonal reflexivity can be visualized as an expansion of unfolding of the "selfing" process.

Mead's notion of role-taking can be made sharper if certain distinctions, which he did not explicitly make, are clarified. One is a cognitive–moral distinction, which I will treat in the next chapter. Another, which I will now explicate, is a communicatee–communicator distinction regarding which aspect of the other's role we are taking. When Mead speaks of role-taking he obviously is not using the term in the contemporary sociological sense of status or social position. By "role" he means standpoint, attitude, perspective, point of view, and so on, including the substantive meanings that go with the role. But in practice he sometimes seems to be speaking of taking the other's role as communicatee or receiver of communication and sometimes as communicator or sender of communication. So I will make a communicator–communicatee, sender–receiver, catcher–pitcher distinction concerning which feature of the other's role we might "take."

In his theory of phylogenesis, i.e. the origin of human nature and language in our line of primates, Mead seems to be saying that role-taking the other (primate) in a communicatee sense was the crucial emergent. In non-significant, i.e. non-symbolic, communication the primate sends a sign of some kind to another primate but does not in any sense understand its own sign. The other primate responds, at least behaviorally, to the sign, regardless of whether this behavior is learned or genetically determined. At some point in evolution, however, the communicating primate learned how to respond to the communication in the same way that the receiving primate did. For Mead this was the birth of meaning. But it can also be called role-taking the other in the other's communicatee role, for the communicating primate now, by taking that role, can understand (or at least "respond to") its own communication.

This kind of role-taking should be distinguished from the variety I am referring to as the communicator kind. In this case one primate is role-taking, not the other's response to, but rather delivery of, a communication. It is the understanding not of a meaning one has sent to another but of one that another has sent to you. It is the understanding of a communication one has received as opposed to one that one has sent.

A similar distinction can be seen in an infant's acquisition of language, for the infant seems to learn how to understand the language of others (communicator role-taking) before he or she learns to initiate speech (communicatee role-taking).

The two kinds of role-taking – communicator and communicatee – are engaged in alternatively during ordinary conversation. I speak to my wife and role-take her response to what I say (communicatee role-taking). This is how meaning is shared and what permits the use of significant symbols. Then, as she speaks back to me, I role-take her communication and thereby understand it (communicator role-taking).

When Mead speaks of role-taking in an interpersonal sense he is referring generically to both kinds of role-taking, for they alternate in ordinary conversation. But when he speaks of the self as defined by reflexivity and of the use of reflexivity in the internal conversation he is basing this concept on communicator role-taking. We can turn back to and address ourselves because we can take the role that the other does toward us when the other communicates with us. We can observe, act on, and talk to ourselves because we can role-take these acts in the other.

To summarize the communicatee–communicator distinction, the birth and use of interpersonal or linguistic meaning is possible because communicatee role-taking emerged. In contrast the origin of the reflexive self, which can be an object to itself, is possible because communicator role-taking emerged. Presumably they emerged together in some sort of bundle of capacities, but nevertheless, in Mead's scheme, the two varieties of role-taking have distinct theoretical functions. In the next chapter I will discuss phylogenesis at greater length, but for now, the distinction I have just been clarifying should be helpful for understanding the distinctions of table 4.1. The two-by-two layout of the table shows the relationship between the two

REFLEXIVITY

	Intra-subjective	Interpersonal
First order	1 Ordinary thought	2 Ordinary conversation
Second order	3 Thought about thought	4 Conversation about conversation

Table 4.1 Mead's modes of reflexivity

modes of reflexivity and the two orders. Each of the two modes of reflexivity can function in either order. I have already shown how intrapersonal reflexivity can either be about ordinary objects or about earlier reflexive acts. This is the difference between boxes 1 and 3 in the table. Correspondingly, first-order, interpersonal reflexivity is ordinary communication or conversation. But when a conversation turns back on itself, e.g. when two people begin talking about the way they communicate, it becomes second order. This is the difference between boxes 2 and 4.

The distinction between the two orders also operates at the upper two semiotic levels, those of social organization and culture, but I will discuss those levels in chapter 6 and 7. Still, at all four of the semiotic or *sui generis* levels the shift to the second order is usually an attempt to solve some problem that appears, but cannot be solved within, the first order.

I have now filled the four boxes of table 4.1 with examples: box 1 is ordinary thought; box 3 is thought about thought; box 2 is ordinary conversation; and box 4 is conversation about conversation. This two-by-two distinction is more structured than Mead's formal thought, but I think it is true to the way he used these ideas. In any case this scheme is useful for the Peirce–Mead semiotic model. Reflexivity is the valence of the semiotic process; the semiotic elements are united by being related, reflexively, to each other. For this reason the four modes of reflexivity represented in the table are also four modes of semiotic. In addition the kind of solidarity is different in each of the four boxes, as I will show in the next chapter.

To clarify the distinction between the two orders I will make a variety of contrasts between Mead's usage and that of several other thinkers. A distinction between the first and second orders is common, but not everyone makes this distinction in the same way, nor does everyone find reflexivity in both orders. But before presenting these contrasts I will quote two philosophers who make distinctions between orders in a way that seems compatible with Mead's.

The first is from Kierkegaard, who is characterizing the highly introspective, self-aware, or "subjective" thinker:

> While objective thought is indifferent to the thinking subject and his existence, the subjective thinker is as an existing individual essentially interested in his own thinking, existing as he does in his thought. His thinking has therefore a different type of reflection, namely the reflection of inwardness, of possession, by virtue of which it belongs to the thinking subject and to no one else. . . . The reflection of inwardness gives to the subjective thinker a *double reflection* (Kierkegaard, 1846/1941, pp. 67–68, [italics mine]; see also Wood, 1990, pp. 108–9).

Kierkegaard is describing a special kind of second-order reflexivity, that of a highly self-analytic person, but his definition of this order is nevertheless about the same as mine (e.g. his "double" is my "second").

The second quotation is from Louis O'Callaghan, who interpreted Aquinas's notion of reflexivity. Although this quotation is somewhat long and uses obsolete terminology, it is important for what it reveals about Scholastic philosophy in the Middle Ages. Despite O'Callaghan's convincing, if neglected dissertation, it is widely believed that, except for minor uses in Plato and Augustine, the concept of reflexivity began with Descartes. The Scholastics are usually regarded as abstractive rather than reflexive. But as O'Callaghan shows, the theory of abstraction draws on reflexivity at every turn. Aquinas all but made my point, given earlier in this chapter, that dialogicity is latent in abstraction. This means the notion of humans as recursive loops is not as post-Cartesian and modernist as is widely believed.

This quotation is in the words of O'Callaghan, not those of Aquinas, but it explains a distinction that pervades Aquinas's theory of knowledge. The distinction is between psychological reflection (my second order) and ontological (my first).

> In the course of this study we shall be occupied with two different types of reflection which will be called psychological and ontological reflection. . . . Psychological reflection is an act of the intellect by which the intellect returns to its act of knowing or willing or sensing,

or to its faculties of knowing or willing or sensing, or to the ultimate knowing or willing principle; this is accomplished by an act which is separate and distinct from the act by which the object is sensed or known or willed. *It designates a second act which returns upon some first act* in order to know this act or to know by means of this act the principles which have entered into the production of this act. It is a return to our interior realities not for the purpose of carrying out an act of direct knowing but for the purpose of perceiving our interior acts and principles for what they are. . . .

Ontological reflection on the other hand is again a secondary act, since it is a reflex act, but it is one by which the intellect returns upon some previous act or upon the principles of this first act in the very operation of knowing some object of direct cognition. *It is not a reflective act which is altogether separate and distinct from some act of direct cognition*, but it is a reflection which is essentially involved in our more complex acts of knowing and which makes these acts of cognition possible. . . . We have called this ontological reflection because it is involved in the very metaphysics of some of our direct acts of knowing (O'Callaghan, 1948, pp. 9–10, italics mine).

The O'Callaghan–Aquinas "ontological" reflection is the built-in or first-order variety. It is not "separate and distinct" but "essentially involved" in knowing. In contrast, "psychological" reflection, like Locke's reflection, is not essential to the knowing process, which is quite complete without it. It is a return to the original act – sensing, willing, knowing – in order to look at it more closely. It is a second look, an instant replay, a retrospection, a meta review, all of which indicate the second-order perspective.

Kierkegaard and Aquinas are at opposite ends of the "schmaltz" or emotional factor in philosophy, the former being suffused with feeling and the latter unusually devoid of it. Still, they are both making the distinction I am making. Distinctions between the first and second orders are quite common in discussions of consciousness and mind generally, but rarely made in relation to reflexivity as such.

Apart from these two supportive quotations, the distinction between the two orders, particularly as applied to reflexivity, can be understood more clearly if I contrast my Peirce–Mead model with the somewhat different views of other thinkers.

Contrasting Views of the First Order

My first order is different from both of Kant's previously mentioned reflexivities. His eavesdropper or implicit self-awareness is more external than my first order. His is an *awareness* of the thought process; mine *is* the thought process. It is not a listening-in to the internal conversation; it is the internal conversation. There may be a kind of implicit character in the nature of this conversation at times, i.e. it might be routinized and built-in to the point of near unconsciousness, or rather preconsciousness. But this implicitness is an internal, not an external, trait. It has to do with the internal communication process itself and not with some external ego auditing the process. Just as with the Scholastics' active and passive intellects, you need both reflective moments before you can have insight. The two together, in dialogical relationship, are both necessary to produce a representation, or in the pragmatists' language, an interpretation. Kant's implicit reflexivity assumed a different theory of knowledge from that of the pragmatists.

In a sense Kant's theory of forms, his second notion of reflexivity, is a smuggling in of a dialogical principle. The dialogicality bounces around in his whole system of concepts; phenomenon vs noumenon; thing-as-known vs thing-in-itself; form vs matter; empirical vs transcendental. Just as the Scholastics went from active to passive intellect and the pragmatists from sign to interpretant, Kant proceeded from matter to form and transcendental to empirical ego. His implicit or eavesdropping ego was outside these two, giving him three notions of the ego. He has the former two in mind in this rather pragmatic-sounding extract:

> That I am conscious of myself is a thought that already contains a twofold self, the I as subject and the I as object. How it might be possible for the I that I think to be an object (of intuition) for me, one that enables me to distinguish me from myself, is absolutely impossible to explain, even though it is an indubitable fact; it indicates, however, a capacity so highly elevated above sensuous intuition that, as the basis for the possibility of understanding, it has the effect of separating us from all animals, to which we have no reason for ascribing the ability to say I to themselves, and results in an infinity of self-constituted representations and concepts. But a double personality is not meant by this double I. Only the I that I think and intuit is a person; the I that belongs to the object that is intuited by me is, similarly to other objects outside me, a thing (1804/1983, p. 73).

To translate Kant's scheme of the three egos – the one outside listening in and the subject–object pair of the above quotation – into that of the pragmatists you would have to get rid of the eavesdropper. This, as indicated in the quotation, would yield a dialogality much like that of the pragmatists. But Kant retained that outside ego, thinking he needed it to give "apperceptive" unity to the self. For this reason neither of Kant's reflexivities is the same as the pragmatists' first-order variety.

Fichte's self-creating ego was an attempt to improve on Kant's notoriously confusing theory of the self. Instead of having that auditing ego unify from without, he had the self-positing ego unify from within. As I mentioned earlier, he and others thought he got stuck in a circularity fallacy, although I think a Hegelian other – which would give recognition to the existence of this self – could have broken the circle.

For present purposes Fichte's first-order reflexivity, circular or not, was a genetic, self-creating explanation, in contrast to the kind I am describing, which is ongoing and systematic. Mead also had phylogenetic and ontogenetic theories of the self, both more social than that of Fichte, but that is not relevant to the present comparison. Kant's eavesdropper model and Fichte's attempt to improve on it by going internal and genetic, then, are both different from the pragmatists' first-order reflexivity.

Finally let me make the contrast with Sartre and his argument against the existence of first-order reflexivity. Sartre's version of the first–second order distinction is his notion of the pre-reflective and the reflective, also sometimes called the non-thetic and the thetic. For the Sartre of the *Transcendance of the Ego* (1936–7/1957), the self simply does not exist when it is not observing itself in a second-order manner. Ordinary first-order consciousness, for Sartre, is "transparent," ego-less and constituted as a kind of "nothingness." Although Sartre's analysis is an effort to refute Husserl's idea of the transcendental ego, the 1936–7 essay is also in contradiction with the Peirce–Mead semiotic. This is because semiotic is always triadic and reflexive, including the kind that Sartre refers to as pre-reflective. Later, in *Being and Nothingness* (1943/1956, p. 103), Sartre altered his position and allowed there to be what amounts to a "sense of self" (Aboulafia, 1986, p. 37) – perhaps reminiscent of Fichte's genetic reflexivity – at the pre-reflective level. For present purposes, Sartre lacks the notion of first-order reflexivity, his only kind, (except for the sense of self) being second order.

Sartre's reflexivity is sometimes referred to as a refrigerator-light theory, for the light goes on only when the door is open. At the pre-reflective level the light is off. Yet I would argue that the refrigerator and its contents are always there, whether the light is on or not. In other words there is a reflexive, quasi-conversational process to thought whether we explicitly watch it or not, and the self is never transparent.

The pragmatists' view of first-order reflexivity, then, has its unique qualities, different from those of Kant, Fichte, and Sartre, among others. These qualities include being intrinsic to the knowledge process, systematic and a necessary condition for knowing anything at all. In other words, just as all consciousness and thought is semiotic, all semiotic is reflexive.

Contrasting Views of the Second Order

Several important theorists use the notion of reflexivity only at the second order, but when they do so, their second order is different from that of the pragmatists. I have already mentioned Descartes and Sartre as lacking first-order reflexivities. Husserl also belongs in this category, for his reflexivity operates only in phenomenological analysis, which is his version of the second order. The three thinkers belong together historically, for Husserl is consciously modifying Descartes, and Sartre is consciously modifying both Descartes and Husserl. The second order of these theorists contrasts with that of the pragmatists in the following ways.

(1) If first-order consciousness is not reflexive it must be intuitive, in some sense of the word. This means it is direct, unmediated, and private. Since second-order reflexivity is, for these theorists, indirect, mediated, and at least quasi-social, this puts it in stark contrast with their first order. The move from first to second is extremely discontinuous and has traces of the gestalt shift or totally new.

Descartes climbed through absolute doubt and presumably some kind of personal crisis to reach his reflexive second order. When he did so it was with a sense of discovering a new continent. He believed that everyone that had preceded him was wrong and that he had, for the first time, discovered indubitable, presuppositionless truth.

Husserl's second order, which he called the phenomenological realm, was announced and brandished much as Descartes' had been. Husserl clearly innovated on Descartes in illuminating and creative ways, yet his sense of having made a great discovery is quite reminiscent of Descartes.

Finally Sartre appears to have made similar efforts to reach his method, which is a modification of Husserl's modification of Descartes. Instead of the doubt, etc. of Descartes and Husserl, Sartre appears to have surmounted intense emotional depression and the hedonistic excesses which, in his case, went along with it (Sartre, 1938/1964; Cohen-Solal, 1987, pp. 77–113).

In contrast to these sharp discontinuities, the second order of the pragmatists is smooth, elisive, and quite continuous with their first order. Peirce, for example, discussed how we can sometimes recover a first-order internal conversation by putting consciousness on hold and re-examining the immediately preceding semiotic stream (Peirce, 7.420; Colapietro, 1989, pp. 116–117). This move from first to second is not the world-shaking event of the previously mentioned thinkers. There is no conversion experience, no new paradigm and no sense of having discovered absolute truth. The pragmatists' second order is an ordinary cognitive tool, certainly capable of unique insights but nevertheless continuous with and built upon their first.

(2) Another difference between this same trio of thinkers and the pragmatists has to do with whether there is a self at all at the first order. If reflexivity is essential to the self, and if there is no reflexivity at the first order, then there would seem to be no self at the first order.

Sartre, for whom the first order of consciousness is pure nothingness, is the clearest case. Yet both Descartes and Husserl privilege the second order so much that the self of that level also looks like the true, if not the only, self. For the pragmatists the self fully exists all the time, at both levels.

A related difference is whether the self is essentially related to a "problem" in some way: as caused by, concerned with, discovered because of, or in some way the result of a problem. Again Sartre is a clear case. On the widespread assumption that *Nausea* was an autobiographical novel, the problem was depression and self-destructive hedonism, and the solution was a second-order self analysis that showed him why he was depressed. He found he was in "bad faith," allowing an identity to masquerade as the self. The cause of the "nausea" was free choice, and the way to cure it was also one of free choice. The problem was located at the first order, but its understanding and cure was at the second. His second-order self, aware of its powers and temptations, was the true self.

The problems that Descartes and Husserl encountered at the first order were not primarily emotional but cognitive. They were matters of uncertainty, doubt and skepticism. For Descartes it was the unconvincing quality of the Scholastic philosophy he had been taught coupled with the challenge of Montaigne's skepticism. For Husserl it was the contradiction among rival geometries and the ensuing crisis in the foundations of mathematics. Unlike Sartre's melancholy these were intellectual problems, but for intense intellectuals like Descartes and Husserl they could discupt the personality just as much as emotional problems could.

Both Descartes and Husserl, in somewhat different ways, found the solution to their problems in a close, second-order examination of the self. Here they found the certainty that was lacking for them at the first order, and this certainty allowed them to find a true and usable self.

(3) A third difference between these same two groupings of philosophers concerns the structure–content distinction and its relation to the two orders. For the pragmatists the two distinctions "cross-cut," i.e. there are two orders in both the structure and the content. This is pictured in table

	First order	Second order
Structure	1 I-you-me structure	2 Restructurings of I-you-me structure
Content	3 Ordinary thought	4 Thought about thought

Table 4.2   Structure-content vs orders

4.2. The examples I have used to fill in the four boxes will already be familiar, except for the second order, structural case of box 2. The term "restructurings" refers to ways in which the structure can rearrange itself so that the "me" or the "you" can occupy the temporal place of, and speak as, the "I." In chapters 2 and 3 I referred to ways in which the me of the past and the you of the future could speak, even though the speaking role is held exclusively by the I, which is the agency of the present. When the podium rule is loosened and the past or future self is allowed to occupy the speaking position of the present, the structure of the self has (temporarily) restructured itself and gone into a second-order stance.

When the contents become second order the thought process interferes with and changes the thought of the first order. And when the structure becomes second order it changes the structure of the first order, specifically by allowing the two non-present agencies – the me and the you – to occupy the structural location of the I.

In the case of the Descartes–Husserl–Sartre grouping there is no difference between the second order and the structure; they are the same thing. For these philosophers there is no reflexivity at the first order, this mode of consciousness being non-reflective and intuitive. The self emerges at the second order, and because of this everything about the self, including its structure, is confined to the second order.

I have now compared both of the pragmatists' orders with those of other positions, using these contrasts as a way of clarifying the pragmatists' views. These contrasts should also show the following advantages of the distinction between the first and second order distinction.

(1) With this distinction the complicated and elusive idea of reflexivity can be divided into two classes, first and second order. This makes for what is at least an initial simplification and permits a more analytically clear and fine-grained use of the concept. The notion of the "meta" level has been used, quite formally, in logic and mathematics, by such thinkers as Bertrand Russell, David Hilbert, Kurt Gödel, and Rudolf Carnap. The second-order idea shows that meta analysis is rooted in and is a normal part of ordinary, everyday consciousness.

(2) The distinction also helps tame the empirical complexity of how we experience consciousness. The self-as-inner-speech appears in complex modalities, differing in such matters as clarity, loudness, linguisticity, attentiveness, dividedness, directedness, emotional loading, closeness to unconscious forces, etc. The first–second distinction begins to sort out these subtle modes of variation.

(3) The distinction also allows one to differentiate the several approaches to both first- and second-order reflexivity, as I have been doing in the last few pages.

(4) Finally the distinction permits one to use the notion of introspection or retrospection effectively. Some notion of introspection, in the general sense of self-awareness, seems indispensable in a theory of human nature. In my terms, introspection is best seen as a second-order process. First-order introspection, insofar as we have it, is normally attainable and usable only by means of a closely following second-order retrospection. Whether and to what degree introspection is accurate is another question and beyond the scope of this book.

So far in this chapter I have reviewed the concept of reflexivity, showing something of its variety in the history of philosophy and how it fits into the semiotic perspective of Peirce and Mead. Then I introduced the orders distinction, its fit into semiotics, and its relation to several contrasting varieties of thought. Next I will review some of the ways the reflexivity concept is currently being used in social theory and philosophy, and finally I will consider the general advantages of the reflexive approach.

Current Uses of "Reflexivity"

I have examined reflexivity in ancient and medieval thought, in Kant, Fichte, and Hegel, and in Descartes, Husserl, and Sartre. This concept has been important for a long time in philosophy, for a moderately long time in logic and mathematics, but for only a short time in social theory. Marx, Weber, and Durkheim made little use of this idea, and it was not until Gouldner devoted 25 pages to "reflexive sociology" (1970, pp. 488–512) that it began to catch on among social theorists. Gouldner used reflexivity in a second-order way to refer to how theorists should be alert to autobiographical forces, personal motives, and domain assumptions, all of which can affect one's conclusions.

Since Gouldner the concept has become increasingly popular, but also increasingly imprecise and blurred. Perhaps the most overt applications are now in anthropology (Spencer, 1989) and the sociology of science (Woolgar, 1988; Ashmore, 1989), although it is also used, with a variety of meanings, throughout social theory.

I think the term is in too much of a state of flux to try to unravel all its possible variations, for example, along all the conceptual dimensions. I have, however, already pointed out two ways in which the term does vary: by the levels of self, interaction, social organization, and culture; and by first and second order. Within each of the four levels and the associated social-science disciplines there are a variety of local uses.

Another important distinction has to do with the medium within which the subject returns to itself. Thus far I have been emphasizing self-knowledge, but there are also the moral, emotional, and agentic media (Rosenberg, 1990). In other words, in addition to knowing and talking to ourselves, we can judge ourselves, have feelings toward ourselves, and act to maintain or change ourselves. Emotional reflexivity will be especially important in the next chapter.

There is also a distinction, within the cultural level, among the various ways in which texts can reflexively contradict themselves, thereby producing paradox. They can do so within a single sentence, as in the famous "all Cretans are liars, said the Cretan." They can do so in short but multi-sentence arguments, such as the paradoxes of infinity and set theory. Or, as has been pointed out by Derrida, they can do so in lengthy arguments, some later stage of which contradicts an earlier stage. In this case a theorist's premises are applied to his or her subsequent reasoning, showing how the latter contradicts the former.

Derrida began his career by applying this method, which is one of his deconstructive tools, to Husserl (Derrida, 1962/1989; also 1967/1973). He has since applied it to a variety of philosophers and social theorists, suggesting that reflexive contradiction is an inherent condition of all theory (Lawson, 1985; Gasche, 1986). In chapter 8 I will refer to this tendency of texts to contradict themselves as the problem of maxim self-applicability. I will show that many philosophies begin with assumptions, particularly

96

epistemological ones, that they later violate. Pragmatism, however, is unusual in remaining consistent with its assumptions. This makes it an exception to the widespread prevalence of the self-contradictory fallacy.

For the Peirce–Mead approach, the main problem with current uses of "reflexivity" is that so many are reductive, either upward or downward, of human nature and the self. It seems as though a (or perhaps *the*) distinctive feature of being human is that we are, in various ways, reflexive. But if this seeming reflexivity can be explained at some lower or higher level, human nature will have been reduced to that level and the self will, accordingly, have been erased.

I will treat the upward reductions, including their concept of reflexivity, in chapter 7 and the downward reductions in chapter 8. Here I will mention these positions and suggest their weaknesses.

Downward reductions use a concept of reflexivity that is too weak to explain this process in human beings. I am referring to arguments from such fields as cybernetics, artificial intelligence, and the various biologisms (e.g. molecular biology, neurophysiology, and sociobiology). As I will show in chapter 8, these conceptualizations describe pre-conceptual and pre-semiotic forms of reflexivity.

Upward reductions use concepts of reflexivity which are built on and presume human reflexivity, and which therefore cannot explain away this process in human beings. The fact that language can talk about or reflect on itself, whether in face-to-face groups, social organizations, or cultural texts, does not explain human beings. These supra-human forms are certainly valid and useful kinds of reflexivity, but they cannot replace the kind that defines the self. On the contrary, it is the self that explains them.

The most famous example of linguistic reduction is the idea that the word "I" is the only I there is. Any experience we may have of being or having a core reality that is designated by the word "I" is said to be an illusion. This is the argument that linguistic reflexivity is what underpins and explains the sense of psychological reflexivity (Benveniste, 1966/1971, pp. 217–30; Muhlhausler and Harre, 1990, pp. 87–105). In contrast I would reverse the argument and say the internal experience of I (psychological reflexivity) precedes and is the model for linguistic reflexivity.

Children, for example, refer to themselves in the third person before they learn how to use the word "I". The pre-"I" self-reference may be crude and inchoate, at least linguistically, but to anyone with experience of small children it is an unquestionable psychological fact. The child is clearly talking about his or her self when he or she yells "Tommy (or Sally) wants candy!" The meaning that is communicated is "I want candy!" even though the word "I," with its special linguistic demands, has not yet been mastered.

97

I will also argue the same order of appearance, first I and then "I," in the evolution of humans from the primates. Before the phylogenetic breakthrough the primates had the pre-semiotic reflexivity that character- izes all non-human animals. They could refer to and know themselves but not as totalities. As I will explain in chapter 8, it was a case of one part knowing another part, not of a whole knowing a whole. Among the animals only humans can reflect on their total or complete selves. They do this by looping through an outside or "other" point of view. This Archimedean lever, so to speak, permits them to become completely uncoupled from or "meta" to themselves. In chapter 5, I will discuss how this might have originated in the primates. Now I simply want to point out that the primates achieved self-reflexivity first, and only then began to use symbolic language. The self-reflexivity was the birth of the I. This birth preceded and was the model for the birth of the linguistic "I".

In chapter 7 I will treat the upward reductions in greater detail. In the present section I only want to touch on the current, upwardly reductive uses of the reflexivity concept, the linguistic versions being a major kind.

So far I have touched upon several current uses of reflexivity, including Gouldner's, Derrida's, Benveniste's, and Rosenberg's. A special case, which is sometimes said to be in direct competition with Mead, is the early work of Garfinkel. His notion of reflexivity is quite subtle and appears to be unique in social theory. Garfinkel's theory is primarily about interaction and not about the selves doing the interacting. His reflexivity therefore appears, at first glance, to be upwardly reductive. In his words:

> [ethnomethodology's] central recommendation is that the activities whereby members produce and manage settings of organized everyday affairs are identical with members' procedures for making these settings "account-able." The "reflexive" or "incarnate" character of accounting practices and accounts makes up the crux of that recommendation (Garfinkel, 1967, p. 1).

This seems to mean that human action, perhaps especially interpersonal conversation, includes explanations or accounts which define and structure that action. Without these accounts, the nature of which are the various ethnomethodological practices (e.g. overlooking inexplicabilities and normalizing deviance), the actions would be meaningless. This bears a similarity to Mead's second order, interpersonal reflexivity, although these distinctions make no sense in Garfinkel's theory.

If one did apply the orders distinction, however, Garfinkel's first order would look quite ambiguous and undefined, almost like Kant's unknowable manifold. The members' accounts, like Kantian forms, would be second-order or reflexive commentary, giving knowability and meaning to the first order.

In a sense Garfinkel is quite close to a semiotic approach in that the interpretation and definition of experience are seen as a constantly ongoing process. He also has similarities with Fichte's self-positing self, although for Garfinkel it is not the self but interaction which creates itself.

In my opinion Garfinkel is complementary to, rather than in competition with, Peirce and Mead. When people role-take or seem to understand each other's communications, the agreement is often more ritual than real. They may not actually understand each other, but nevertheless go through the motions. There is often side-talk and commentary which, for all practical purposes, creates a "sense" of agreement where very little is present. I think of this constructive or ethnomethodological process as a matter of degree, sometimes a minor and sometimes a major component of agreement. Nevertheless in Mead's concept of role-taking he emphasized actual agreement too much, and Garfinkel's insight is a necessary corrective. What I am saying then is that Garfinkel's reflexivity may be interpreted not as a replacement but as a supplement to the semiotic kind.

Advantages of the Reflexive Approach

Throughout this chapter I have been showing how the concept of reflexivity fits into the theory of self, both historically and systematically. I see four basic advantages to this concept.

First, it makes sense out of the various kinds of reflexivity in language. I have already pointed out how language, as a system of meaning, is a field or medium for intra- and interpersonal reflexivity. In addition it has specific reflexive words, usually ending with the suffix "self," e.g. itself, myself, etc. Some words, notably the much-disputed pronoun "I," are reflexive without the suffix. I will discuss the disputed referentiality of the word "I" again in chapter 6. I am now mentioning it merely to illustrate the reflexivity of language.

The pronouns not only encode and designate reflexivity, they are also a useful instrument for analyzing its empirical process. In particular the explicit internal conversation, as I showed in chapter 3, constantly makes use of the words "I," "me," and "you," among other pronouns.

In addition to the two linguistically based reflexivities already mentioned, language can refer back to itself in the variously sized reflexive loops I mentioned earlier. It is possible to argue that, although language is reflexive in several ways, consciousness is not. Yet there is a strength in the position that reflexive language is isomorphic with the reflexivity of consciousness. Not only does language then make more sense; the data of language also help to explain the data of reflexive consciousness.

A second advantage of the reflexivity perspective, as in Mead's case, is that it can offer a unique theory of universals. The classic theories of the universality of ideas are: Platonic or extreme realism; the opposite position of nominalism; and the mediating position, associated with Aristotle and Aquinas, of moderate realism. Kant's conceptualism or theory of forms, by virtue of which the mind inserts the universality into ideas, is a modern position, as is Mead's theory of reflexivity.

According to the latter, the cognitive agreement among the reflexive poles – self and other, or (for Mead) I and me – is the foundation for the universality of the particular response or idea at issue (Miller, 1973; Lewis and Smith, 1980, p. 126). In this theory the particulars, which are united by the universal, are not the members of a class in the usual sense. They are the members of a response to a class. In the case of a biological species, such as dogs, the universal is not found in the shared properties of all dogs but in the shared properties of all responses to dogs. In the case of artifacts, such as chairs, the universal is not in the shared features of chairs but in those of chair-users.

Each of the five theories of universals has its strengths and weaknesses, but Mead's is uniquely supported by the concept of culture. If reality is, at least in part, filtered and defined by culture, the meanings of ideas must be similarly based on our cultural response to reality. It is possible to combine Mead's theory of universals with one of the other four, my own preference being for moderate realism. This would entail the combining of a consensus theory of truth with one of correspondence, although this line of thinking is too fine-grained for the present context.

A third advantage of the reflexive approach is that it can explain both cognition and freedom with the same concepts. In the first chapter I explained freedom of choice as a function of the semiotic process, particularly its capacity to give unique definitions and interpretations to situations. Once made, these interpretations can require and, in effect, determine a certain choice. But the process of forming the interpretation is itself free. I kicked the notion of free will back a step to semiotic cognition.

Looking at the same process with the concept of reflexivity, free choice is a reflexive act in which the I uncouples from the me. Routine semiotic reflexivity, in which distinct acts of choice are not made, entails less reflexive distancing between the I and me, and no uncoupling. In the act of choice the reflecting pole, the I, stands back from and scrutinizes the me, the locus of memory, habit and earlier definitions of the situation. The I reviews previous responses to situations similar to the one being faced, and, from these materials of the past, constructs a completely new definition.

In the literature on volition and desire, there have been two ways in which these processes are said to be reflexive. One is the previously mentioned Hegelian–Baldwinian–Lacanian idea that humans, in addition to wanting specific objects, have a desire "for desire." The other is the idea that an act is free if the desire it is intended to satisfy conforms to a higher or second-order desire (Frankfurt, 1971; Neely, 1974). The reflexive theory of freedom, which I am drawing from Peirce and Mead, is a third, although it could be combined with elements of the previous two.

The reflexive approach, then, not only permits a theory of universals but also one of freedom. The parsimonious quality of this theoretical strategy – many explanations from few concepts – is part of reflexivity's strength.

Still another strength of the reflexive approach is that it helps explain the "blind spot" of all reflexive relations, including those of the self and consciousness. The reflecting pole can see only the other pole, the reflectee, and never itself. The self has a permanently unknowable blind spot. Kant postulated a transcendental ego to explain away the blind spot, but he was not convincing. As one Kantian commentator put it:

> Immanuel Kant put the problem in another manner. There are three factors in a knowing relationship: subject, act, and object. In the case of self-knowing the subject and the object appear to be identical. The ego knows the ego. But this, said Kant, is impossible; for whenever the knower tries to know the knower it thereby turns the knower into the known. The knower knows the known, but not the knower. Or to express this in another fashion – the "I" cannot know the "I," it can only know the "me." And the "me" and the "I" are not identical. The "I," the self as knower, said Kant, cannot be the object of knowledge; it is transcendental to knowing. Kant appears to have made sure that the "I" could never be known by christening it "the original transcendental synthesis unity of apperception!" (Organ, 1987, pp. 114–115).

In contrast, the approach I am using merely accepts the blind spot as a structural feature, both of reflexivity theory and of the empirical reality it sets out to explain.

In the analysis of cultural, as opposed to intra-personal, reflexivity – whether in the formal sciences of mathematics and logic or in theory generally – a reflexive meaning can be regarded as applying to itself. In other words the blind spot can be filled with self-reference and self-application. When this is done, the blind spot can turn into contradiction and paradox, for, when applied to itself, the meaning can contradict itself. This can happen indirectly, when a theoretical proposition refers to a class of entities that include itself (Russell's fallacy of "types"). And it can happen directly, when a thesis refers to its own meaning. Such cultural reflexivities fill the blind spot with contradiction, making it look better, kept empty. Gödel (1931) was the only one who could find not contradiction but permanent uncertainty in cultural reflexivity. I think this is because he modeled this reflexivity more closely on that of the self than others had done.

We have now encountered several ways of handling the reflexive blind spot. It can be filled in by a transcendental ego as Kant does. It can be filled by infinitizing the self, fusing subject and object and making it into a God, as Hegel does. It can be filled in by contradiction, as the formal theorists – Russell, Hilbert, and Carnap – or, in another way, Derrida, do. This option is complicated, however, by Gödel's non-contradictory filling-in of the blind spot. It is also possible to deny there is a blind spot at all, but to do this one needs an upwardly reducing, mechanistic theory of consciousness. Finally, it can simply be accepted as an unavoidable, built-in feature of the human being's psychological make-up. Although the I may attempt to talk to itself, it can talk only to the you, and, in a more indirect way, to the me. It cannot talk to or know itself.

The reflexive approach's handling of the blind spot is one of its strengths, for it neither denies nor explains it away in some unsatisfying manner. Instead it simply accepts and shows the structural reasons for its unavoidable existence. This interpretation also helps to explain the experience of a divided self, which is a pathological expansion of the blind spot. In addition it helps to explain Sartre's bad faith. In that situation a person repressed the memory of their free choices by burying their freedom in their blind spot.

Summary

This chapter has been an attempt to enrich Peirce–Mead semiotic theory by relating it to two concepts: reflexivity and orders. I sketched the history of philosophy, showing the genealogy of the pragmatists' reflexive self. Then I showed how the reflexive circuit fitted into and was the same as that of the semiotic triad.

After that I introduced the distinction between the first and second orders showing how it clarified the difference between two modes of reflexivity. I also showed how my two orders differed from those of various other theorists. I followed this by listing the advantages of the orders distinction.

Then, with the concepts thus far developed, it was possible to look at some current uses of reflexivity, relating them to the way I am using the term. Finally I reviewed and discussed some advantages of the reflexivity approach, showing its utility for organizing, if not solving, a wide range of intellectual problems.

5

Solidarity

So far my notion of the semiotic self, both in structure and content, has emphasized the cognitive side. This is reasonably true to both Peirce, who gave emotion a minor role in his semiotic, and Mead, who gave it no role at all. My notion of reflexivity, including its two orders, has also been primarily cognitive. It is possible for the self to reflect on and relate to itself emotionally too, although so far I have been saying little of that possibility. This cognitive bent is in tune with the dominant way the self has been theorized in recent years, in psychology and sociology if not in psychiatry and psychoanalysis.

But the cognitive approach was not always dominant. Around the turn of the century, an emotional theory of the self, defined by William James, was the more important. This approach, which he called "self-feeling," was further developed by Charles Horton Cooley in sociology. But that theory was opposed by Dewey and Mead, whose more cognitive leanings prevailed in the social sciences.

Nevertheless there have always been two theories of the self: emotional and cognitive. The emotional approach dominated until about the 1920s. Then the cognitively reflexive approach dominated for several decades. But in recent years the emotional approach has been making a comeback. I will refer to the emotional approach as the "solidarity" theory of the self, for I will interpret self-feeling as a kind of solidarity. I will show what solidarity means in Durkheim's macro theory and then show how this idea can be "lowered", not only to the level of interaction but also to that of the self. Then I will work my way through James, Cooley, and the other self-feeling theorists.

After that, having laid out the two approaches side-by-side, I will look at their complementarity and the problems that can be clarified with this complementarity. The main problems I will consider are those of semiotic bindingness or necessity, master–slave fights and recognition, and the phylogenesis of the self.

My major purposes, then, for this chapter are: formalizing the self-feeling theory of the self and showing that it is a continuing tradition; filling a hole in the Peirce–Mead semiotic theory by inserting emotion and thereby explaining semiotic power; showing the complementarity of the two traditions; showing that in synthesis they can shed new light on various problems; and explaining, via the concept of solidarity, how the micro and macro levels can be integrated.

Durkheim and Solidarity

In social theory the major use of the concept of solidarity has been that of Durkheim, particularly in his *Division of Labor* (1893/1964). He, of course, located this property in the society or social structure, not in the individual. I will relocate this concept at the individual level, showing how this macro idea can be applied at the micro level as well. I will not be claiming to use the concept exactly as Durkheim did, for there are certain transformations entailed in the movement from one level to another. In addition, as I describe Durkheim's use of this concept I will be entering disputed scholarly territory. In Durkheim there are usually enough gaps and ambiguities to create significant disagreement among interpreters. I will try to remain reasonably close to Durkheim's actual views, imprecise and inconstant as these sometimes were. But my primary purpose will be in building my own theory, with Durkheim serving as means to an end.

Durkheim drew the concept of solidarity from an ongoing French discussion, in which the term was used in a loose ethical or ideological sense (Hayward, 1959). He narrowed the concept, not without some debt to Comte, to mean social cohesion or unity (Alpert, 1939/1961, p. 178). He also added the quasi-evolutionary distinction between mechanical and organic solidarity.

I will not examine the many difficulties with this distinction, not least the misleading overtones of the two terms (the "signifiers"), but I must mention their asymmetrical quality. Mechanical solidarity is the unity of a shared culture, itself pictured as highly ritualized, morally dense, and symbolically thick. Organic solidarity is not primarily cultural at all, but industrial, economic, and logistic. This asymmetry creates problems for transferring these concepts, particularly the latter, to the intra-subjective level.

There is a related ambiguity about what might be called the surface and deep meanings of "solidarity." Most of the time Durkheim uses the term to mean the moral unity of a society, whether based on the modern division of labor or the pre-modern absence of this division. But some of the time, especially in *The Elementary Forms of Religious Behavior* (1915/1965), at least as I read this book, he uses the term more comprehensively and profoundly, to mean something like the meaningful or semiotic bondedness of a society. He argues that ritual creates social bondedness, which in turn provides the underlying energy, force, and "necessity" for cultural power. In my terms deep solidarity creates "semiotic power."

Once ritual produces cultural or semiotic power the latter expresses itself in the forms of meaning, specifically truth, goodness, and beauty. The semiotic definition is deeper than the moral for several reasons: it includes the (cognitive and esthetic) non-moral as well as the moral forms of meaning; it points to the force that underlies the forms of meaning; it identifies the ritual process that produces or constitutes this force; and it hints at the genesis or self-assembly of this force in the primates-becoming-humans.

The deeper interpretation of Durkheim's "solidarity" is also hinted at in *Suicide* (1897/1951). In that work the states of the collective consciousness that could produce high suicide rates are at the extremes of two continua: egoism vs altruism and anomie vs fatalism (Westby, 1991, pp. 294–303). These two continua or variables are sometimes said to be properties of organizational and normative integration respectively. All four pathologies – egoism, altruism, anomie, and fatalism – weaken unity and integration, although Durkheim was imprecise about the exact ways in which they do this.

On the face of it, integration and solidarity, both defined as unity, look similar. It is therefore surprising that Durkheim did not take his use of "solidarity" through from *The Division of Labor* to *Suicide*. It would have stitched those books together more effectively and deepened the argument of *Suicide*. But on the other hand it would have forced him to face the theoretical ambiguities of that book.

In particular Durkheim was never clear enough about the two continua: about what they measure and how they differ from each other. He never explained or clarified the two underlying properties. He also failed to name or even mention the healthy mid-points of the two continua. He gave us the four pathological terms as though they were a free-standing and self-explanatory network of concepts. Yet they make sense only in comparison with the two unnamed mid-points: the one between egoism and altruism, and the one between anomie and fatalism.

At this point no attempt to improve on Durkheim will please everyone, and I realize there are several arguable interpretations of *Suicide's* logical structure, but the one I think works best, particularly in the context of this book, is the following. The underlying property of the egoism–altruism continuum is the cognitive culture, and more specifically the locus of cognitive authority. At the egoistic extreme this authority (and responsibility) is thrust upon the individual. For Durkheim the Protestant rule of individual interpretation of the Bible exemplified this extreme. In contrast the altruistic pole locates cognitive authority in the larger society, the individual being dependent on and subordinate to this structure for access to truth. The Catholic church exemplified this mode of cognitive authority. When Durkheim locates the Jews on this continuum he sometimes seems to vacillate between the cognitive and the moral, for the Jewish community had both kinds of integration. This vacillation is a limiting factor for my interpretation.

In contrast to egosim–altruism the anomie–fatalism continuum seems to be based unambiguously on the moral culture, i.e. on normative or moral integration. The reason I am contrasting this mode of integration with the more cognitive one is that the contrast leads back to deep solidarity. Moral solidarity is relatively superficial, for it assumes a pre-existing linguistic or semiotic solidarity. Cognitive solidarity is deep because it assumes nothing. This form of solidarity is the great human "differentia," for it is the means by which our line of primates entered the world of abstract meanings. Later in this chapter I will explain how I think the phylogenetic breakthrough may have happened, again using Durkheim in a somewhat innovative manner. For now I merely want to point out that *Suicide* suggests the moral-cognitive contrast and the correspondingly deepened concept of solidarity that I will be using.

Returning to the two continua, egosim–altruism and anomie–fatalism, the optimal mid-points might be called cognitive solidarity for the former and moral solidarity for the latter. Alternatively they could both be called modes of "semiotic solidarity." The identification and naming of the mid-points plugs the four pathological states back into reality, i.e. into the universe of cultural possibilities of which they are members. In addition it connects *Suicide* and *The Division of Labor*.

The two mid-points also have clear counterparts in pragmatist theory. In relation to cognitive standards the pragmatists' self is neither completely private ("egoistic") nor completely absorbed by society ("altruistic"), but at a kind of mid-point. In relation to moral standards it is neither anomic nor fatalistic but at a similar mid-point. The pragmatists would not deny that culture can be at Durkheim's four pathological extremes, or that these conditions can influence the individual. But the self, both in its structure and in its healthiest milieu, is characterized by the two mid-points.

107

Although I think this interpretation has a reasonable fit with *Suicide*, it does reveal still another problem: both cognitive and moral bondedness are primarily matters of mechanical solidarity, not organic. The argument works best with undeveloped, mechanical societies with little or no division of labor. But most of Durkheim's data on suicide are derived from 19th-century European societies, which were characterized primarily, at least as Durkheim saw it, by organic solidarity. For present purposes, however, all I want to show is how *Suicide* can be read as using the concept of solidarity in a comprehensively cognitive-moral or "deep" way.

When Durkheim introduced the concept of solidarity, including the mechanical–organic distinction, he used the anaology of friendship (1893/1964, pp. 54–6). Once he had formalized the concept, however, he did not use it on the levels below social organization, i.e. on interaction *sui generis* (including friendship) or the self. More recently, though, others have begun to do so. Both Goffman (1967) and Collins (1982, pp. 53–9) have applied his notions of ritual and solidarity to the interaction order, dropping these concepts down one level from where Durkheim had located them. Collins (1989) has also suggested a way in which these ideas can be dropped still another level, into the self, and, in a somewhat different way, I have made this suggestion as well (Wiley, 1989).

Yet it is also possible to see traces of Durkheim's solidarity at his own level of the self, lurking behind his notion of the sacred individual. In mechanical society, as he saw it, sacredness was primarily a characteristic of the overall society and, only in a derived and limited way, of the individual. In his organic solidarity, however, sacredness became increasingly attached to the individual, forming the centerpiece of organic's morality, limited as that was.

He explained the sacredness of the society as generated by face-to-face ritual and mediated by solidarity. But he did not explain the sacredness of the individual in a parallel way, i.e. by internal semiotic processes. Instead he explained it externally, as derived from the society, much as he did for the individual of mechanical solidarity. He did not allow the individual to self-create his or her own sacredness, via ritual and solidarity, as he did for the society.

Given that Durkheim's assumptions privileged the social over the individual, it is understandable that he would use a double standard to explain how each got its sacredness. Yet it is at least as reasonable to explain the sacredness of the modern individual, not just as an extension of society's sacredness, but by processes internal to the individual, specifically those of intra-subjective ritual and solidarity.

One improvement Goffman made on Durkheim was to see sacredness, not just in the individual in general, but in concrete individuals. For Durkheim sacredness was confined to the generic citizen, to the rights, the inviolability, the holiness, etc. It did not extend to the individual as such, except in an indirect and derived way. It was the public society, particularly the state, that constructed and guaranteed the morally sacred individual. By restricting sacredness to the idea or category of the individual, Durkheim restricted its ritual production to the society, for it was society that gave sacredness to the abstract class or role.

If he had seen the importance of everyday, face-to-face ritual, as Goffman did, he would have noticed that sacredness is in the concrete as well as in the abstract individual. Individuals do not just borrow it from their species on public holidays. They also create sacredness, its rituals and solidarities, at their own, concrete interactional level, as in birthday parties, handshakes, kisses, vacations, dates, family gatherings, etc. (not to mention the more indirect effects of negative or conflictual ritual). They do this with their own semiotic resources, without any help or derivations from the state or other societal agencies.

Goffman's fleshing-out of Durkheim's sacred individual leads right to the question I am bringing up: whether ritual and solidarity operate, not only in Durkheim's society and Goffman's face-to-face group, but also inside the minds of concrete human beings. My view is that the internal conversation can create intra-personal rituals that, in turn, produce and maintain the internal solidarity. This solidarity is the basis for the sacredness and also for whatever standards of truth, goodness, and beauty might animate this individual. The interaction order and the society are, of course, not completely uninvolved in this internal process. But the heart of it is internal to the person (Hilbert, 1992).

To transform Durkheim's macro-level solidarity into a micro-level variable I had to make two adjustments: deepening and semioticizing his notion of solidarity; and transferring this variable from the societal, via the interactional, into the level of the self. I am also arguing that, although Durkheim did not explicitly say these two things, his thought implied them. I have shown the semiotic version of solidarity in both the religion and suicide books, and I explained how, with the help of Goffman, the ritual scheme can reasonably be inserted into the self.

If the Durkheimian scheme of solidarity, ritual, and collective consciousness, is lowered into the level of the self, interesting theoretical possibilities appear. A solidaristic theory of the self becomes available, and the insights of several, now unrelated theorists begin falling into place. In addition a solidarity-driven self fits neatly into the reflexive semiotic scheme, supplying the dynamic force it needs.

The Self-Feeling Theorists

William James's theory of the self was quite eclectic (Cravens, 1978, pp. 72–5), but it centered on a unique kind of feeling. A quotation cited in chapter 2 bears repetition at this point:

> *In its widest possible sense*, however, *a man's Self is the sum total of all that he CAN call his*, not only his body and his psychic powers, but his clothes and his house, his wife and children, his ancestors and friends, his reputation and works, his lands and horses, and yacht and bank-account. All these things give him the same emotions (James, 1890/1950, vol. 1, p. 291).

Or in the same book:

> *The words* ME, *then, and* SELF, *so far as they arouse feeling and connote emotional worth*, *are* OBJECTIVE *designations, meaning* ALL THE THINGS *which have the power to produce in a stream of consciousness excitement of a certain peculiar sort* (p. 319).

James's self was multi-dimensional, and it certainly included cognition, although its central, organizing feature was a kind of ownership, ownness and, one might say, self-love. This usage is close to what I am calling "emotional reflexivity," in contrast to the more bloodless cognitive reflexivity of George Herbert Mead.

Cooley, who studied his children, moved beyond James in some respects (Mead, 1930, p. 699). He worked with incipient notions of reflexivity, both interpersonal (the "looking-glass self") and intra-personal (thought as a conversation with an imaginary playmate, who gradually became a kind of generalized other). Nevertheless his core position was one of self-feeling, much like that of James. Here is Cooley on the first-person pronouns:

> The distinctive thing in the idea for which the pronouns of the first person are names is apparently a characteristic kind of feeling which may be called the my-feeling or sense of appropriation. Almost any sort of ideas may be associated with this feeling, and so come to be named "I" or "mine," but the feeling, and that alone it would seem, is the determining factor in the matter (1922/1964, pp. 169–70).

The feeling-self of James and Cooley seems nested or layered in degrees of intimacy. They use an ownership or property metaphor, but one that is not quite uniform from layer to layer. Starting from the innermost layer, they seem to move from the psychological parts of the self, to the body, to other people, to physical property. The inner layer is not so much ownership as ownness and, in my terms, solidarity. I am suggesting that the James–Cooley self-feeling, particularly at its core, is not an emotion in the ordinary sense but rather an energy or force (or "proto-emotion"), similar to Durkheim's semiotic solidarity. The force created at the inner layer is strong enough to hold and contain the outer layers.

A close look at the preceding quotations will reveal an imprecision in the central concept. For James the self seems to be both a kind of feeling and the things that cause that feeling. For Cooley it is also a feeling, but in addition it is the "ideas" that may be associated with that feeling. For the present study I will just gloss over these differences, since they do not affect the way I am using the concept.

But in the case of James the word "excitement" does have interesting Durkheimian echoes. For Durkheim, of course, the sacred produced collective feelings of effervescence, electricity, and other forms of excitement. James's self-feeling, as an "excitement of a certain peculiar sort," sounds like Durkheim's solidarity.

An admirer of James, who also preferred an emotional to a cognitive theory of the self, was Alfred North Whitehead.

Mere existence has never entered into the consciousness of man, except as the remote terminus of an abstraction in thought. Descartes' "Cogito ergo sum" is wrongly translated, "I *think*, therefore I am." It is never bare thought or bare existence that we are aware of. I find myself as essentially a unity of emotions, enjoyments, hopes, fears, regrets, valuations of alternatives, decisions – all of them subjective reactions to the environment as active in my nature. My unity – which is Descartes' "I am" – is my process of shaping this welter of material into a consistent pattern of feelings (1938/1966, pp. 165–6).

Although James, Cooley, and Whitehead were all three aware of the self's cognitive processes, they all thought feeling was the more encompassing, self-defining activity.

Before continuing with the self-feeling tradition, let me consider the objection Mead made to the James–Cooley approach.

Emphasis should be laid on the central position of thinking when considering the nature of the self. Self-consciousness, rather than affective experience with its motor accompaniments, provides the core and primary structure of the self, which is thus essentially a cognitive rather than an emotional phenomenon. . . . Cooley and James, it is true, endeavor to find the basis of the self in reflexive affective experiences, i.e. experiences involving "self-feeling"; but the theory that the nature of the self is to be found in such experiences does not account for the origin of the self, or of the self-feeling which is supposed to characterize such experiences. The individual need not take the attitudes of others toward himself in these experiences, since these experiences merely in themselves do not necessitate his doing so, and unless he does so, he cannot develop a self; and he will not do so in these experiences unless his self has already originated elsewhere (1934, p. 173).

Mead is here claiming that the self could not originate, presumably ontogenetically but possibly also phylogenetically, by emotional causes. He thought some cognitively reflexive cause was needed to get the process started. He also thought self-feeling could not be explained without cognitive presuppositions. For him James and Cooley were superficial thinkers, missing the obvious. Although he granted them a phenomenological "feel" for the way we experience the self, he claimed that this feel presupposed the pathway of cognitive reflexivity. By the time Mead wrote his evaluation of Cooley (1930), restating his earlier objections to the self-feeling approach, the shift to cognitive reflexivity in the social sciences had already taken place.

Mead had a point, but he overstated it. Self-feeling does not explain the cognitively reflexive dimension of the self, but it does not depend on it as much as he thought, either. Each process is somewhat independent of the other.

For one thing, in Cooley the socially reflexive basis of self-feelings, in contradiction to Mead, clearly entails the taking of other's attitudes toward oneself. This is quite explicit in his notion of the "looking-glass self." The weakness of Cooley's emotional mirror is that it cannot capture cognitive reflexivity and therefore misses much of the self. But the strength, which was inaccessible to Mead's approach, was that it explained emotions we have toward our self in a way that is both social and reflexive. As he put it:

A self-idea of this sort seems to have three principal elements: the imagination of our appearance to the other person; the imagination of his judgment of that appearance, and some sort of self-feeling, such as pride or mortification. The comparison with a looking-glass hardly suggests the second element, the imagined judgement, which is quite essential. The thing that moves us to pride or shame is not the mere mechanical reflection of ourselves, but an imputed sentiment, the imagined effect of this reflection upon another's mind (1922/1964, p. 184).

Cooley's mention here of how we imagine our appearance to others and how they judge us refers to taking the attitudes of others toward us.

Mead's cognitively tilted theory of meaning makes him want to deny intersubjectivity or shared response to the experience of emotion. He wants to deny it reflexivity, particularly the interpersonal variety, and privatize it inside the self. But this works only for some of the emotions some of the time. Ego's anger may be accompanied, not by alter's shared anger but by alter's fear (of ego's anger). Some emotions create opposite emotions in others. But many emotions are shared, at least at times. Examples are joy, fear, grief, guilt, triumph, ennui, and virtually all other emotions, including anger.

In addition, in the preceding quotation, Mead both affirms and denies reflexivity to the James–Cooley self-feeling. On the one hand he says, "Cooley and James, it is true, endeavor to find the basis of the self in reflexive affective experiences," but then he contradicts this with "The individual need not take the attitudes of others toward himself in these experiences, since these experiences merely in themselves do not necessitate his doing so." If an emotion does not entail taking the attitudes of others toward oneself it cannot be reflexive, since the latter implies the former. For Mead, "reflexive" means looping through the other and back to the self in a social manner, even if the "other" is internalized in oneself in a Peircean you or a generalized other. If self-feeling is, as in the first comment, reflexive, then it must entail taking the attitude of the other toward oneself. Of course the attitude in question is not Mead's cognitively tilted habit or dispositional. It is the emotional attitude that Cooley's others have toward us, and which we discern with the looking-glass process.

In other words, if emotion is treated more socially than Mead does and is accordingly inserted into the structure of meaning, it can fit nicely into the theory of reflexive semiotic. Peirce saw this (5.475; 5.292) even though Mead did not. Similarly, the things that Mead's self-feeling could not do – account for the origin of the self or of self-feeling itself – the theory of reflexive semiotic can, to some extent, do.

Later in this chapter I will argue that the origin of the self, both phylogenetically in the primates and ontogenetically in the human infant, is caused partly by emotions. A version of Cooley's looking-glass, as a way of perceiving the caretakers' emotions, is obviously related to the birth of the self in the infant. Phylogenesis is more obscure, but I will show how the

113

emotion of solidarity may well have been central to the birth of the self in the primates.

Having now laid out the James–Cooley position, Mead's critique of that position and my evaluation of that critique, I can go on to state my belief that both positions are partially correct, i.e. they complement each other. The self is constituted in a cognitively reflexive manner, but in addition it is powered by a kind of emotion, itself also reflexive. This emotion, which is the psychological counterpart of biological life, is the solidarity that creates semiotic power. Without the reflexive triad this power is blind, but without the power the triad lacks cognitive force and is therefore meaningless. I will show the advantages of recognizing this complementarity later in the chapter.

I am now about to show how self-feeling is used in psychiatry, and particularly in the thought of Heinz Kohut, but I first want to list the most important meanings of the term "self-feeling." Both "self" and "feeling" are difficult concepts, and it should be no surprise that their combination is also difficult. Even James and Cooley used self-feeling with imprecision and relative abandon, and I can think of at least half a dozen ways in which the term is being used today. But if I describe the major four, this will be enough to put some order in the concept.

I have already mentioned the James–Cooley "property" metaphor and the loose way in which those two theorists use it. The main thing that is "mine" is the "I" or self-as-present. This is much like the concept of personal identity. This self is mine and nobody else's, and it is the one I have always been. The other semiotic elements of the self, namely the me and you, are also intimately "mine." With this starting-point the property metaphor fans out to include the body, one's family and friends, and one's physical property. This notion of self-feeling is somewhat like the notion of the "first-person point of view," though neither James nor Cooley said that.

Second, when I translate the James–Cooley self-feeling into internal solidarity and semiotic power I am blowing up one aspect – the most intimate one – of their concept. I used Durkheim's energy metaphors of effervescence, electricity, etc., to get at the dynamic quality of this self-feeling. This notion is a little like Freud's "Lust-Funktion" or joy in being mentally healthy, for it is a natural brimming of semiotic energy that flows from a well-operating self.

Third, when Cooley is talking about the looking-glass self he seems to be talking about how we construct our level of self-esteem. If we think others approve of us it will be high; if we think they disapprove it will be low. This is the notion of feelings toward or about the self. It is perhaps the clearest and most literal notion of self-feeling.

Finally there is the notion of reflecting, or looking back in some way, on

114

our emotions. We might want to take a close look at our emotions for some reason. Or we may even want to guide and regulate them. I have not discussed this notion of self-feeling or emotional reflexivity yet, but it is important enough to belong here. Rosenberg (1990) pointed out three ways we might want to bend the cognitive self back onto our emotions: since emotions are often ambiguous we might want to reflectively identify them; we may also want to regulate or display them in some preconceived manner; we might want to deliberately experience certain emotions, such as grief at a funeral.

The above four notions of self-feeling and emotional reflexivity show what a fertile area of conceptualization this is. It is not necessary to attempt to clarify these concepts further for all I want to do is funnel these meanings through the concept of intra-psychological solidarity.

Earlier I suggested that psychiatry and psychoanalysis have always defined the self in a primarily emotional way. It was in psychology and the social sciences that the more cognitive pragmatists had their influence. But the precise notion of self-feeling has recently been developed in psychoanalysis by Heinz Kohut, chiefly known for his theory of narcissism (1971). For Kohut narcissism was caused by a flaw in self-feeling, itself resulting from either too little or too much attention (his "mirroring") in the pre-oedipal years. Kohut believed that his paper on introspection (1959) represented his theoretical breakthrough, for it was at that point that he departed from mainstream psychoanalysis and began developing self theory, although he never got around to explicitly connecting introspection with reflexivity and the self.

In the mind of one Kohutian "the concept of the self was derived from empirical data as a clinical matter of necessity; it was not invoked as an abstract scientific concept" (Palaci, 1980, p. 323). When Kohut was using standard, psychoanalytic "drive theory" with his patients, several of them claimed that he was not listening to them. In orthodox Freudianism this sort of complaining is usually interpreted as "resistance." Kohut mentions one patient in particular ("Miss F") who insisted that her experiences of herself be given more weight than any inferences that might be derived from mainline theory (Kohut, 1971, pp. 283–4; Ornstein, 1978, pp. 52–4). It looks to me that Kohut's notion of introspection, both direct in the self and especially "vicarious" in others, was his response to these patients' insistence. In other words the "clinical matter of necessity" was the voice of patients insisting that he credit their introspections and use them, vicariously and empathetically, as valid clinical data.

Kohut's therapeutic shift to the self, then, although not "invoked as an abstract scientific concept," appears to have been a response to his patients' experience of the self. This experience was reflexively introspective, justifying the shift to the word "self." Kohut's definition of introspection is clearly reflexive.

> The inner world cannot be observed with the aid of our sensory organs. Our thoughts, wishes, feelings, and fantasies cannot be seen, smelled, heard, or touched. They have no existence in physical space, and yet they are real, and we can observe them as they occur in time: through introspection in ourselves, and through empathy (i.e., vicarious introspection) in others (1959, p. 459).

Kohut is not explicitly in either the cognitive or the self-feeling camp, but I think his working notion of emotional reflexivity ("introspection") bridges the two. Kohut's self, like that of Mead, is an "object to itself," but emotionally rather than cognitively. Kohut's self is defined and energized by its reflexive feelings toward itself. Of course the self-feeling of James and Cooley branched out, vaguely, into the whole spectrum of emotions one could have toward oneself. The only unifier was the "mine" or property theme. Kohut's self-feeling is primarily one of self-worth or esteem, which of course also branches out into modalities. But self-esteem is much more clearly reflexive than the property metaphor, since it has to do with a clear and tangible emotion that the self has toward itself.

Kohut improved on James's and Cooley's self theory, and showed how to connect them to the (cognitive) reflexivity theory of Mead. In addition Kohut is getting us closer to the solidarity theory of the self. His narcissist is the person whose internal solidarity is in jeopardy for some reason. To explain narcissism, particularly in the insistent patients I mentioned earlier, he had to shift from the linear concept of personality to the non-linear and reflexive concept of self, using the process of introspection as his bridge. With these Freudian revisionist premises he created a unique theory. This theory explains how the infant's self-solidarity originates in the family, why it sometimes runs amiss, and how, via his version of psychoanalytic practice, it can be got back on track again.

In the recent symbolic interactionist turn to emotion, there are ideas which resemble the James–Cooley self-feeling approach. As I mentioned earlier, Rosenberg (1990) has shown how reflexive processes modify and define the raw physiological experience of emotion. He is not discussing emotional reflexivity in what I take to be Kohut's sense, but rather a cognitive aspect of emotion. But his work does draw attention back to the James–Cooley tradition.

Norman Denzin's theory of emotion explicitly uses the term "self-feeling" (1984, pp. 50–51) and reconnects with the James–Cooley tradition. For Denzin all emotions, not only Kohut's self-esteem, are feelings that the self has about itself. In other words Denzin's central analytic concept is emotional reflexivity. This concept integrates the insights of James and Cooley, Kohut and Mead.

In this section I have discussed a long-standing theory of the self, defining it as emotional reflexivity, which runs parallel with Mead's more cognitive version of reflexivity. My argument is that the two traditions can be integrated, emotion with cognition and, correspondingly, solidarity with reflexivity.

Lacan and Solidarity

Lacan's theory of the self has similarities with that of the self-feeling theorists, although he is even more obscure than they are. In chapter 7 on the reductions I will discuss Lacan's overall theory. Now I only want to point to the role of Lacan's "father" in relation to intra-subjective solidarity. I am placing "father" in quotation marks because I am using the word to mean not the biological male but the one who performs the function of "fathering." Lacan was careless about this word, as he was about the word "phallus," sometimes using them physiologically and sometimes psychologically or functionally (Macey, 1988, pp. 177–209; Sprengnether, 1990, pp. 181–223).

My "fathering" is parallel with Nancy Chodorow's "mothering" (1978, p. 3), which was also used in a purely functional sense. In principle both genders can "mother" and both can "father," although empirically, women tend to do the former and men the latter.

Lacan's "father" forces the pre-oedipal child out of symbiotic solidarity with the mother (or "mother"), into communal solidarity with "him," and, by that fact, into the wider community. For Lacan the "father" brings the child the first meaning, the first "signifier," and thereby introduces the child into the worlds of language (truth) and law (goodness) (Lacan, 1966/1977).

As I read Lacan, the first signifier (his ambiguous "phallus") or entry into the universe of public meaning is the same as Durkheim's "mana" (see Lévi-Strauss, 1950/1987, pp. 56–66 for the idea of mana as the "floating signifier;" and Mehlman, 1972, for an attempt, not completely successful, to integrate the semiotic meanings of Lévi-Strauss's mana and Lacan's phallus). In the oedipal transition the "father" (aided by the "mother") pushes the child into the public semiotic community, itself based on the solidarity of shared mana, thereby removing the child from the pre- or semi-semiotic bond with the "mother." Although this separation brings gain it also brings loss, for a precious kind of meaning (or what we vaguely and semi-consciously think was precious) is lost forever, and "desire" for a return to this early meaning will never be satisfied. The gain, however, is in

117

participation or solidarity with the public, semiotic community, and thereby in the means to develop as a normal human being.

With the entry into the collective consciousness or semiotic world, I would argue that the child, for the first time, also has internal mana, semiosis, and solidarity. This is manifest in internal language (the internal conversation) and internalized law (conscience), although, underlying these capabilities, is the same semiotic force that Durkheim saw operating in the public community. This internalized solidarity operates in the same way as do the James–Cooley self-feeling and the Kohutian emotional reflexivity. What Lacan adds is a theory of how internal solidarity is first produced, in the matrix of the oedipal family.

At this point I want to mention Sprengnether's objection to Lacan and, by implication, to the way I am interpreting Lacan. (Sprengnether, 1990, pp. 233–9). Sprengnether thinks the mother (or "mother") alone can teach the child language and morality. In other words "fathering" can be part of "mothering," and both can and usually are done by the same person. She thereby demotes the importance of the oedipal transition and of the line that separates pre- and post-oedipal. Her ideas also question what I said above about how the pre-oedipal meanings that the child shares with the mother are merely pre- or semi-semiotic.

I think Sprengnether has a kind of conceptual correctness here but the scenario she is describing would be a rare and inefficient case. The "fathering" role is certainly indeterminate. It can be done by one or many, males or females, straights or gays. It is a psychological rather than a biological function. But the idea that this whole job can be done, routinely, by a single person, usually a woman and sometimes even a "single Mom," boggles the mind. There are almost always other people interacting with the infant, and they are bound to exercise some of the "fathering" role. For Sprengnether to be right, the "mother" would have to keep other people away from the child. I think Sprengnether's objection to Lacan is based largely on the careless way he throws the word "father" around. If Lacan's father is de-biologized, as I am doing, Sprengnether's objection loses much of its force.

Given, then, that Lacan bears a resemblance to the self-feeling or solidarity approach, he is also suggestive for the Peirce–Mead, semiotic approach. The triad of the three family positions or functions – "mother," "father," and "child" – bears a similarity with the semiotic triad (see Peirce W1: 503 for a comparison of the semiotic triad with the quasi-family of the Christian Holy Trinity). As I view it, the child is the sign or I position, the mother the object or me, and the father the interpretant or you. When, in the oedipal period, the father-function is added to the mother–child dyad of the pre-oedipal, the semiotic triad is completed and, in addition, mana or semiotic solidarity is released by way of the father's position. This mapping of the family roles onto semiotic space seems like a useful way of theorizing the family, although the distinction between the biological and the psychological, which I have borrowed from Chodorow and applied to all family roles, would complicate the analysis.

Garfinkel, Wittgenstein and the Solidarity of Procedure

Both Garfinkel and his close cousin, Wittgenstein, have theories in which there is no clear place for the concept of the self, and at first glance they therefore seem irrelevant to this analysis. Garfinkel (1967) pretty much replaces the self with the ethnomethods of interaction. Wittgenstein (1953), at least according to many interpreters, also tends to empty the self and place all meaning in public language. Yet at the level of language and interaction both tended to find meaning more in shared procedure and the resulting solidarity than in semantic content or, to say the same thing, "intentionality." Since neither works with intra-subjective meanings, intersubjective meanings tend to be matters of procedure, consensus, and relatively syntactic agreement. In other words both seem to rely on some notion of cognitive solidarity – not at the level of Durkheim's social structure or the Peirce–Mead self but at the interaction order *sui generis*. For both, shared meaning is a procedural matter: a "sense" of agreement for Garfinkel (according to Turner, 1988, p. 51, Garfinkel's actor seeks a "sense of facticity") and a usable or working agreement for Wittgenstein.

For my argument they are perhaps a contrasting case, for what I want to place inside the self – semiotic solidarity – they place exclusively in the interaction order. But I would like to push a step further and ask, in the spirit of a thought experiment, what a theory of the self would look like if either of these two theorists were forced to internalize their interactive theories of meaning into the self. If so, the selves of both theorists would be characterized primarily by a sense of solidarity.

Garfinkel's self would be unified by an internal conversation of ethnomethods, i.e. procedural agreement. What research there is on the internal conversation shows it to be even more ethnomethodological than the interpersonal conversation. Wittgenstein's self would, in turn, be unified by a set of working or practical agreements. These would be linked together by what I called a "semi-private" language. Neither theorists' self would have reflexivity or perhaps even intentionality, but both would have a semiotic or procedural consensus.

I have now reviewed the notion of solidarity – treating it primarily as an intra-subjective quality – as it originates in Durkheim, appears in the self-feeling theorists, gets elaborated in Lacan, and resides implicitly in Garfinkel and Wittgenstein. There are many other, closely related concepts in social theory, e.g. Erik Erikson's notion of trust, Anthony Giddens's concept of ontological security, Ralph Turner's notion of identity motives, Thomas Scheff's notion of pride (vs shame), Guy Swanson's theory of commitments and ego defenses, and, for that matter Sigmund Freud's notion of the mentally healthy person. I have included both cognitive and emotional kinds of internal solidarity because I think they merge under the broader and deeper notion of internal semiotic.

My concept of solidarity has several advantages over the closely related concepts mentioned above. It is semiotically comprehensive, underlying and animating all the forms of meaning. It fits into both the reflexively semiotic and the self-feeling theories of the self. And it transfers the macro Durkheim into the micro world, showing how his hard-won armamentarium of concepts – mechanical and organic, repressive and restitutive, anomic–egoistic–altruistic–fatalistic, negative and positive, sacred and secular, etc. – can be applied to the solidarity of the self.

I will now turn back to reflexive semiotic to show the theoretical possibilities that appear when this concept is combined with solidarity.

The Complementarity of Reflexivity and Solidarity

To consider the connection between reflexivity and solidarity it will be useful to turn back to Table 4.1 on the four modes of reflexivity. First-order, interpersonal reflexivity (Mead's "role-taking") starts the process off in the infant. Gradually the infant internalizes this interactive relation and develops the capacity for intra-personal reflexivity. In other words, the infant first learns to take the role of the other (presumably the close caretaker) as communicatee, which permits the sharing of meaning. Then comes the role of the other as communicator. This allows back-and-forth conversation of some kind. Once these interpersonal role-taking skills start taking hold, the infant can use them for the internal conversation, i.e. thought. The move is from passive to active communication and from inter to intra.

In chapter 7 I will show that the infant's self-recognition in a mirror, which I think Lacan misinterpreted, may speed up the move from inter to intra. Given the priority, then, of the inter- over the intra-personal, the temporal and causal order in table 4.1 goes from right to left. On the top-down dimension in the table the causal and temporal primacy goes to the first order, second order being a derivative reflexivity. Thus box 2 gets filled first, then box 1, and only later boxes 4 and 3.

120

The history of philosophical discovery, as described in chapter 4, is misleading, because it followed a different order. The philosophy of reflexivity, officially beginning with Descartes' "cogito," was the discovery of second-order reflexivity. Descartes then used this "thought about thought" to work his way back to the first order, i.e. to the routine contents of consciousness. This reversed the order in which these two reflexivities appear in the life of the infant, including the infant Descartes, and perhaps explains why some theorists, such as Sartre, think of second-order reflexivity as the only kind.

The modes of solidarity follow similar orders of time, causation and perhaps importance. Once the human being is formed, i.e. fully socialized, the ordering among the solidarities may become more systematic and circular, i.e. second-order solidarity has feedback effects on the first order and intra on inter.

But this fine-grained comparison of solidarity and reflexivity is more detailed than I want it to be. Instead I will approach the relation between these two concepts freely and generally, using table 4.1 as a background resource and applying the synthesis of the two concepts to a series of problems.

Solidarity and the "Bindingness" of Reflexivity

I am using the term "bindingness," as a generic term for more specific ideas. These include the necessity of truth, the oughtness of moral obligation and the "constraint" of Durkheim's social facts. This is actually "semiotic power" again, but looked at from the point of view of the knower or interpreter. Linguistically speaking any predicate that is tied to its subject and forces our assent, regardless of how, has bindingness.

Mead and Peirce both had theories which rested on the notion of reflexivity, but since Mead was the more explicit about that concept, I will relate bindingness primarily to his semiotics. Mead's concept of reflexivity, as a theory of how cognition works, lacked a clear explanation of bindingness, in any of its forms. He invented the notion of role-taking, the first of the reflexivities, to explain how humans differed from the other animals. His goal was to explain the shared, abstract, and universal features of meaning, in contrast to the unshared, concrete, and particular qualities of animal communication. This gave him only a partial semiotic, for it contained universality but not necessity. The closest thing he had to the latter was the effectiveness or workability of an idea for solving problems (Mead, 1929/1964), a kind of utilitarian persuasiveness, which is a feeble substitute for necessity.

As Randall Collins put it: "What is lacking in Mead is precisely what

Durkheim put at the center of his picture: a strong drive for solidarity with others, or at least a strong susceptibility to human belonging in a group, as an end in itself" (Collins, 1989, p. 14). This end in itself is part of reflexivity's power. Mead's theory of role-taking, as it stands, over-promises. It assumes an equivalency or isomorphism between two responses or meanings: that of the communicator and communicatee. This, it will be noted, is a good deal more static than Peirce's equivalent relation between sign and interpretant.

Accordingly, Mead's universality, as indicated in chapter 4, is in the sharedness of the two responses (and those of other possible participants). But the sense that the role-taking is accurate and "true" can hardly come only from the alleged structural isomorphism between the two responses, for research on this process shows only an approximate isomorphism and plenty of downright inaccuracy in role-taking (Shrauger and Schoeneman, 1979). In addition, Garfinkel's ethnomethodology shows how this sense of mutuality, when it appears at all, is laboriously and, in a sense, fictitiously, produced. Instead the truth or bindingness must come largely from the solidarity between the communicators, or, in Hegel's terms, from the mutual recognition.

Let me put the reflexivity–solidarity relation into a metaphorical picture. This is only a rhetorical device and not an explanation, but it does suggest how the two processes interpenetrate. Reflexivity is the uniting of two "poles:" self and (external or internalized) other. The circuit between the poles is a kind of ellipse or loop. Mead referred to this loop as "triadic," for it always has a three-point, self–other–self or I–you–me recursivity. In contrast, the usual picture of solidarity – and Durkheim's favorite – is that of a field of force, e.g. a magnetic field. Mead's reflexivity supplies the bi-polarity or ellipse, and Durkheim's solidarity the force-field itself.

I think Mead always assumed solidarity within reflexivity, in a kind of peaceful, nuclear-family setting, but he was unaware of it. A closer acquaintance with Hegel and recognition might have made him conscious of this tacit assumption. In any case, solidarity can explain the puzzle of reflexivity's bindingness.

This does not imply that there is no truth, beauty, or goodness, or that bindingness is purely "relativistic." Rather it means that, whatever absolutes or necessities may exist, they are mediated and energized by social solidarity. An idea of this kind has always been present in the notion of "culture," that broad paradigmatic assumption that unites all the social sciences. The "externality" of culture is in its abstractness, universality, and reflexivity, but its power and "constraint" arise from the solidarity of cultural communities. Just as reflexivity and self-reference are "concealed" within Durkheim's concept of solidarity (Luhmann, 1982, p. 7), solidarity is implicit within Mead's notion of reflexivity. Combining these two ideas, then, produces a more workable theory of meaning than either can give alone.

Up to now I have primarily been addressing bindingness and inter-personal reflexivity. When we turn to intra-personal, the overall argument remains the same, but this mode of communication has nuances of its own. The two poles are still self and other, but this is now the internalized other, a more elusive concept than the real or free-standing other.

Recall the distinction between the two orders, first and second, of internal reflexivity. If all thought is a conversation with oneself, as Mead and Peirce both argued, what is the difference between a first- and second-order internal conversation? I would say that in the first order conversation is with the self about external objects, and in the second order talk is with the self *about the self*.

This "about" notion should be regarded as wide-ranging. In particular one can talk about "part" of the self or about the whole (Rosenberg, 1979, pp. 19–22). Earlier I defined second-order internal reflexivity as thought about thought, or, as we might now say, (internal) conversation about (internal) conversation. To talk to oneself about oneself, then, is either to talk about part of one's internal conversation or about its entirety (the "whole" self). Second-order self-talk ranges from relatively unimportant bits of introspection to the most intense and global self-examination.

With this distinction between the two orders of self-talk at hand, let me return to the place of solidarity in internal reflexivity. The internal conversation is primarily between the I and the you, although indirectly and reflexively it is also between the I and the me. There can also be various "visitors," as discussed in chapter 3.

In all these varieties of the internal conversation the "role-taking" formula of interpersonal reflexivity, in both its communicatee and communicator aspects, continues to hold. The speaker or communicator (the "I") talks to the "other" (you, me, or visitor). This other is perceived as understanding the communication, and the perceived understanding is captured reflexively (communicatee variety), in the manner of Mead's significant gesture. In other words mutuality of response or meaning is perceived. This is the cognitive side of internal reflexivity or role-taking.

In addition, however, there must be a certain solidarity between the two communicative poles for meaning to have its energy, force, or necessity. This assumes a certain amount of mutual recognition between the poles or aspects of the self. As Hegel pointed out, to have mutual recognition among parts of the self, there must first be mutual recognition between the self and an intimate other or others, the former being derivative of the latter. Just as intra-personal reflexivity is derivative of the interpersonal, internal solidarity is derivative of the interactive.

Accordingly, just as the isomorphism in interpersonal role-taking is partly a fabrication of solidarity (and ethnomethodological practices), the sense of mutuality of meaning in the internal conversation is also, in part, solidaristically (and again ethnomethodologically) driven. The "bindingness" of both conversations then, internal and external, is largely the result of solidarity.

At the second order, there is an additional way in which solidarity is implicated in the two conversations. So far, I have discussed solidarity primarily as a driving force or efficient cause. But it is also a goal or final cause in both conversations. Much second-order interpersonal conversation is either ritual or "repair-work," both being attempts to increase solidarity. Anniversaries, birthdays, holidays, vacations, etc, are examples of the former. Explaining what one meant, trying to patch up an earlier fight, or even going into couples' or family therapy, are examples of the latter. These second-order reflexivities require a good deal of solidarity to begin with, and without this they can be abysmal failures. But when they succeed, they build up the solidarity of a relationship.

Much internal conversation also has a bearing on solidarity. Some depressed people seem to get stuck in a flow of negative thoughts, thereby systematically lowering their internal solidarity. Cognitive therapy is often an attempt to redirect the internal conversation into solidarity-building channels.

In more normal circumstances, the internal conversation, like the interpersonal conversation previously mentioned, is often an attempt to repair, maintain, and build up internal solidarity, even in the absence of mood disorder. The self spends much of its flow soothing, reassuring, congratulating, and daring itself. This is a variant of Collins's "strong drive for solidarity," mentioned earlier in this chapter. This kind of conversation is a pure transformation of Durkheim (1915/1965), replete with rituals, totems, solidarity, and (the intra-subjective version of) collective consciousness. Moreover, just as communal ritual gave Durkheim's aborigines semiotic power, bondedness, and energy, ritualized self-talk can do these things for the "community" which constitutes the self.

The idea of internal ritual also lends support to Durkheim's notion of the sacredness of the individual, a quality he thought constructed solely by the public community. In addition to the influence of civil liberties, the rule of law, the democratic vote, and the welfare state, the sacredness of the individual is constructed in face-to-face interaction. But beyond all those factors, the self, by internal ritualizing and solidarity-building processes, generates its own sacredness. In fact these processes, and the political expectations which they may underlie, helped force (some of) the modern states to recognize the sacredness of the self.

Hegel's Recognition and Solidarity

On several occasions I have referred to Hegel's master–slave struggles, which are over "recognition." The attainment of solidarity at any semiotic level assumes a resolution of these fights and a resulting mutuality of recognition. The achievement of political peace between the two combatants opens the channel of meaning between them. But more than that, it already gets a certain proto-meaning or readiness for meaning into the bond. This is one aspect of the Durkheimian–Lévi Straussian "mana" I referred to earlier.

The idea that master–slave fights are multi-leveled is inadequately developed in Hegel, as well as in the secondary literature. Nevertheless there are suggestions in his *Phenomenology of Spirit* (1807) of three different struggles: intra-personal, interpersonal, and intergroup. The first can produce psychological problems, ranging from bad faith to complete psychoses. The second can lead to faulty face-to-face relationships, such as those between males and females. The third can lead to problems of social structure, especially class conflict. In addition there is a fourth master–slave struggle at the cultural level, especially between the colonizer and the colonized.

In the case of ordinary semiotic processes in human beings, it is the first two levels that are crucial. The infant must receive recognition, which is a variant of simple love, from the major caretaker or caretakers. Without this recognition the semiotic possibilities of the infant will never be kindled. And if the caretaker's recognition is extreme, either with over- or under-attention, Kohut's narcissistic problems will interfere with semiotic growth in the infant. But beyond these caretaker skills and contingencies, the infant also needs to grant appropriate recognition in return. To create the bond of semiotic solidarity the recognition must be mutual.

Related to the problem of interpersonal mutuality there is an intra-personal one. The internal agencies of the growing child must also avoid damaging master–slave fights and find the stability of mutual recognition. In Freudian terms the dominating internal master can be either superego, ego, or id, any one of which can derail the personality by getting too much power. In semiotic terms the dominator can be the I, me, or you, any one of which can disequilibrate the balance of the semiotic triad and prevent normal growth.

Neither Peirce nor Mead had a good appreciation of recognition in the child's semiotic life, even though both were familiar with Hegel. Peirce's theory was primarily meant to apply to full-grown adults and did not attempt to explain childhood socialization. Mead's did make this attempt, but it is so cognitively biased that it missed the role of emotion. In particular the love and recognition that caretakers give to human infants are crucial to their developing semiotic selves. Mead thought the caretaking "other" was primarily a kind of cognitive mirror, allowing the child to gradually share intersubjective meanings. He did not see that these meanings depended not only on semiotic reflexivity but also on semiotic solidarity, itself an achievement of mutual recognition.

The complementarity of solidarity and reflexivity, then, opens the door to Hegelian recognition. Neither the self-feeling nor the reflective semiotic traditions alone can explain mutual recognition, but together they can not only explain but build on it.

The Origin of Self in the Primates

A third implication of the reflexivity–solidarity combination, which I will treat at some length, concerns the origin of the self, language, and meaning, in our line of primates, i.e. the phylogony issue. At present there is no serious theory of human origins. The issue is usually either ignored, denied (by minimizing the gap between animals and humans), relegated exclusively to extra-scientific explanation, or given over to vague guess-work. Recently biologists have talked a great deal about the evolution of language and mind after they originated, but they are relatively silent about the origin itself (see, for example, Alexander, 1989, and the collection in which his essay appears).

Nevertheless there are several phylogenetic hypotheses, spread through various disciplines. These hypotheses single out the following factors: primate dreams; the wakeful internal conversation; sexuality (masturbation, intercourse, the sexually evolved body, the incest taboo); the problem-solving process; rituals; meaning-generating factors (mana, solidarity, the "phallus"), and biological factors (e.g. genes, brains, and speech organs). This list seems rather scattered, but much of it can be ordered around the classical theory of the four causes (Aristotle, 1984a, Book II, part 3, pp. 332–4 and Book II, part 7, pp. 338–9; 1984b, Book I, part 3, pp. 1555–7 and Book II, part 2, pp. 1570–72). The sexual factors, which intensified consciousness, are efficient causes (or at least facilitators). The three biological factors are material causes. The meaning-generating factors are formal causes. And the problem-solving process is a final cause. A systematic theory would probably need to use some such combination of causes.

My own hypothesis will draw primarily on the concept of ritual. I will also touch on several other factors, although, rather than attempting a systematic explanation, I will merely construct a framework for thinking about the issue.

Regarding sources, Peirce himself has no theory of phylogenesis, nor does he seem to have been interested in one. He was both a believing Episcopalian and a Darwinian, although according to Corrington (1993, pp. 199–200) he interpreted divine creation as so drawn-out and indirect a process that it was compatible with Darwinism. I will draw on Peirce's semiotic triad, particularly as it defines human nature. Phylogenesis was a transition from a dyadic to a triadic medium. In other words the birth of the self was the birth of the symbol, the distinctively human interpretant.

Mead, who was an atheist as an adult, did have a theory of phylogenesis, but it was not very powerful. It leaned heavily on the usefulness or functionality of thought for the primates. This is a teleological or finalistic explanation, and it explains little by itself. Many things might be useful for humans, but that does not make them come into existence. Mead also referred casually to the "cortex," which played the role of a material cause. But he had no productive or efficient cause and he was vague about the formal cause. He also liked to compare, side-by-side, the pre-human and human cognitive capacities (the non-significant and the significant gesture) but he did not explain how the one evolved into the other.

Mead thought of phylogenesis as the origin of role-taking between individuals, which was one of his reflexivities. I will also draw on his other reflexivity, the kind that defines the self and structures the thought process.

Durkheim is useful because his *Elementary Forms of Religious Life* (1915) is virtually a theory of human origins. It is an attempt to explain the beginnings of religion, which makes it phylogenetic. In a sense his religion and self are born together (see Bellah, 1970, p. 25, n. 13 for a similar argument), although he did not pay much attention to the birth of the self. Nevertheless his idea that religion was born in a ritual that symbolized communal solidarity may also apply to the self. In particular I think the force or cutting edge of solidarity, which Durkheim usually referred to as "mana," may be one of the formal causes of human phylogenesis.

I should mention that I am not going to pay much attention to materially causal explanations, such as those involving genes, brains, and speech glands, although this is the usual way biologists approach the question. I am going to take those for granted and, like Clifford Geertz (1973, pp. 62–3), assume that phylogenesis had genetic changes in the background. These new conditions may have been necessary, but they were not in themselves sufficient.

The symbolic birth was a distinct causal process, differing from the material base as form from matter. In this process the human gesture

127

"stretched" or "leapt" from the non-significant to the significant, from the concrete to the abstract, from the dyadic to the triadic. The moment of formal, as opposed to material, change is what I am after. Mead does not say much about the leap itself. He gives a better, though not totally clear, idea of how the ontogenetic leap occurs in the human baby, but that assumes the leap in the primates.

My interpretation of emergence will not be pragmatic in the purposive sense, but rather ritual and expressive, in the manner of Durkheim. There is a clue in Durkheim's idea that the concept of "category" or "class" is the master concept. Durkheim never gave a formal list of what he thought to be the key, socially generated concepts, but at various times he included the following: time, space, number, cause, substance, personality, universe, totality, being, God, left–right and non-contradiction (Coser, 1988). In addition he included category (also known as group, class, kind, or type) as a kind of over-arching or meta concept, since all concepts, including those in the preceding list, fall under the scope of this one.

If we were to look for a master concept in Mead, I do not think it would be the class or category, whether anchored in the group or not. Mead is certainly quite social, particularly in his theory of knowledge, but nowhere near as much as Durkheim. Mead's version of Durkheim's architectonic concept seems to be reflexivity itself. For Durkheim, all knowledge is in categories; for Mead all knowledge is in reflexive symbols. Like that of Descartes, Durkheim's knowledge is linear, intuitive, and direct, fitting neatly into classes. For Mead (and Peirce) knowledge is non-linear, semiotic, and reflexively indirect, fitting not into classes but triads.

To continue with Mead, the primate, energized by a new gene, discovered a reflexive capacity or quasi-mirror within. This was not the mirror of sensation but the much more abstract mirror of signification. With reflexivity, both as capacity and category, the primate could see not only the outside but the inside of objects, i.e. their abstract properties. For Mead, the primate's first significant act was problem-solving and instrumental. It was to reach more effectively for something material and practical.

Yet these two master concepts, Durkheim's category and Mead's reflexivity, may be compatible. Let me sketch a ritualistic, as opposed to a food/sex-seeking situation, in which significance may have first appeared. I will make this happen all at once, for the convenience of the thought experiment, even though it must have happened gradually, over a long time, in fits and starts (Goodenough, 1990).

Imagine a band of primates, all in the same place at the same time, much as Durkheim's primitive clans were sometimes assembled. They cannot be engaging in a significant ritual yet, since significance is what I am trying to

128

get to. Nor can they be engaging in ethnological, instinctive rituals, since primates do not seem to have such rituals. Instead it was a pre-ritual, in which some elements of ritual were present and some absent. Let us assume only assembly and some sort of focused attention, still at the animal level. There is also the presence of that new gene, not yet activated but available for the new capacity. These primates are potential talkers, neurologically equipped but not yet experienced with significance.

The attention had to be focused on something. It could be something external, such as a common danger, but I will make it internal to the group. This means it is embedded in the sociality proper to social animals, i.e. solidarity without symbolic significance (Kroeber, 1948, p. 9). The thing attention is focused on is a pre-signifier. It could have reference to food or sex, but not in an immediate, instrumental manner. It could also be a vocalization, body movement, or even some physical object of emotional importance. I am trying to name things that could have had the totemic function of solidarity symbols.

This stimulus, whatever it might have been, is the same one that formerly, before the new gene, had no significant meaning. It had been an animal signifier, rooted in animal sociality and without symbolic significance. But this time it starts making the leap, referring to something outside the previous limits of concrete or animal gestures.

On this occasion, powered by the new material base, the signifier begins referring to the group itself, its power, consciousness, and emotionality. In other words the signifier turns back on itself, reflexively, giving these primates a new consciousness of the group.

For this to happen, returning to Mead, some kind of role-taking pathway had to open. For the human infant the caretaker is the pole and external pathway for the first act of role-taking. Significance comes from a kind of looping from non-significant infant self, through significant caretaker, and back again to the newly significant infant self. That birth of the self, again unrealistically sped up, is via an individual other.

But the first act of reflexivity or role-taking in the primates did not loop through an individual but through a corporate or group other. The signifier or ritual element created a stronger group unity than had previously been possible. This unity created a group self or, in Durkheim's terms, a collective consciousness, which could "carry" the first act of role-taking. The individual primates looped through the group, and by means of this role-taking or reflexing, they all arrived at the first concept more or less at the same time. This concept came as a species-changing moment.

The first concept, however, was not only arrived at "via" the group, as a role-taking pathway. It was also "of" the group. It was a representation or symbol of the group, remembering that this is the social basis for

Durkheim's concept of category. Presumably the two came together, concrete group (significantly encountered) and the general concept of class, kind, or category. Once the non-significant signifier bent back on itself, allowing the first concept, it changed. Now the signifier was full of meaning. The first word or concept, then, must have been something like "Us!, Us!, Us!" (or "Ugh!, Ugh!, Ugh!"). When this breakthrough occurred the primates must have taken a long look at each other, especially into each other's eyes, to corroborate the experience. There are similarities here with Lacan's one-year-old, achieving self-recognition in a mirror (Lacan, 1966/1977).

In Peirce's terms the first concept had the following triadic elements: the ritual signifier (object, vocalization, etc.) was the *sign* of the group; the community of assembled primates was the *object* of the signifier; and the newly emergent, social solidarity was the *interpretant* of the group. The first two elements had always been there, although not in their upgraded semiotic roles. The new element was the interpretant, which is the source of meaning, language, self, solidarity, and, of course, Durkheim's religion.

Another way of saying this is that the group now has mana. This was Durkheim's name for the general form of meaning, which divides into truth, beauty, and goodness. In pragmatist language mana is semiotic solidarity or power. In Lacan's (perhaps incautious) language the corresponding term was the "phallus," by which he meant the first or breakthrough signifier. These concepts are all attempts to capture the distinctive symbolic power of the now talking primate.

I have laid out a conceptual division of labor between Mead and Durkheim, with the former supplying the *process* of role-taking or reflexivity and the latter the specific *pathway*. Only the group could have the power to open this first reflexive channel. This group can also be viewed as Mead's generalized other, often thought of as purely moral, but surely also cognitive.

My argument differs from Mead's in the way the gesture gets upgraded. Mead's animal or non-significant gestures are one-way, i.e. the effect or meaning accrues to the recipient but not to the maker of the gesture. The clucking hen just clucks, and knows not that the chicks will come to her. In contrast, two-way or significant gestures are supposed to have the same effect on the gesturer as on the recipient.

Mead tended to think dyadically on the phylogenetic issue and not about the larger group, except as it provided the background or enabling power to the dyad. But in my scenario we do not have a situation in which ego learns to respond to his or her own gestures as others do. Everyone has to start again, gesturee and gesturer alike. This is not a dyadic but a group situation, and the response is new to all members. The group's first reflexive experience of itself, although distributive to each member, was a collective experience.

This account differs from Mead's then in several ways: the situation is ritual and expressive, not instrumental and purposive; reflexivity is merged with the non-reflexive concept of category; the reflexive pathway is accordingly social, not individual; and the upgrading of communication is not merely the feedback of the old gesture's meaning onto the gesturer. It is an entirely new kind of gesture, the meaning of which was never experienced by either party to the dyadic, animal communication. It is an entire community, shifting as one, from animal solidarity to the semiotic, human kind.

The self which was born of this process combines reflexivity and solidarity. Not only are these two traits constitutive of the ongoing self. They were also, on my argument, indispensable to the self's origin in the primates.

Conclusion

I have now shown the compatibility, complementarity, and, perhaps, logical interdependence of two key concepts in self theory: solidarity and reflexivity. Once these two are combined, they can be used to explore a variety of theoretical issues.

An important logical issue, not currently discussed in social theory but important in philosophy, is whether the notion of reflexivity is inherently contradictory, or at least "paradoxical" (see Bartlett, 1992 and Bartlett and Suber, 1987 for comprehensive bibliographies). This question has been discussed primarily at the level of reflexive discourse, as opposed to reflexive entities, such as the self. In addition, however, the reflexive approach to the self has been pronounced inadmissibly paradoxical by several contemporary German philosophers, as I mentioned in chapter 4. In my view the bases of human reflexivity in solidarity, both interpersonal and intra-personal, explains how the self evades paradox. The reflexive poles of the self, subject and object, do not violate Aristotle's principle of contradiction because they are ontologically different. The reflexive triad or I–you–me (self–other–self) loop places the reflecting self in the place of the "other," real or internalized. This otherhood, itself based on solidarity with other human beings, provides the difference which evades paradox.

Another theoretical issue, which arises in gender theory, is whether males and females have basically different symbolic styles (cognitive, moral, and emotional). This discussion, which was started by Chodorow (1978) and the object-relations feminists, has continuously grown. The

Lacanese feminists (Marks and Courtivron, 1981; Moi, 1987) take a quite different position from the object-relations one. And a third position (Sprengnether, 1990), opposed to both the previous two, has been added. There is also a broader, less psychoanalytic discussion of gender and epistemology, metaphysics, methodology, and the philosophy of science (see Harding and Hintikka, 1983 and Harding, 1987 for representative collections).

Much of this discussion draws, at least implicitly, on the concept of reflexivity. There was a hint of this when Janet Lever concluded her study of gender and childhood play by saying, "In Meadian terms, it may be that boys develop the ability to take the role of the generalized other while girls develop empathy skills to take the role of the particular other" (Lever, 1978, p. 481). The concept of solidarity, which is implicit in Lever's hypothesis, is in the background of the entire discussion.

Durkheim distinguished several solidarity variables, such as mechanical vs organic, altruistic vs egoistic, anomic vs fatalistic, among others. These concepts have been little used for research, particularly at the levels of interaction and the self. Nevertheless, they add to Lever's reflexivity distinction as possible resources for gender analysis. I think much of the discussion of gender and the symbolic processes, including their relation to the master–slave schema, could be reformulated in terms of the reflexivity–solidarity relationship.

This chapter has continued the ongoing discussion of the Mead–Durkheim connection. Stone and Farberman (1967) initiated this discussion by showing how the later Durkheim (1913–14/1983), despite his antipathy toward the more individualistic forms of pragmatism, was "on the edge of rapprochement" with Mead. Habermas pointed out how Mead jumped from the cognitive to the moral in an unexplained manner, arguing that Durkheim could help fill this gap (Habermas, 1981/1987, pp. 1–76). Rochberg-Halton (1986, pp. 51–7) clarified the relation between Mead's generalized other and Durkheim's collective representations. And Collins (1989) showed a way in which Durkheim's solidarity could be inserted into Mead's internal conversation. The present chapter shows how reflexivity and solidarity can be formally integrated, further arguing that Durkheim's solidarity has always been implicit in Mead's reflexivity.

Summary

This chapter described, compared, and integrated two major theories of the self: reflexive semiotic and self-feeling. The latter is often thought to be a dead idea, confined to the era of James and Cooley, but it is a tradition which, with ups and downs, extends to this day. In addition I showed that

132

the self-feeling tradition is an intra-personal version of Durkheim's solidarity, suggesting that the entire Durkheimian theory can be applied at the level of the individual.

I then showed that if solidarity and reflexivity are combined, a number of theoretical issues can be treated more effectively. These were semiotic bondingness in all its forms, the Hegelian master–slave scheme, the phylogenesis of the self in the primates, and, more briefly, paradox and gender.

6

The Self as a Level

I have now laid out the Peirce-Mead model of the semiotic self fairly comprehensively. This chapter and the next two will not be about the self viewed internally, but about its relations to the other ontological levels. They will contextualize the self within the larger field of the sciences.

The present chapter will introduce the concept of *sui generis* levels and show the status of this concept in sociological theory, both past and present. Chapter 7 will discuss specific levels, showing how the psychological differs from the others and how the fallacy of upward reduction works.

In the contemporary intellectual scene it is common to see human beings explained away or reduced to some other kind of reality. At present the two most influential downward reductions, which reduce the self to a lower level, are probably those of artificial intelligence and molecular biology. I will discuss these in chapter 8. The most influential upward reductions, which reduce the self to a higher level, are those of post-structural and post-modernist, French social theory. I will discuss these and other reductions – also called displacements and decenterings – in chapter 7, although the levels scheme of the present chapter will be the foundation for that discussion.

It is widely (though certainly not universally) recognized that reality is stacked into organizational levels, from simple to complex. Human beings or selves, I will argue, constitute one of those levels. The importance of the levels scheme has been well put by William Wimsatt:

> One of the most ubiquitous phenomena of nature is its tendency to come in levels. If the aim of science, to follow Plato, is to cut up nature at its joints, then these levels of organization must be its major vertebrae.

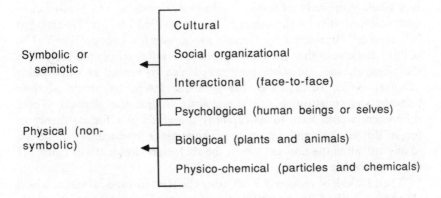

Figure 6.1 The hierarchy of ontological levels

They have become so major, indeed, that our theories tend to follow these levels, and the language of our theories comes in strata (1981, p. 148).

There is no consensus in philosophy or social theory on the list of levels: how many there are, the nature of each, or their interrelations. And the mono-leveled approach, particularly that of physicalism, is quite important. For purposes of understanding the autonomy and irreducibility of the self, however, it is useful to single out what might be called the major competing levels. Figure 6.1 is a six-level scheme with the self at its center. Below and above are the major levels to which the self tends to be reduced.

Below are the physical or non-symbolic levels: the biological and the physico-chemical. These two are often further divided, but for the purposes of this chapter, further division would be distracting. Above are the other symbolic levels: the interactional, social organizational, and cultural. The four symbolic levels taken together do not have any name in the social sciences, although White's "symbolate" was an attempt, unsuccessful as it turned out, to give them one (White, 1959/1977, pp. 177–8).

When the primates evolved into selves, these higher symbolic levels, themselves based on the now-human primates, emerged too. In other words, when the human or psychological level emerged, it did so in a batch of four, symbolic levels. The list of levels is therefore grouped into two clusters, the physical and the symbolic. Humans, being both bodies and selves, are included in both clusters.

135

The physical and symbolic clusters have important differences, in addition to the presence and absence of symbolism. The physical emerged in a slow, temporally extended, evolutionary process. The symbolic, to quote Lévi-Strauss on the origin of language (1950/1987, p. 59) emerged "all at once" (translated by Derrida as "in one fell swoop," 1967/1978, p. 291). Because of this, the symbolic cluster is not as crisply hierarchical as the physical, and, for some purposes, it can be viewed as side-by-side (Yinger, 1965). In addition, the symbolic levels, by virtue of their non-physical constitution, are more abstract than the physical. These differences would have to be carefully unpacked in a formal theory of levels. But for the simpler purpose of showing the irreducibility of the self to any and all of the non-self levels, the six hierarchical levels of figure 6.1 are a serviceable scheme.

When I speak of reduction I am using the term in a special sense, which should be clarified. In the philosophy of science Ernest Nagel (1961) gave the classic, though much disputed, statement on reduction. For Nagel, who was critical of the notions of emergence and levels, reduction was the replacement of one theory by another, the latter usually being more inclusive or accurate. His statement spawned, and continues to spawn, an enormous literature, refining and correcting his formulation.

Nagel leaned toward the mono-leveled, physicalist position, and therefore his reductions, in the absence of a vertical dimension, were always "horizontal." I am working with a multi-leveled position, and the reductions I am talking about are "vertical." Vertical reductions are arguments in which what may appear to be an autonomous level is said to be non-autonomous and, in fact, part of some other level. Within the multi-leveled scheme there can also, in a subordinate sense, be horizontal reductions. For example, within the level of social organization Marx reduced politics to economics, arguing that the former is derivative of the latter. But when I speak of reduction I will normally be talking about the vertical kind, e.g. the kind that explains away the human person as derivative of some lower (or higher) kind of reality. I call reductions from below, such as physicalism, "downward," and those from above, such as cultural determinism, "upward."

The vertical or inter-level reductions, then, abound in contemporary intellectual life. The DNA biochemists, for example, argue that traditional organic biology, which assumes an autonomous biological level, can be subsumed under and be reduced to the physico-chemical level. Closer to the theme of this book, neurophysiology or brain science is attempting a reduction of psychology, including the philosophy of mind. The neurophysiological position, of which there are several variants, is that psychological processes, such as sensation, thought, emotion, and volition can be explained physiologically, thus making the field of psychology unnecessary.

136

Within the symbolic cluster of levels there are also several would-be inter-level reductions. Each of the four symbolic levels is sometimes claimed to explain away, i.e. reduce, one or more of the other three. Some anthropologists and students of culture, for example, claim that culture can explain the other three symbolic levels. Some social organization positions claim that culture can be reduced to their level. Some interactionist positions would reduce social organization and culture to their level. And all of the supra-individual positions, i.e. those of interaction, social organization, and culture, sometimes claim that the level of the self is explicable and reducible to their higher level.

The inter-level reductions are also, to speak more concretely, power struggles among sciences and disciplines. These struggles bear some resemblance to the paradigm fights within sciences and disciplines, although the two differ much as wars do from revolutions. To perceive the full force of inter-level reduction it is necessary to consider the "external" as well as the "internal" dimension of science. The latter is the formal content of science: the ideas, methods, research findings, theories, etc. The former is the more informal context: the money, jobs, alliances, ideological implications, career opportunities, historical pressures, and the like. In the USA one of the major external influences on inter-level reductions is the funding agencies, particularly those of the federal government.

When I talk about the various reductions of the self I will usually be talking about the internal forces of science and the other disciplines. But I will sometimes touch on the externals as well, particularly in the last chapter, when I return to the public policy implications of self theories.

With the concept of inter-level reduction and the scheme of levels on which it is based, this chapter will be devoted to issues preparatory to a consideration of the reductions. First I will clarify a terminological problem, the term "levels" and the many ways this term is used, so that my own use is properly understood. Then I will discuss the self and its irreducibility in classical American sociology. After that I will look briefly at the general form of the argument that characterizes the reductions of the self. And finally will treat the problem of the symbolic levels in general. In the next chapter I will turn to the upward reductionist arguments themselves, while chapter 8 will treat the downward reductions.

The Concept of Levels

The notion of levels is one of those spatial metaphors that tends to be used quite loosely in social theory. There are at least four important ways the term is used, along with several less important.

137

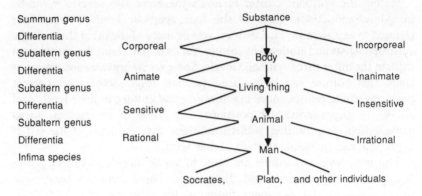

Figure 6.2 Tree of Porphyry

(1) When the notion of level is applied to the degrees of *abstraction* it refers to the generality of a concept. Logic books often explain this idea by presenting an "abstraction ladder," e.g. Fido, mutt, dog, animal, organism, physical object, entity. Extension or applicability increases as intention or semantic content decreases. There are more animals than dogs because the former is a thinner concept.

The classic portrayal of these logical levels is the ancient Greek "Tree of Porphyry," reproduced in figure 6.2. The semantic flow of this diagram goes both upwards and downwards. The words "abstraction" and "generalization" emphasize the upwards flow, but the notion of *sui generis* levels, which are the kind I have been talking about, is best seen on the downward slope.

The epistemology of the generalization process seems to be a permanent problem for philosophy, but the simple logic of it has been fairly clear since Aristotle. The distinction between the theoretical and the empirical is often said to be a difference in degree or level of abstraction. This notion of levels, then, is certainly important to the logic of sociology, but it is too inclusive an idea for my purposes. It has to be narrowed to become equivalent to Wimsatt's levels of organization, i.e. *sui generis* levels.

(2) The notion of *meta* levels is another use of the spatial metaphor, although now the space has back-loops. Meta levels are not only higher than first-order levels. In addition they react back on them, cognitively. Earlier I defined a meta level as an intellectual perch from which you can examine a lower level, seeing meanings that are not visible from within that level.

One famous such vantage point was the meta-arithmetic from which

Kurt Gödel (1931/1962) looked down at "Formula G." That proposition, which asserted its own indemonstrability, could not be proved at the first-order level, although it could be seen, intuitively and glaringly, to be true at the meta level.

Another famous, but less successful, use of the meta level was the one from which Bertrand Russell hoped to escape from Wittgenstein's critique of logical atomism (Janik's and Toulmin's "Indian rope trick," 1973, p. 189). In the *Tractatus* (1921/1922, p. 26) Wittgenstein had pointed to atomism's fallacy. The totality of logical atoms could never be compared and equated with the totality of ontological atoms, as the theory required, because new logical atoms (words) would have to be created to do the comparing and equating. This would mean the "totality" was not a totality after all (nor could it ever be). Like the blind spot Gödel would later find, this one would require an infinity of meta-languages to escape from.

This notion of levels is also important for social theory, especially for meta-theory, and I have frequently used the concept of meta levels throughout this book. However for analyzing inter-level reduction it has the wrong specification, back-looping being the wrong logical lens.

(3) There is also the notion of *historicist* (time–space) levels. In contrast to abstraction, which widens into larger classes of cases, this is the widening of a single class. Historicist thinking has recently been re-emphasized in sociology: at the macro level by comparative historical research and at the micro by Garfinkel's "indexicality" and kindred ideas, which resist generalization.

These widening time–space perimeters are sometimes called levels (Mouzelis, 1991), but they are perhaps better called continua. This notion of levels is quite useful for single-case, historical, and context-sensitive research, but not for the present, more analytic treatment of reduction.

(4) Finally there is the notion I am using, that of *sui generis* or *emergent* levels. The term "sui generis" refers to a species whose differentia is so novel and important, relative to those of the other species of its genus, that it gets singled out for closer analysis, thereby becoming its "own genus." The Tree of Porphyry not only depicts, on the upward slope, generalization and abstraction. It also singles out, on the downward slope, the emergence of the highly innovative differentiae, i.e. the *sui genera*.

The four notions of levels – abstractive, meta, historicist, and *sui generis* – are not as crisply separated as I am making them out to be. In the concrete practice of social theory the kinds of levels often cross-cut, and theorists may use all four conceptions at once. Nevertheless I will make primary use of the *sui generis* concept, keeping the other three in reserve.

There are several competing lists of levels in the philosophy of science and social theory, as I will consider later. Durkheim worked, at least in his explicit statements, with a list of five: the physical, chemical, biological, psychological, and social (1897/1951, p. 325). If we compare Durkheim's list with the one implicit in Porphyry, the constructed or semi-arbitrary character of these lists is apparent. Durkheim does not use Porphyry's "corporeal vs incorporeal" or even his "sensitive vs insensitive." On the other hand, Durkheim adds the chemical, and, in his boldest stroke, subalternates the "rational," not to concrete individuals (Socrates, Plato, etc.) but to two species of rational being: the individual and the social.

I will work with Durkheim's general approach but add two additional levels: interaction and culture. This gives four rational or symbolic levels above Durkheim's three sub-human ones. Figure 6.3 shows how this expansion of the rational would look if added to the Porphyrian tree.

Following Durkheim, I subalternate the rational, not into concrete individuals, but species. The advantage of placing all the symbolic levels into the context of Porphyry's "twigging" is that it disciplines thought, particularly about the nature of the differentiae and their relations to each other. Interestingly the diagram now not only flows toward the subject or human being. In addition it flows away from it (though now on the far side).

The Irreducible Self in Classical American Sociology

It might be wondered why the discipline of sociology, which appears to be the study of the "social," would be concerned with the individual at all. More pointedly, why would a sociologist write a book on the self? If the disciplines were what they appear to be, psychology, and perhaps philosophy, would study the human individual, and the social sciences would simply rely on the findings of those disciplines.

But the social and behavioral sciences have never had clear borders, and territorial disputes are central in their histories. The discipline of sociology, which slowly originated during the 19th century, has always addressed human nature and the self, both implicitly and often quite explicitly. Among those who are considered founders of this field, some, most notably Emile Durkheim in France, excluded the study of the individual, while others, especially W. I. Thomas and Florian Znaniecki, included it. Sociology's concern for the self eventually became formalized in the sub-discipline of social psychology, a field shared to this day by sociology and psychology.

A related factor is that psychology originated in the USA as an offshoot of

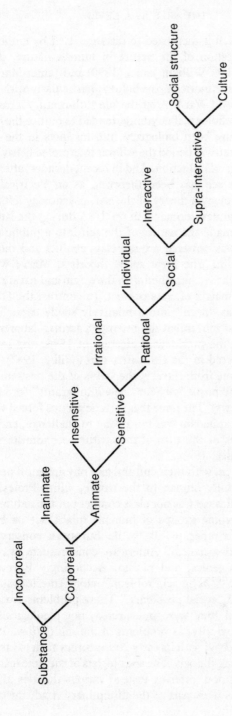

Figure 6.3 The Porphyrian Tree with the addition of the rational (symbolic) genera

philosophy, from which it then tried to distance itself by emphasizing its scientificity. The question of the nature of human nature, despite the ground-breaking work of William James (1890) and James Mark Baldwin (1899), was ignored in American psychology, particularly with the rise of behaviourism after World War I. After the late 19th-century introspectionist period, American psychology, if anything, tended to reduce the human self to lower levels. Having been biologized into instincts in the early 20th century, during the inter-war period the self was interpreted behavioristically, another kind of biological reduction. And in recent decades, after the rise of cognitive theory, the self has been theorized as an electrical machine. Instead of giving sociology a theory of the self, psychology left a vacuum.

Moreover, historical developments in the USA during the late 19th and early 20th centuries made the nature of the self into a public issue. The Europe of the time was centered around class conflict and the unsettled transition to capitalism. The great social theorists, Marx, Weber, and Durkheim, were primarily concerned with the origin and nature of modern capitalism, itself the matrix of class conflict. In contrast the USA had no feudal period and was "born" into a relatively stable capitalism. Some leaders of the Populist movement did attempt a farmer–laborer coalition, but this fell apart in the presidential election of 1896, and serious class conflict never reappeared in the USA after that (Wiley, 1967). The more enduring conflicts came from slavery, the status of the post-emancipation blacks, and that of the post-Civil War "new immigrants" (predominantly Italians, Poles, and Jews). The issue these ethnic groups forced was not one of class conflict, for capitalism was too strong to challenge, and the timid anti-capitalist theories of the turn-of-the-century economists were ruthlessly punished (Furner, 1975).

Instead, these groups, with their cultural and physiological peculiarities, did not seem quite fully human to the native, white Protestants. The underlying theoretical issue was not class conflict but the nature of human nature and whether some groups of humans might not be biologically inferior to others. In other words, while European conservatism was centered around anti-socialism, American conservatism was centered around biologism, eugenics, and racism. Accordingly European social theory was oriented to "*The* Social Problem," while American social theory was organized around "social problems." These problems arose from the ethnic pluralism, and they were interpreted, not ideologically as class conflict, but psychologically, as problems of the self (Wiley, 1986).

The field of psychology, with its early 20th-century turn to instincts, was the leader in biologizing the self. The sociologists of the time leaned toward an anti-biological position, offering instead various theories of the self as symbolic. These ideas were part of the disciplinary triad, the coalition of

142

pragmatic philosophy, anthropology, and sociology, as mentioned in the first chapter.

Sociology's early self theories were usually couched within an anti-reductionist framework, since biological reduction was so powerful at the time. But the early sociologists were also conscious of the upward reductions, based on culture and nationalism, coming from European social thinkers. The Americans wanted to theorize an autonomous, politically egalitarian self, and to do so they had to fight a two-front war: against downward reductions, coming from the biological level in the USA, and upward reductions, coming from the socio-cultural levels in Europe.

What gradually developed in American sociology was a theory of the symbolic and irreducible self, constituting an autonomous level between the physical and the socio-cultural. This image of the self gradually overcame biological reductionism, giving the USA the theoretical resource it needed to manage ethnic pluralism in a more-or-less democratic manner.

This intellectual "template" – the symbolic, irreducible self in an anti-reductionist framework – was introduced, inchoately, by Charles Horton Cooley (1902) and William Graham Sumner (1906). Cooley's *Human Nature and the Social Order*, highly influenced by William James's theory of the self, pictured a symbolically constituted self, distinct from the biology of the body and the symbology of the social. Cooley's actual theory of the self, which I touched on in chapter 5, was an unclarified combination of affective and cognitive processes. Nevertheless his overall meta-theory, which is at point here, was an early form of the template.

Sumner's *Folkways*, centering more on culture ("folkways" and "mores") than on the self, also helped to form the template. Sumner, along with Franz Boas in anthropology, did much to invent the great concept of culture. Rather than relying on the biological determinism of the time, Sumner argued for the force of culture on human behavior. His theory of the self was poorly developed, but his two-way anti-reductionism was clear, and his self could only be symbolic. As Robert Park summed up Sumner's contribution:

> Sumner . . . was trying, by analysis of existing cultures, to describe and classify their different and typical forms in such a way as to make these the objects of systematic investigation and explanation. What he did was to revive an interest in the study of human nature based, not upon instincts, physiology, and the lower animals, but upon the study of man and society (1931, p. 162).

After Cooley and Sumner created this framework it was strengthened by the three most influential books of inter-war American sociology: W. I.

	Thomas and Znaniecki	Mead	Parsons
Upward reduction (from above)	German folk psychology Durkheim's sociologism	German idealism Mentalism	German idealism Durkheim's sociologism
The self	Self as meaning ("attitude")	Self as reflexive	Self as voluntary action
Downward reduction (from below)	Instinct theory	Behaviorism (Watson)	Utilitarianism (rational choice) Positivism (behaviorism)

Table 6.1 Three anti-reductionist theories

Thomas's and Florian Znaniecki's *The Polish Peasant in Europe and America* (1918–20), George Herbert Mead's *Mind, Self, and Society* (1934) and Talcott Parsons's *The Structure of Social Action* (1937). These three books each had a somewhat different theory of the symbolic self, but they all fit the template. Robert Park's and Ernest Burgess's *Introduction to the Science of Sociology* (1921 and 1924), the highly influential textbook-reader of the period, was also central to the template though not relevant for comment here.

Table 6.1 schematizes the three positions. These classics are all, rather explicitly, fighting the two-front, anti-reductionist war, although the precise terminology differs from case to case. The definition of the self, the central level of the scheme, varies somewhat, and for some purposes these differences would be important. For present purposes, however, it is the implication of autonomy, which all the definitions share, that matters.

The contents of both the lower and upper levels also vary, though not much. The lower levels are primarily the forms of biological determinism. At the upper levels the various German idealisms are in all three. Durkheim's sociologistic side would also be in all three, but Mead does not appear to have been familiar with Durkheim's work. If the scheme were revised for today's politics of levels, which I am implicitly doing in this chapter, Durkheim's descendants, the French decenterers, would have to be added. Otherwise not much has changed.

What I have been calling a template could also be called a frame of reference or a meta-theory. The cumulative effect of Cooley, Sumner, Thomas and Znaniecki, Park and Burgess, Mead, and Parsons was a set of taken-for-granted premises or deep structure, that has informed sociological thinking ever since. This convergence in anti-reductionism is only visible from the standpoint of presuppositions, themselves viewed from a meta perspective. If you look from the standpoint of substantive theory, or, still worse, ideology, the deep structure will be invisible. Instead you will see Parsons opposed, theoretically, to the Chicago school, and Sumner opposed, ideologically, to almost everyone else. But if you look at the presuppositions or frame of reference, the continuity of American sociology becomes evident.

Since World War II, American sociological research and much of its theory has tended to be quite positivist, particularly in method. If this positivism were completely thought out, it would imply the reduction of the self to a lower level: biological, physical, or perhaps even mathematical. In practice however the positivist orientation in contemporary American sociology is not deeply or consistently thought out – it is largely a research methodology – and as a result, the classic template continues to prevail. The predominant meta-theory of human nature is still that of an autonomous self, interposed between lower and higher levels.

To return to the question with which I began this section, an American sociologist would write about the self because this is traditional in American sociology. The Americans never centered on any specific theory of the self but rather on the outside boundaries or parameters of such a theory. I think the two-way anti-reductionism of the Americans is extremely relevant to today's intellectual climate, and the notion of the self as symbolic is equally so. The Americans developed this orientation, in default of psychology, in the face of a crisis in American democracy. As I pointed out in chapter 1, the founding father's democratic paradigm had become obsolete, the new immigrants had produced a new crisis for democracy, and the social sciences, in concert with pragmatic philosophy, created a new democratic paradigm.

I have discussed the sociological approach to the self in some detail because there is insufficient awareness of its historical significance, or, for that matter, of its contribution to American civil liberties and democracy. The great European macro sociologists – Marx, Weber, and Durkheim – also worked with autonomous versions of the self, but their main interest was in the social structure. As a result they had undeveloped, eclectic, and sometimes inconsistent theories of the self. All three also had tendencies – *de facto* if not *de jure*, in Weber's case – to upward reductions. To theorize the power of the macro institutions they had a tendency to let these

145

institutions swallow up the self. There is a sense, then, in which the European macro and American micro contributions are complementary, i.e. each is strong where the other is weak.

At present there are new and influential reductions of the self, both upward and downward. These reductions do not have the explicit anti-democratic political implications they had in the early 20th century, yet it seems to me they have this potential, as I will discuss in chapter 9. In addition the classic, libertarian template of early American sociology has been living off its capital for a long time and badly needs renewal. In particular the inner sociality of the self – its dialogism, reflexivity, and semiotic quality – needs theoretical clarification. One purpose of this book is to strengthen the classic template by bringing it up to date.

The General Form of the Reductionist Argument

The three classics of table 6.1 all posed their argument in a relatively common-sense manner. The technical vocabulary of reductionism was not available to these authors at the time, nor did they confront the logic of reductionism. Yet Parsons did provide an interesting clue, and I will use an insight of his as the point of departure for my own analysis. In looking for similarities between upward and downward reduction, I am trying to find a common denominator or "general form."

Before examining Parsons's clue, I will mention an ideology or perhaps mood that the two kinds of reduction have in common. Both regard themselves as emancipatory, libertarian, and pro-human. In other words both reductions define themselves in the same terms as I am using for anti-reductionism.

The upward reductions regard the notion of the autonomous self as an historically oppressive idea, used to promote elites and to dominate non-elites. As I pointed out in chapter 1, such theorists as Foucault and Derrida regard the self as a manufactured idea, concocted by some (small) groups to dominate other (large) groups. In my opinion, this is true only for faulty theories of the self. If instead the theory of the self is adequately open and flexible, it is liberating. It can not only explain human freedom and equality, but can also provide a ground for human rights, both moral and legal. But despite my counter-view, the usual self-appraisal of upward reduction is one of liberation and concern for human values.

Interestingly the downward reductionists, basing their position on physicalism and biologism, have worked with a similar self-evaluation. Their naturalism (Taylor, 1985, pp. 1–12) is a moral quest aimed at maximizing human values. Their approach assumes that natural science is

146

the only way of reaching truth, and that all other methods inevitably distort and misconceive. Of course there have been times in history, particularly in England, when positivism *was* politically liberating. At those times natural science, including its application to human topics, had an emancipatory effect. This was because humanistic and social studies were proceeding in illiberal and, I would say, erroneous ways.

Both reductions, then, usually regard themselves as occupying the high moral ground, and sometimes – when the theory of human nature is proceeding in irrational or politically harmful ways – they are right. This they share. But if the theory of the self is healthy, then both reductions are themselves irrational and can be politically troublesome.

Apart from this dubious sense of moral superiority, there is also a logical weakness, suggested by Parsons, in both reductions. For Parsons, the crucial components of human action, in addition to the actor and the end, were: the material situation or conditions, including the human body; and the standards or norms, in view of which actors form actions. The appropriate grasp of the human level, in his view, required both components. For Parsons, reduction consisted in omitting one of the two. Reduction from below, from what he called the positivist cluster of positions, consisted in omitting the voluntarist or normative property. Consideration was narrowed to the material conditions, especially the human body. Reduction from above consisted in the opposite error, i.e. omitting the material conditions and retaining, in some manner, only the moral component.

In addition to seeing both reductions as based on an incomplete frame of reference, Parsons also saw them as methodological errors. An adequate explanation, which he identified with his position of voluntarism, required two kinds of explanation together: cause and meaning. Upward reduction, which omitted the material conditions, based explanation solely on meaning. Downward reduction, which omitted the normative property, based explanation solely on cause. Reduction was then both an ontological and methodological error.

Parsons's analysis of reduction, which was quite sophisticated for the 1930s, nevertheless had serious limitations. It was embedded in the particular concepts he used, some of which seem poorly chosen to me. In particular his self seems too morally based, too much the superego, and insufficiently cognitive. He also had an undeveloped notion of the self's reflexivity and how this might underlie its cognitive capacities. Nevertheless his overall anti-reductionist argument, his logical design, seems correct and useful to this day.

Let me reframe Parsons's argument. A human being, as the ancient Greeks said, is a rational animal, the latter trait being the genus and the

147

former the differentia. To properly apprehend the human species or level, you need both the genus and the differentia, i.e. both the animality and the rationality (which becomes "reflexivity" in my scheme). Reduction from below, as in the Parsonian formulation, retains the genus but snips off the differentia, the reflexivity. Reduction from above commits the opposite fallacy: it drops out the genus, the animality, and focuses exclusively (and, in philosophical terms, "idealistically") on the reflexivity.

As an example of the latter, consider the currently widespread practice of reducing human beings to the cultural level, particularly to the formal system of language (Saussure's and Hjelmslev's *langue*). On this view, which I mentioned in chapter 4 and will consider in more detail in chapter 7, language "speaks humans." They are only an extension of the cultural code, and their individuality or autonomy is a linguistic illusion. This reduction does recognize the rationality or reflexivity, but envisions it as only an expression of the formal language.

To further pinpoint the example and return to an issue I touched on in chapter 4, the word "I," which is the most disputed single word in the contemporary discussion of the self, can be understood in (at least) two ways. If the human level is recognized, i.e. given autonomy, "I" refers to the person doing the speaking. The Peirce–Mead self, in which "I" is the sign element of the semiotic triad, is an example of this. This reflexive reference is possible because of the temporal and spatial localization of the speaker, because it refers to that person in that body. If the body, i.e. the genus, animal, is omitted from consideration, the word is still reflexive of the speaker, but not to some particular, individuated speaker, made so because of the body. Instead it now refers to the role of the speaker or the generic idea of a speaker, for it is the body that gives particularity.

The word "I" is indexical, i.e. contextually defined, in two ways. For one the word refers to the person saying the word. Whoever says "I" is the one to whom the word refers. But in addition, the person saying the word is indexical, in time and space, to his or her body. Upward reduction can approximate the first indexicality but not the second.

The self is a property of the organism (Colapietro, 1989, pp. 69–70), and without the organism it cannot exist at its *sui generis* level. In addition it is in large part the body and its desires that motivate language and meaning.

When detached from the body, reflexivity and the semiotic triad in which it is embedded becomes a purely cultural or linguistic relation. The logical genus has been uncoupled and removed from the differentia, and, by that fact, upward reduction has been accomplished. The other two, upward reductionisms, interactionism and structuralism, also focus on a disembodied reflexivity, although they construe the latter in the manner in which it operates at their level.

The general form of the reductionist argument – by which I am referring to fallacious, inter-level reductions of the self – is one of omitting an essential property of human nature, either the genus or the differentia. This formula does not explain any particular reductionist argument, because each requires further specification. Nevertheless it captures what they all have in common. Another way of saying this is that materialism (downward reduction) and idealism (upward reduction) both omit important features of human nature. Parsons's theory was an attempt to be adequately inclusive. He was attempting to apply the similarly inclusive position in philosophy, the "philosophy of the via media" (Kloppenberg, 1986, pp. 15–63), to social theory.

The general form of reductionism can also be explained in other ways. In Peircean terms both are semiotically "dyadic," meaning they lack one of the essential triadic elements. Downward reduction lacks the interpretant and upward lacks the sign. Both dyadicisms have the effect of omitting the "person," for downward lacks personhood altogether and upward substitutes corporate for individual personhood. I will return to the Peircean analysis of the two reductions later.

The Symbolic Levels

Earlier I mentioned that the symbolic levels, perhaps even more than the physical, are a matter of scholarly controversy. There is disagreement over how many there are, the nature of each, and their interrelations. In social theory the closest thing this cluster of issues has to a name is the "micro-macro" question, itself located within the broader issue of "meta-theory." Within sociology these issues have tended to come to the fore at two times of crisis: the birth trauma of the discipline's founding, which has never quite settled down and ended, and the paradigm struggles that have run through its history.

The Founding

The founding of the discipline was largely concerned with the levels problem. This process, which extended from the early 19th century to the early 20th, was an attempt to find, claim, and legitimize intellectual territory or space. In the system of disciplines and universities of the time there was no fresh, unoccupied space for sociology. Both in Europe and the USA the established disciplines claimed all the would-be sociological space and were accordingly resistant to the rise of that discipline. There was no obvious entry point. In particular, there was no single, symbolic level at which sociology could enter the system of disciplines. As a result there were scattered attempts at doing so, based on a variety of levels entries.

Auguste Comte (1798–1857) in France and Herbert Spencer (1820–1903) in England were two of the earliest to make these attempts. They relied primarily not on a theory of ontological but logical levels, that is on the division of the sciences, to legitimize the new field. It may be that the public demand for the discipline of sociology, itself based on accumulated social problems and tensions, was not great enough until the late 19th century. But an additional factor in Comte's and Spencer's quite limited success as founders was the lack of a clear theory of levels. Nor did it help that the two disagreed on the classification of the sciences.

Emile Durkheim in France was the first founder to use an explicit and well-developed theory of ontological levels. His attempt, which continues to be sociology's classic claim to disciplinary legitimacy, was quite successful in the French educational system, at least during Durkheim's lifetime. His "social" level, however, in my terms, was an unanalyzed amalgam of the interactional, social organizational, and cultural.

In Germany, Max Weber used the individual, viewed in social context, as his entering level, although in practice his methodological individualism tended to lapse into a *de facto* social structuralism. Also in Germany, Georg Simmel used the level of interaction as his entering wedge (Levine, 1989, p. 114). This symbolic level was the least claimed in the system of the sciences and perhaps the most promising for sociology's entry. Although Simmel's essays on interaction were quite influential, particularly with the Chicago school, he lacked an explicit and formal levels theory and had only modest success in founding the field on this space. Only very recently, as I will discuss in the next chapter, has the *sui generis* level of interaction come to be recognized meta-sociologically in social theory.

In the USA W. I. Thomas and Florian Znaniecki, reacting to Durkheim's earlier founding in France, used a bi-level entering scheme. They based the field on the joint effects of the individual and social organizational levels, referred to by them as the domains of "attitudes" and "values." Their multi-level strategy, which created a successful American version of sociology, had the advantage of allowing the field to spread across more than one symbolic level. In practice, American sociology also used Simmel's interaction level along with Thomas's and Znaniecki's individual and society (Levine, Carter, and Gorman, 1976). Thomas's and Znaniecki's scheme had the advantage of providing a workable explanation to the problem of the "individual and society" (currently called the agency-structure or micro-macro problem), giving their founding a strength that Durkheim's lacked.

Finally Talcott Parsons, in a late version of the founding, followed Weber in entering at the individual level (1937). Eventually he found this level confining, and he re-entered the field with the tri-level scheme of personality, society, and culture (1951). For several years this scheme competed successfully with the Chicago school's scheme of the individual, interaction, and society, their unanalyzed mixture of Thomas and Znaniecki and Simmel. In effect Parsons substituted culture for interaction. But somewhere around the late 1960s the Parsons–Merton, Harvard–Columbia school of functionalism declined, and the personality–society–culture scheme became less important. In retrospect these foundings look like attempts to get "above" biology and psychology and "around" economics, the latter having been already established at the social level. Sociology needed to stake out a territory which was at least partly above the individual and, in addition, more socially inclusive than economics. In addition the solution had to be viable, not only "internally," i.e. intellectually, but also "externally," i.e. institutionally and politically. The intellectual justification never quite crystallized, for sociology continues to have several competing foundational arguments. Instead the discipline gained *de facto* legitimacy by becoming institutionalized in universities and other scientific institutions. This unsettled and unending founding is one reason the symbolic levels remain an area of controversy.

Paradigm Disputes

In addition the levels issue is kept unsettled by paradigm disputes. The founding of the field was an attempt to establish what might be called paradigm space, by which I mean some domain of reality that needs theorization. The finding and claiming of the domain, the space, is not the same as its theorization. Space could be successfully claimed but never adequately or convincingly theorized, i.e. there could be no paradigm or there could be too many, either situation producing inconclusive theorization. A space can be all of a level or, more commonly, part of one, depending on the scientific history of the level. Physics and chemistry both have paradigm spaces on the physico-chemical level. There are several life sciences at the biological level. Sociology is one of several social sciences occupying the "social" level. But anthropology is the only field that has successfully claimed the cultural level. To claim a space, a field need only point to something important enough to merit scientific investigation. The pointing out might be merely an ostensive definition or one based on examples; it might be a preliminary and partial theorization; or it could be a quite sophisticated theorization. All that is required is that the claim be recognized by important audiences and authorities. In the USA the best

151

form of recognition is institutionalization in universities, above all getting one's own "department."

Thomas Kuhn's theory of science (1970) has no distinction between paradigm space and paradigms themselves. In effect he fuses these two ideas, thereby making his approach to scientific history relatively useless for the social sciences. He also blunts analysis by referring to the social sciences as basically "pre-paradigmatic," implying that they are not (yet) scientific and that they therefore do not have scientific histories. His ideas are useful for the histories of the physical sciences, which generally lack and do not need the space–paradigm distinction, but they need to be modified for the social sciences.

The situation in the history of sociology has been one in which intellectual space or "turf" was gradually legitimized but never clarified, particularly in relation to the system of levels; theorization was attempted but no conclusive paradigm or theory was ever produced; and specific but relatively weak paradigms or quasi-paradigms had *de facto* hegemony for certain historical periods, but without commanding stable recognition or decisively overcoming their competitors.

The discipline of sociology has been most firmly established in the USA, and the preceding three-point description applies best to that case. In other places (Wiley, 1979 and 1990) I have described the history of American sociology as the rise and fall of two quasi-paradigms: the Chicago school, from World War I until the mid-1930s; and the Parsons–Merton, Harvard–Columbia functionalists from World War II until about 1970. The period before these two I call a "pre-regnum," the periods between and after "interregnums." The first interregnum lasted about a decade; the second has lasted far longer, with no end in sight (Wiley, 1985).

During sociology's interregnums, the levels issue comes to the fore. Any group claiming paradigm status for its ideas needs to clarify the space in which the paradigm is to be erected. These spaces are located in levels, so the clarification of a space requires a levels scheme. At present there are would-be paradigms based primarily on the level of the individual, e.g. the quasi-economic theories of rational choice and neo-Weberian versions of methodological individualism. There are theories based primarily on the level of interaction, including symbolic interaction, exchange theory, and ethnomethodology. And there are several paradigm claimants based on the level of social organization or structure. Paradigms based explicitly on the level of culture are rare, perhaps because anthropology has laid claim to that level, although some versions of French sociology are culturally based. In addition to single-leveled schemes there are several that are multi-leveled, in the spirit of Thomas's and Znaniecki's bi-leveled scheme or Parson's and Sorokin's tri-leveled.

Interregnums in sociology, then, resemble the long founding process in the salience they give to the levels issue. During an interregnum the quest for a new paradigm, an ontogeny, reproduces to some extent the problem of the founding, a phylogeny. This is because the space–paradigm gap is unusually wide during both historical moments. At present, during sociology's long interregnum there is a heightened consciousness of levels, of the micro-macro issue and of meta-sociology generally.

Current Levels Schemes

Turning from these historical issues back to the substantive analysis of the symbolic levels, I will look at the question of their number, i.e. how many there are. A great many other questions are attached to the matter of number. At present there are schemes that recognize up to four levels. I do not think there are any current schemes that work with more than four, although Gurvitch's rather imprecise scheme used eight (Gurvitch, 1964).

I have already mentioned rational choice and neo-Weberianism as mono-leveled schemes, based on the individual or self. The most common bi-leveled scheme is that of the "individual" and "society," the one that Durkheim formalized. He saw that this distinction could not be merely quantitative, i.e. society had to be more than just a plurality or multiplicity of individuals. Plurality does not create a qualitatively new level, but just multiplies the old. The difference had to be qualitative in some sense of the word "emergence." He approached this emergence with the notions of exteriority and constraint, two traits which he thought were lacking at the individual level but emerged at the social.

Durkheim's analysis is still at the heart of contemporary bi-level schemes, despite the highly equivocal manner in which he used "exteriority" and "constraint." In addition his bi-leveled scheme was simply not fine-grained enough to map out the symbolic field. Not only did he fail to distinguish social organization from culture, he also smuggled in the missing level of interaction in an unmonitored, uncontrolled manner (Liberman, 1985, pp. 26–7). The current two-level scheme is still pretty much as Durkheim left it.

The most common tri-level scheme, to move one step beyond Durkheim, is the personality–society–culture triad of Talcott Parsons (1951, pp. 3–23) and Pitirim Sorokin (1962, pp. 3–18) in sociology and Alfred Kroeber (1952, pp, 118–35) in anthropology. This model, which reigned during the functionalist hegemony of approximately 1950 to 1970 and continues as an option today, was never subject to careful analysis. The scheme, roughly a three-step stairway, has two rises: from person to society

153

and from society to culture. To be logically adequate the two rises, the two distinctions, should fit together under some overall basis of division, or if not, the incommensurability should be faced.

The first rise was sometimes treated as a plurality, which offers no explanation of emergence, and sometimes as exteriority and constraint, which offers an equivocal one. To be logically adequate the second rise, from society to culture, should have used the same basis of division as the first, i.e. some modification of the exteriority–constraint idea. In their co-authored note, Kroeber and Parsons defined society as "relational systems of interaction among individuals and collectivities" and culture as "patterns of values, ideas, and other symbolic-meaningful systems" (1958, p. 583). The "patterns" vs "relations" distinction was never clarified, nor did it reflect the actual practice of anthropologists and sociologists. As a result the classic, three-level scheme had, and still has, an under-analyzed, *ad hoc* quality, which weakens its meta-theoretical usefulness.

At present the major four-level scheme in sociology is the person–interaction–organization–society scheme of Niklas Luhmann (1982, pp. 69–89). His scheme differs from mine by the presence of an organizational (roughly, bureaucratic) level, interposed between interaction and society, and by the absence of a cultural level (which Luhmann sees suffused throughout the other levels). Luhmann's general approach, which uses the unlikely combination of cybernetics and phenomenology, is one of the few totally new ideas in recent sociological theory.

He was the first sociologist after Simmel to explicitly recognize the domain of interaction as a formal "level." He also uses a uniform "basis of division" to map out the symbolic field, namely, rules of inclusion or membership rules. For interaction, the rule of inclusion is time–space co-presence; for organization, contract or voluntary decision to become a member; and for society, residence in some specific territory. Luhmann has the clearest and most sophisticated levels theory in sociology today, although he is sometimes ambiguous about whether his levels are hierarchical or side-by-side. And of course he bases all his thought on a mechanistic version of cybernetics.

My own theory of levels will stress the basis of division, a weak spot in most discussions of this issue. In general I differentiate the four symbolic levels on the basis of their distance from the subject, i.e. the person or self. Accordingly the level of the self is intra-subjective; interaction is inter-subjective; social organization is collectively subjective and culture is extra-subjective. The presence of the subject thins out from level to level.

At the level of the self, meaning is within the self, and the subject is, by definition, fully present. In interaction the meaning is not within but between and among selves. In social organization the meaning is encoded in abstract, generic, or collective selves. And in the culture the meaning is completely removed from selves, including the collective variety.

My four-level scheme is built on the Peirce–Mead model of the self. The other three symbolic levels are, like the self, composed of semiotic elements. But these elements, in contrast to the I–you–me model, are not parts of or "intra" to the self. Rather they are "inter" (interaction and social organization) or "extra" (culture) to the self. Yet, as I will show in table 7.1, all four symbolic levels have their version of sign, interpretant, and object. The four levels, although dissimilar in substance, are nevertheless alike or homologous in formal structure. One reason it is possible to formulate an upwardly reductionist argument at all is the structural similarity among levels.

Conclusion and Summary

This chapter has described the concept of level and the corresponding conception of inter-level reduction. I had to disentangle several different notions of "level" – abstractive, meta, historicist, and *sui generis* – to clarify my own use of the term. I then showed that a concern with levels, and particularly with protecting the level of the self, was the most important single theoretical, or rather meta-theoretical, issue in classical American sociology. These sociologists were predominantly, if only moderately, left of center in their ideological orientations. They knew that the downward biological, as well as the upward socio-cultural, reduction of the self was in anti-democratic conflict with their politics. But, in addition to this altruistic motive, they had a professionally selfish one. If biology (including psychology's "instinct" theory) were to succeed in reducing and annexing the self, the social would go with it. If psychology became biologized, sociology would also become biologized. This meant their discipline and jobs were threatened. In any event, regardless of motives, the early American sociologists, in connection with the anthropologists and philosophical pragmatists, used the levels issue to redesign the theory of democracy.

I also showed how the levels issue continued to be salient in the ordinary dynamics of sociology as a discipline. Successfully founding the field required that it "locate" itself within some theory of levels along with a corresponding theory of sciences. Historically, sociology has used a variety of levels arguments for legitimizing its scientific status, although no single one has proved decisive. In addition to the founding problem, which is one of finding paradigm space, sociology has also had the problem of establishing a successful paradigm on this space. American sociology has seen the rise and fall (or some would say "ebb and flow") of at least two quasi-paradigms, though no highly successful paradigms have ever been established. The constant clash of would-be paradigms has also kept levels theory in a continuous state of instability. The importance of the levels issue has brought a great deal of attention to the larger micro-macro issue, and that in turn has focused attention on meta-sociology (Ritzer, 1991).

Finally I touched on contemporary levels theory, looking at it from the standpoint of number. There are theories of one, two, three, and four levels. My own version, building on the Peirce–Mead semiotic approach, recognizes four.

For the most part this chapter has attended to levels in general, though it paid more attention to the symbolic four than to the non-symbolic two. My purpose has been to develop the concepts necessary to look more closely at particular levels, especially the symbolic. In the next chapter I will look at the upwardly reducing levels – interaction, social organization, and culture – in more detail. My purpose will be to show why the reductions are in error. In chapter 8 I will discuss the downward reductions from the physico-chemical and biological levels. These reductions are better understood in the social sciences (Wolfe, 1993), and they do not need lengthy analysis. Nevertheless both kinds of reduction, upward and downward, are issues in the current theorization of democracy, and when I return to that issue in the final chapter, I will build on my critique of the reductions.

7

Upward Reduction

The four symbolic levels are all semiotic and therefore composed of semiotic triads, though in different ways. Neither Peirce nor Mead had explicit theories of levels, particularly in the symbolic range, so they supply only limited guidance for this chapter. I will rely partly on what they said and partly on extrapolations from what they said. Table 7.1 shows the sign–interpretant–object triad by symbolic level. For each level I have divided the object into two aspects: structure and content. This is what I did in chapter 2 for the level of the self, and it constituted a basic premise of the Peirce–Mead synthesis.

The level of the self is, of course, composed of the I–you–me triad. The object is further differentiated into the structure and content. This is familiar from earlier chapters.

The triad constituting the level of interaction, to continue the semiotic unfolding, is made up of the ego, alter, and we. Alternatively this triad could be called I–you–we, remembering that now "I" and "you" are not aspects of the self but free-standing persons.

Social organization, as I am using the term, is also a unique semiotic level, but its elements are generic or collective. Its version of the self's I or interaction's ego is the "collective agent" or actor. This agent can be an actual individual, defined primarily as a role-incumbent, or it can be a group of actual individuals, again defined as role-incumbents. Examples of these two kinds of agent would be the president and board of directors of an organization. I am referring to the receivers or recipients of this action as the collective "patient," meaning the audience, interpreters, or alters of the communication. Again the patient can be an organizationally defined individual or a set of them. The purpose of using these generic terms is to fit

157

	Sign	Interpretant	Object	
			Structure	Content
Culture	Sign	Interpretant	Meaning	Concrete referent
Social organization	Collective agent	Collective patient	Collectivity or organization	Concrete referent
Interaction	Ego	Alter	We	Concrete referent
Self	I	You	Me	Concrete referent

Table 7.1 Semiotic triad by symbolic level

the concept of generic subjectivity which I used to define this level. In other words I am using the notion of collective agent to mean the same as collective subject.

Finally at the cultural level the distance from the subject is maximal. Here we have only the abstract inner triad of Peirce's semiotic. Culture is composed of pure meanings, divorced from the individuals who, in any concretely meaningful act, are required to think or feel these meanings. Culture is our concept of an abstract world of meanings, located "above" concrete or abstract individuals. There is a sense in which culture has less ontological status, i.e. less existence or reality, than the other three symbolic levels. This is because culture is there only because we disembody meanings from the other three symbolic levels and pretend they could exist in isolation from those levels. Number and language exist primarily in concrete psychological and social actions. Still we do think of these semiotic systems as abstract and isolated, and often with great profit. Therefore, even though culture is there only because we think it is, its *de facto* reality is important enough to treat it as an autonomous level. Peirce, of course, developed his theory of semiotics largely at the extra-subjective or cultural level. For the names of culture's semiotic elements I have simply used Peirce's sign–interpretant–object, which is the way he described culture's triadicity.

158

	Point of View	Reflexivity	Solidarity	Materiality
Culture	Extra-subjective ("it")	Virtual	Ritual symbols	Virtual (as "carriers")
Social organization	Generically subjective ("we" to "they")	Collective consciousness	Social solidarity	Time-space elasticity
Interaction	Inter-subjective ("we")	Role-taking	Interactive solidarity	Time-space indexicality
Self	Intra-subjective ("I")	Internal conversation ("I" - "me")	Inner solidarity	Embodiment in organism

Table 7.2 Profiles of the four symbolic levels

The first or sign elements of the four semiotic levels are I, ego, the collective agent, and the sign. The interpretants are you, alter, the collective patient, and the interpretant. And the objects, looking at the triad structurally, are me, we, the collectivity or organization, and the overall meaning. For the content aspect of the object, i.e. the concrete object, I have just used the term "concrete referent" for each level.

Table 7.1, then, is a first approximation at defining the four symbolic levels. Upward reduction consists in imposing an inappropriate triad on the level of the self. If you argue that the human level is absorbed or explained away by one of the supra-individual levels you have to erase or "efface" the I–you–me triadicity of the human being and superimpose some other version in that empty space. The three major ways of doing this are interactional, organizational, and cultural.

The semiotic differentiation of the four levels can be made clearer by comparing the semiotic properties of each level. Earlier I talked about nestedness, ordering, reflexivity, and solidarity as the major properties of the semiotic self. Of these, reflexivity and solidarity are the more important for distinguishing the four levels. In addition I will introduce two other properties, point of view and materiality, as a further means of specifying how the four levels differ. These four properties, by level, are shown in table 7.2. Table 7.1 showed the semiotic structure of each level. Table 7.2 builds on table 7.1 by showing how four general or across-the-board

159

semiotic properties vary by symbolic level. I will discuss each of the four properties, beginning with point of view. Like table 7.2, table 7.1 shows what goes wrong, or what mistake is made, in each upward reduction, but it does so in more detail.

(1) *Point of view* is a concept of several dimensions. In grammar it refers to the first (I, we), second (you), and third (he, she, it) persons. In table 7.2 I divide the third person between humans (they) and non-humans (it). By point of view I also mean "relation to subject," in the sense in which I use this concept to differentiate the symbolic levels. For early Peirce, as I pointed out in chapter 2, the concepts of "I," "you," and "it" were the most basic categories of reality. This system of categories has a pre-oedipal ring to it. "I" is baby; "you" is the main caretaker, usually the mother, and "it" is everything else, particularly if it is extraneous to the dyad. Father is the most notorious "it." The pre-oedipal child's categories might well be Peirce's early categories right on the button. Then as father, i.e. the "fathering process" of chapter 5, intrudes into the pre-oedipal dyad, the categories are broadened and universalized. Peirce did this broadening by renaming the categories "firstness," "secondness," and "thirdness." These numbers are the same as those of the three points of view and of the pre-oedipal categories, but they suggest greater abstractness.

I am taking Peirce's early categories and distributing them by semiotic level. All signs have points of view built into them. These depend on what kind of communication system the sign is in. If it is in the intra-subjective system, i.e. if it is something that the self communicates to itself, its point of view is the one we find at the level of the self. That point of view is the first-person singular or I. If the sign is used in a face-to-face, interpersonal communication, it is in an intersubjective semiotic system; and the point of view is the first-person plural or "we."

If it is used in a social organization, the group is too large for face-to-face or time–space unity. Instead abstractions are needed to organize communication and relationships. This means the organizational communicators, i.e. the collective agents and patients I mentioned earlier, often relate to each other impersonally, as though to a "third" person. Even though the corporate agents, e.g. the official leaders and authorities of the organization, may be communicating with the patients, they may face them, not as "you," but as "they." The generality and impersonality creates such emotional distance that the I–you or we–you bond may be too difficult to sustain. Similarly audiences, non-authorities or patients in social organizations may receive communications from the agents but nevertheless regard the agents, not as you, but as "they." Both poles of communication may regard the other pole as they.

The word "we" also belongs in table 7.2 because social organizations can have successful rituals and generate a "we feeling." Durkheim was the expert in explaining how unity rituals work. But these rituals are expensive to produce and they "run down" rather quickly. Also some social organizations are simply too stratified to allow for unity rituals. Once in a while, then, a social organization can adopt a "we" point of view, but its normal condition is to be, not in the inclusive "we," but the more divided "we vs they."

When I speak of "social organization" I am talking about a social level that can exist in any technological setting from primitive hunting and gathering societies to contemporary industrial. All that is needed is enough size and complexity to transcend face-to-face unity. My social organization includes two of Luhmann's levels, organization and "society," in addition to other kinds of social organization (Luhmann, 1982, pp. 69–89). This wide inclusiveness requires the relatively abstract terminology.

(2) I have already discussed *reflexivity* at the levels of the self and interaction, but now I will look at it in the other two levels as well. The internal conversation and role-taking are the names for reflexivity at the levels of self and interaction. Within the self, I and you talk directly with each other and indirectly or reflexively with the me. Within interaction, ego and alter converse directly with each other and indirectly or reflexively with the "we" or "us." The we is what family therapists call the family's or group's system, and it functions at the interpersonal level much as the me functions at the intra-personal. It carries the past, the memories, the habits, and it may even be visualized as having the whole Freudian apparatus of unconscious memories, repressed desires, (shared) neurotic symptoms, etc. I will not analyze the interactive we or us, but it is clearly a concept that has been under-theorized in social theory.

At the level of social organization reflexivity is shaped by the nature of communication in that medium. Reflexive consciousness at this level is neither intra- nor inter-subjective. Instead the subjects are corporate or collective, so the reflexivity must be similarly collective. The term "collective consciousness" is associated with Durkheim, though I am using it more broadly than he did. His collective consciousness was the shared meanings of a collectivity, particularly that of the whole society. The term consciousness can refer to either the process or its contents. Accordingly the collective consciousness can be either the activity of being collectively conscious or the object of this consciousness. Durkheim usually used the term in the latter sense, whether the French term be translated as "consciousness" or "conscience." Luhmann pointed out, however, that if Durkheim is to have social consciousness, he is also, at least tacitly, drawing on group self-reference or reflexivity as well (Luhmann, 1982, p. 7).

This kind of social reflexivity applies well to Durkheim's ritualized unity or we experience, but not to the more routine and divided condition of social organization. In the latter case there is also collective consciousness, but it is that of a "we" communicating with a "they." In the former case the implicit analogy is with the self, assuming the relatively solidaristic unity of the normal (non-psychotic) self. In the latter, it is with dyadic interaction, and at that, fairly distant and constrained.

Finally, at the cultural level I refer to reflexivity as "virtual." By this term I mean that, since this level is removed from the subject or self, including the thinned-out varieties of collectivities, it cannot have reflexivity in the usual sense. If the cultural element were re-embedded in one of the lower, symbolic levels it would automatically be part of a reflexive loop. But at the cultural level, this loop is only a possibility or virtuality. Purely cultural symbols do however have a kind of reflexivity in the relation among their triadic elements. As I mentioned in chapter 4, the interpretant is responding to and reflexive of the sign. This is not virtual but actual, even though no subjects are involved. Still, to capture the special relation to reflexivity that characterizes the cultural level, I will call it virtual, understanding that this term is not completely adequate.

It should be noted that the mode of reflexivity follows from the point of view. At the level of the self the point of view is the intra-subjective, first person of the I. The corresponding reflexivity is that of the intra-subjective, I–you–me self. Similarly the face-to-face or interactive level has the point of view of the we. The corresponding mode of reflexivity is that of role-taking. This same, determining connection between point of view and kind of reflexivity continues at the other two symbolic levels.

(3) The nature of the *solidarity* is also differentiated by level. Chapter 5 was devoted primarily to intra-subjective solidarity. In that chapter I took Durkheim's theory of social solidarity and lowered it into the level of the self. I also showed that there is a lengthy tradition in social psychological theory that leads to the solidaristically defined self. It is relatively easy to go up the levels ladder with this idea. Durkheim introduced the concept at the social organizational level, and it is much more familiar there than at the intra-subjective. Nevertheless, since my purpose is to show that one kind of semiotic solidarity cannot be reduced to another, I will briefly go up the ladder.

Interactive solidarity appears in the sociological literature mainly as Erving Goffman's and Randall Collins's interaction rituals. These joint symbolic acts can, if done effectively, increase interpersonal solidarity.

Goffman also described negative rituals which can decrease solidarity and create conflict. This kind of solidarity, like that of the other levels, can be analyzed with Durkheim's various solidarity variables. All four kinds of solidarity have a great deal in common. Still, they are distinct, and all of the upward reductions entail the substitution of some supra-personal solidarity for the variety that is indigenous to the self.

Durkheim worked with the vaguely socio-cultural level or levels, not distinguishing the social from the cultural. In fact all of European classical sociology blurred the social and the cultural, this latter concept being a slightly later, American contribution. But if you divide Durkheim's solidarity into its social organizational and cultural aspects, you have something like what I specify in table 7.2. The social solidarity itself is present in the social organization, but the ritual symbols that are used to create this solidarity exist at the cultural level. The social solidarity is an emotion which links people, not only making them feel united but also letting them be on the same semiotic wavelengths. In other words this solidarity underlies the various forms of semiotic meaning.

But when we confine our attention to the cultural aspect of this process, the relevant solidarity is in the symbols themselves, divorced from people and relationships. The various 20th-century dictatorships that attempted to absorb individuals into the solidarity of political parties, nations, and their "isms" substituted social and cultural solidarities for the individual variety. The American founding fathers and the pragmatists were well aware of these non-democratic ways of handling solidarity. The similar upward reductions of today are not necessarily non-democratic and may even be regarded, by their adherents, as ultra-democratic. Still they are reductions, and they explain the solidarity of the inner self by substituting some external variety.

(4) In technical terms, *materiality* comprises everything contained on the physico-chemical and biological levels, including the human animal, but I will use the term more loosely. In relation to the symbolic levels, materiality has more specialized meanings, as suggested by table 7.2.

At the level of the self the most important relation to materiality is embodiment. The self is an organism, although the human organism has such subtle and comprehensive semiotic powers and is so far ahead of the other organisms that it is in a class by itself (*sui generis*). I will consider the biological component of human beings more extensively in chapter 8. Now I only want to show that each symbolic level has its own relation to materiality. In particular the upward reductions have to substitute their more attenuated materialities for embodiment, resulting in a disembodied human being.

163

It is very difficult to think about, and even more so to talk about, humans as animals and nothing more. They are, relatively speaking, so smart and so different from the other animals that they seem to be something over and above their animality. The European tradition of the "soul," and the more general animism of human cultural history favors separating the self from the body. But beyond religious tradition, the simple social psychology of the question also makes it difficult to think of humans in a completely embodied manner. Both Peirce and Mead regarded the self as no more than a property of the organism, yet both of them used the term "selves" at times as though these entities had complete autonomy from the body. From another viewpoint, Cooley shows that Shakespeare's uses of "I" and "me" in *Hamlet* hardly ever refer to the body (Cooley, 1922/1964, pp. 176–7).

Be that as it may, humans *are* bodies, however intelligently so. In figure 6.1 I placed humans in both the non-symbolic and symbolic levels, since they have both aspects. And I also placed them in an ontological level of their own. Still, among the four symbolic levels, theirs is the most sunk into matter. The materiality of the other three becomes increasingly distant as you go up the ladder.

Interaction, in the face-to-face sense of the word, is also embedded in matter but less intimately so than is the human being. I have defined interaction as the intersubjective, meaning the semiotic forms that exist in the relations among (face-to-face) human beings. This mode of meaning lies "between" rather than within humans. Of course when people are interacting they are still thinking, in a somewhat private way. Part of them is in the interactional semiotic and part is not. But for present purposes the private meanings, which are in the embodied self, are irrelevant. Interaction refers only to the shared meanings. Thus interaction is not materialized in the bodies of the interactants. It is a notch above the biological. Instead its relation to matter has to do with the face-to-face co-presence of the interactants.

Their co-presence is materially located, in the sense of being in the same place at the same time. These are indexical coordinates i.e. they have meaning only in relation to the thing that is in the time and place. The temporal and spatial borders of an interacting group are not precise. People may be half in and half out, and groups may be half alive and half dead. The loose borders do not detract from my point.

An interacting group may also be related to matter in other, more instrumental ways. In addition to time–space location, groups may use material objects, such as food, residences, automobiles, money, etc. All four symbolic levels use artifacts, although, except for some cultural elements, these are relatively outside and "environmental" to the semiotic structures in question.

If we stick with intrinsic or close connections with matter, the interacting group's major materiality is in the time–space positioning. In this respect the group is less embedded in matter than is the self, but more so than is the level of social organization.

At the level of social organization the time–space co-presence of the face-to-face group does not operate. Instead the members of the group or groups may be quite distant from each other, both temporally and spatially. Still there will usually be some boundaries, both in time and space. A country as large as France, for example, is too big to be considered as an interacting, face-to-face group. Still, it is loosely bounded, both by its territorial borders and by the lengthy time period during which it has existed. This relation to time–space materiality is not indexical, for the group is not located in some single space at some specific time. Instead it has a highly changeable, "stretchable" location. For this reason I am referring to its time–space status as "elastic" (Giddens, 1979, pp. 198–233) rather than indexical.

On the cultural level materiality is almost completely absent. Cultural elements are pure, semiotic symbols. They are abstracted, not only from agents (human and corporate), but also from all forms of matter. Matter includes the physico-chemical and biological levels, along with all artifacts made from these materials. It also includes the time and space containers that coordinate the two material levels. The sign–interpretant–object triads of culture are removed from all these forms of matter. Nevertheless these meanings are in the culture only because we have put them there. We uproot them from their psychological, interactional, and social organizational settings and pretend they exist by themselves.

The natural settings, at the lower three symbolic levels, entail closer relations to materiality. When meanings are extracted from these levels and placed in the culture, they are still virtually material, for the levels which actually carry these meanings are in some way material. The virtuality here is parallel with the kind I mentioned in describing culture's relation to reflexivity.

In the case of material artifacts ("material culture") some scholars would include the matter itself, and not just its design, in the culture. This is an extremely intimate materiality, almost like the kind the self has for being embodied in an organism. I am taking the position that only the design or semiotic component of a material artifact is in the culture. This is an arbitrary decision to some extent, although I think this approach yields a less cumbersome theoretical scheme.

The overall argument of table 7.2 is that upward reduction imposes ill-fitting properties on human nature. The self is a property of a physical organism, which engages in an internal conversation, from the first person

165

point of view, with a certain mimimum of inner solidarity. Upward reduction discards those properties and attributes inappropriate ones to the self. Table 7.2 describes three other sets of semiotic properties – those of interaction, social organization, and culture. Upward reductions substitute these other sets for those that actually define the self.

Having looked at reduction, particularly the upward variety, from several points of view, I will now turn more concretely to the way upward reduction works. To do this I will go from the interactional to the social organizational to the cultural levels.

Interactional Reductions of the Self

The notion of upward reduction has not been clarified in the scholarly literature, so my treatment will have to be somewhat tentative and exploratory. My division of this kind of reduction into the three varieties – interactional, social organizational, and cultural – has both strengths and weaknesses. A strength is that it fits the levels scheme I have been working with and it is also knit into my approach to semiotics. It uses existing concepts. On the other hand a weakness is that it may occasionally be overstructured. Several upward reductions reduce the self to language, but it is not clear whether the language is *parole* (interaction) or *langue* (culture). They do not fit easily into my scheme. It would be easier to treat them as vaguely upward without trying to pigeonhole them. Nevertheless, some classification, however imperfect, seems better than none (particular reductionist positions that are difficult to classify will be pointed out).

The notion of interaction itself, as I previously indicated, has become more sharply defined. George Simmel discovered the theoretical power of interaction *sui generis*, but he did not formally locate interaction within a meta-theory of levels. Goffman followed Simmel in mining the vein of interaction, but he too did not theorize it as such, nor did he clearly distinguish it from social organization or the self. Luhmann was the first to formally claim interaction as a level (1975, pp. 9–20), but his mechanistically cybernetic approach was so foreign to the other social theorists that his discovery went unnoticed. Anne Rawls (1987) was the first to theorize interaction both as a level and in its intersubjective interiority, thereby building on the insights of Simmel, Goffman, and Luhmann. In this section I will be referring to interaction in roughly Rawls's sense of the word.

In American pragmatism and the closely related interactionist sociology there has always been some blurring in the distinction between the self and interaction. There has also been imprecision in the distinctions between interaction and social organization and between social organization and culture, but that is not of present concern. Interaction was not clarified in meta-theoretical or levels terms until Rawls's 1987 paper, and the pragmatist approach to the self has not been clarified to this day.

The problem has been one of distinguishing the two kinds of interaction: the kind that goes on within the self, intra-subjectively, and the kind that goes on between selves, intersubjectively. Peirce's dictum that humans are "words" gave a misleadingly linguistic and interactionistic view of the self. Umberto Eco, in fact, used Peirce's dictum to argue for the cultural–linguistic reduction of the self (Eco, 1976, pp. 314–18). Mead, in turn, was not articulate enough about the difference between inter- and intra-personal interaction. It seems to me you need both interaction as a *sui generis* level and the self as a unique kind of semiotic triad to distinguish the two levels crisply. The self is a "word" but it is not like the other words. To rephrase, you need a clear distinction between the two semiotic triads: the ego–alter–we of interaction and the I–you–me of the self.

Because of the self-interaction blur there has always been a slight tendency in American sociology to reduce the self to interaction. Even the template was fuzzy on this question. The anti-reductionism of Cooley, Sumner, Thomas and Znaniecki, Park and Burgess, Mead, and Parsons was quite clear about the lower and upper extremes. The self was not the biology below nor was it the community, nation, or culture above. But the distinction between the self and interaction went unanalyzed. No one was reducing the self to interaction in any anti-humanistic or anti-democratic sense, so this kind of reduction was irrelevant to the discussion of the times. In addition these early theorists did not have the conceptual resources to clarify this distinction. Therefore, since they were, after all, sociologists and not psychologists, they tilted a bit toward interaction in visualizing the self. In other words there has been an occupational tendency in the history of American sociology to reduce the self to interaction, even though it was rarely done explicitly. This tendency, which I am consciously trying to counteract in this book, is another reason why interactional reduction is difficult to conceptualize.

Among contemporary sociologists interactional reduction continues to be a tendency. In ethnomethodology, the idea that meaning is primarily located in interpersonal interaction makes the self seem somewhat epiphenomenal to interaction. At times Garfinkel speaks this way, although at other times he seems to be assuming an autonomous self. (See Knorr-Cetina, 1981, for another ethnomethodological statement of interactional reduction.)

Among contemporary symbolic interactionists there has also been a tendency for interaction to swallow up the self. Herbert Blumer felt uncomfortable with Mead's I–me distinction (Athens, 1993, p. 186) which was the main plank of Mead's self theory, but Blumer never constructed an alternative self theory of his own. He felt comfortable and creative with the concept of interaction but not to the same extent with the self. Therefore, by dint of emphasis and theoretical attention, he seemed to lean quietly toward an interactional reductionism. Many other symbolic interactionists use Blumer's concepts and have followed his interaction-leaning lead.

As a third example of the interactional tendency I will mention German critical sociology, particularly as represented in the work of Jürgen Habermas. Habermas has been influenced by Henrich's analysis (1982) of reflexivity as circular. Therefore, in the absence of a non-reflexive theory of the self, Habermas seems to be accepting the idea that the self has been effaced. He has replaced this category with interaction and specifically with speech act theory. Habermas's interactionist reduction is not fully explicit and, as with the previous two cases, I would call it a tendency rather than a fully articulated theoretical position.

The widespread tendency in sociology, then, to be careless if not completely reductionist with the self-interaction distinction, has created an atmosphere in which these kinds of reduction are difficult to identify and understand. Nevertheless I think there are some unambiguous cases, if not in sociology then in other disciplines. The two cases I will use as my examples are those of Wittgenstein in philosophy and Lacan in psychoanalysis. Many others have worked in the shadow of these two interactional reductionisms.

In chapter 3 I looked briefly at Wittgenstein's views of inner experience, the I, the self, and internal language. At that time I was not so much looking at his interactionist tendencies as his views on the internal conversation. His thesis that all language, including the kind in the internal conversation, is public, is in conflict with the Peirce–Mead synthesis. The self is a "community" to some extent, consisting of communicators and their communications. These communications – barring people's thinking out loud – are private. This privacy, along with the semiotic peculiarities and short-cuts of inner speech, creates a measure of uniqueness in each person's interior language (for Vygotsky's analysis of the short–cuts see Wertsch, 1985, pp. 121–8 and 223–31). This uniqueness is not completely private, in Wittgenstein's strict sense, nor is it public either. I called it semi-private, by which I mean not some vague, in-between category, but one with a nature all its own.

Turning to Wittgenstein's interactionism, I will look at two of his linguistic claims: that the word "pain" has no referent; and that the word "I" has none either. The comment on pain is in the context of the private language argument. If we actually did have distinct experiences of pain, such that we could describe these experiences in some way, the door would be open to private language. The experiences would obviously be private, but more importantly the descriptions might also be at least part private as well. A private referent is an argument for a private or semi-private language.

Accordingly Wittgenstein argued that pain does not have any clear experiential qualities and that we would be unable to describe this experience without public language. This view of pain is in contrast to Peirce's, for whom pain tells the child that it has a self in the first place, i.e. it leads to the discovery of the self.

The argument that the word "I" has no reference, i.e. that the person is not an I and has no I, has much the flavor of the anti-pain argument. Again something that people think is interior is claimed not to be so, and the self — whatever that might be for Wittgenstein — is explained by external language. Both arguments also have a counter-intuitive, almost outrageous quality, bumping against common sense and ordinary experience. Nevertheless Wittgenstein does make a kind of gestalt shift in the way he empties out the self. It "feels" wrong to think you have no private experience and no I, but Wittgenstein's linguistic argument provides a strong counter-explanation. His counter-gestalt is also attractive to various scientistic positions, which want an emptied self. I am treating Wittgenstein's reductionist tendencies as upward, but his general argument can also be used by such downward reductionists as behaviorists and artificial intelligence psychologists.

The thread that links Wittgenstein's anti-pain and anti-I arguments is his criticism of consciousness ("intra-subjectivity") as such, including the first-person point of view. We experience pain privately, in the first person, and in ways that cannot be completely reduced to words. Yet the biology of pain may be uniform enough to make even the non-verbalizable aspect of the experience familiar to everyone. To argue that there is no private or semi-private concept of pain you have to get rid of the I, which is what Wittgenstein did. Then there is neither first-person experience nor a first person having these experiences.

This view of the I contrasts with the one Bertrand Russell (Wittgenstein's teacher) had, at least in *The Problems of Philosophy* (1912). In his discussion of knowledge by acquaintance he takes positions that conflict with those of Wittgenstein, both on the privacy of consciousness and on the referentiality of the word "I." On the first:

> We are not only aware of things, but we are often aware of being
> aware of them. When I see the sun, I am often aware of my seeing

the sun, thus 'my seeing the sun' is an object with which I have acquaintance. When I desire food, I may be aware of my desire for food; thus 'my desiring food' is an object with which I am acquainted. Similarly we may be aware of our feeling pleasure or *pain*, and generally of the events which happen in our minds (Russell, 1912/ 1959, p. 49; emphasis added).

Russell's distinction between knowledge by acquaintance and knowledge by description was roughly equivalent to that between the first- and third-person points of view. On this issue Russell opted for common sense and the first-person perspective. Accordingly he affirmed inner experience, the private perspective on this experience, and specifically the private awareness of pain.

On the "I" Russell said:

> We have spoke of acquaintance with the contents of our minds as *self*-consciousness, but it is not, of course, consciousness of our *self*: it is consciousness of particular thoughts and feelings. The question whether we are also acquainted with our bare selves, as opposed to particular thoughts and feelings, is a very difficult one, upon which it would be rash to speak positively. When we try to look into ourselves we always seem to come upon some particular thought or feeling, and not upon the 'I' which has the thought or feeling. Nevertheless there are some reasons for thinking that we are acquainted with the 'I', though the acquaintance is hard to disentangle from other things (1912/1959, p. 50).

Russell went on to wrestle with the problem that ran through British empiricism: the human inability to introspect the I. The I is what is doing the introspecting or reflecting and, because of the blind spot, it cannot see itself. In other words, there is no humunculus or little person inside the self, visible to the inward glance. This fact led Hume to say there is no self, but Russell was more impressed with the underlying agent or subject of experience. He concluded by saying "it is probable, though not certain, that we have acquaintance with Self, as that which is aware of things or has desires toward things" (1912/1959, p. 51).

We have now seen three positions on the existence of the I, or to put it another way, the referentiality of the word "I": The Peirce–Mead position that there is an I, and that it is the sign element of the semiotic self; the Wittgensteinian position that there is no I and the word therefore has no reference; and Russell's position that there "probably" is an I. I mentioned that Peirce had a position on pain and the self that seems to be in sharp contrast with Wittgenstein's. As I pointed out in chapter 2, Peirce thought the self was not discovered directly and intuitively, as Descartes seems to have said. For Peirce everything, including the self, is known indirectly, i.e. through signs. The child is unaware of having or being a self until a certain kind of sign appears in its experience. This sign is ignorance and error. To expand a quotation given in chapter 2:

> A child hears it said that the stove is hot. But it is not, he says; and, indeed, that central body is not touching it, and only what that touches is hot or cold. But he touches it, and finds the testimony confirmed in a striking way. Thus, he becomes aware of ignorance, and it is necessary to suppose a *self* in which this ignorance can inhere. So testimony gives the first dawning of self-consciousness (W2:202).

Peirce does not get around to dividing this moment of discovery, or "sign" of the self, into its semiotic triad, but it would seem to have to be as follows: the pain is the sign; the awareness of ignorance and error is the interpretant; and the self, which is inferred as underlying this error, is the object. Peirce is here arguing against Descartes, but his argument is also an answer to Wittgenstein.

For Wittgenstein the experience of pain was so indeterminate and fuzzy that it could be understood and talked about only after people had explained it to you. Pain was, in effect, a public experience. For Peirce it was the opposite. The pain of ignorance and error pierced through the veil of public experience and revealed the private sphere, which, in turn, is the sphere of the self. For him the private meaning of pain was so insistent that it opened the door to a whole new dimension of being, the interiority of the self.

I have now contrasted Wittgenstein's interactional reductionism with the views of Russell and Peirce. To reach interactionism, Wittgenstein had to deny the first-person point of view of table 7.2 and the "I" of table 7.1. Once the I was effaced there was an existential "hole" in the levels hierarchy, and he could use linguistic *parole* or interactionism to fill in that hole.

I am not claiming to have refuted Wittgenstein (or the views that many people have attributed to him). Whether or not you have private experience, an I and a first-person point of view is itself a matter of first-person experience. If someone denies having this experience, there is no public evidence with which to refute him or her. This is one of those things you have to point to or "show," to quote the more interpretive side of Wittgenstein. Still, I think the Peirce–Mead position, which is the common–sense position, explains a lot more and creates less "strain" for the person doing the philosophizing.

My second example of interactionism is drawn from Lacan (1966/1977), who had two arguments against the personal self: the mirror-stage idea and the linguistic interpretation of the oedipal complex. These two arguments, the latter building on the former, both empty the self, reduce it to some form of otherness and thereby lead to interactional reductionism. I will present his arguments in condensed form, for my purpose is not to fully air them but only to show how they lead to downward reduction.

Lacan's essay on the mirror stage (1966/1977, pp. 1–7) argues that the bits-and-pieces, self-less infant identifies with the mirror reflection, building an ego around this fictive, external element. Lacan uses "identify" in the strong sense, meaning not merely that you want to be like the object of identification but that you think you actually are that entity. The child, according to Lacan's theory, does not think it is the cause of the reflection but rather that it *is* the reflection. Of course the child, or at least its body, is the cause of the reflection. The reflection itself is merely a sign of the child, much as a photograph or tape recording is a sign. Therefore this identification is a mistake or, in Lacan's terminology, a "misrecognition."

To me Lacan's interpretation appears to be simply a bad guess about what happens to an infant when he or she first recognizes his or her self in a mirror. Lacan had no empirical data of his own, although he referred casually to some early child development researchers. But even though there is now a great deal of careful mirror research, both with infants of all kinds and with various other animal species (Anderson, 1984), no one knows what happens to an infant upon self-recognition.

My alternative interpretation, however, which seems more congruent with experimental data, is that self-recognition leads not to the fictitious invention of a self, but to the *discovery* of an inchoately developing self. The usual thing that happens with an infant at the mirror is that it initially thinks the reflection is another child, a sort of playmate. The playmate stage leads to the discovery of peculiar matching behaviors between the self and the other. The child frowns and the playmate frowns. The child sticks out his or her tongue and the playmate does too. The child touches the playmate and the playmate seems to be touching the child. Not only is the duplication uncanny, the touch of the playmate is unrealistically hard and unyielding. In Peirce's terms, the hypothesis of the playmate is beginning to prove in error.

In my opinion the child finally figures out the mystery by eye contact with the playmate. I base this interpretation on my childhood memories and on having observed my own six children at the mirror, although I will use these informal sources of data only as a background resource. The eyes start pairing, just as the hands did. The uncanny matching continues, although now it is so subtle and nuanced that the child begins to realize he or she not only controls the playmate but in some way is the playmate. This resembles Lacan's notion that the child identifies with, i.e. thinks he or she is, the reflection. The difference is that for Lacan this identification was the final result of the mirror experience, freezing the self into a misrecognition for life. In my interpretation, however, this identification is merely one stage in the series, ending not with Lacan's glassy ego but, as I will show, with the pragmatist's dialogical self.

The eye dance breaks the bubble. Seeing your own eyes in the mirror, but thinking they are someone else's, gradually becomes a self-refuting experience. The matching is too good, the pairing is too close, and the emotions in the eye conversation are too much one's own to be those of a playmate, or even of a second you. The child realizes, all at once, that the person in the mirror is his or her self. At the same time he or she realizes that the duplication is not some parallel, or even less the primary, reality, but a harmless representation.

By now, somewhere between 12 and 24 months, the child usually has some command of language, including meaningful baby talk. This means the child can think to some extent, and, with these linguistic resources, can experience an early form of the internal conversation. In other words before the child has Lacan's mirror experience it will usually be experiencing an early version of its own internal semiotic processes. This means it is not quite as unintegrated or in bits and pieces as Lacan thought. Presumably the child does not yet have complete control of the thought process, both because of linguistic inadequacy, and because internal privacy has not yet been clearly discovered. Some uninvited guest may be in there listening, and even the person at the other end of the conversation may not yet be known with certainty to be the self. There are also complications coming from the fact that children of this age think out loud some of the time, thereby losing privacy.

On my interpretation of the mirror experience, then, the child discovers that the person at the other end of the internal conversation is his or her self and, in addition, that the conversation is private. No one else is in there, and the communicative partner is always and only oneself. In other words the child discovers not the armoured and paranoid Lacanian but the dialogically decentered Peirce–Mead self.

This discovery fits Peirce's hunch concerning how the child first realizes that it has a self. For Peirce this came from ignorance and error, leading to the realization that there was a self in which this error inhered. Since his main example had to do with finding out that the stove is hot after all, just as the parents insisted, I used this analysis of pain against Wittgenstein's. But Peirce is also useful in correcting Lacan's interactionism.

The child's playmate theory is gradually proved to be a mistake. Instead

173

the playmate turns out to be a representation of the self. I think this representation is perceived as the "other" of the internal conversation, or at least as a strong metaphor of this other. At the same time, however, the discovery of error also leads to the self as the repository of error. The anxiety ("pain") of the pairing process is relieved by the self-recognizing gestalt, and at the same time the cause of error, and of the anxiety–pain, is located in the self. There are then two Peircian routes back to the self for Lacan's mirror child. One is the realization that the mirror dialectic, between viewer and viewed, is a visible picture of the internal conversation, or, in other words, that the mirror's reflexivity is an outward expression of inner reflexivity. The other is the anchoring of the playmate error in the self, itself now known to be dialogical.

Lacan's linguistic version of oedipal theory is his second argument against the personal self. According to this the child, around age three, loses a castration battle with the father, or fathering figure(s). In defeat the child internalizes language, law, and the kind of self that these institutions create. Sometimes, by "castration," Lacan seems to mean simply taking the child out of the exclusive pre-oedipal bond with the "mother." Strained as this metaphor is, it does have approximately the same meaning for both male and female infants, and it explains the nature of their defeat (Ragland-Sullivan, 1986, pp. 55–7). At other times he seems to mean something more like what Freud meant by the term, i.e. amputation of the male genitals, in which case the term cannot be applied to males and females in the same way. Lacan is often unclear whether he is using this, and other, terms literally or not, but the reductionism of his oedipal theory is independent of these terminological ambiguities.

The post-mirror self, as it proceeds through the oedipal crisis, has no real content. It is based on an identification with its mirror reflection and, in addition, its closeness to the mothering one. Some commentators have interpreted Lacan's mirror as somehow turning into the mother, but Lacan does not say this and it does not fit his overall theory. In any case, when the child loses the oedipal fight, it has no inner structure, no defense, against whatever the father might do to it. What the father does is to force the institutions, language and law, into the child, or (better said) the child into the institutions. This insertion into the institutions is gender-specific, for each gender is placed into a different "position" in the language-law institutional field. There are male and female ways of being located in and internalizing these institutions, and the two positionings define the genders. But for purposes of explaining Lacan's reduction, the important point is that the self continues to be defined by something external.

Now, on top of the specular, glassy self the institutions are overlaid. The reflection of the body in the mirror is replaced by the law and language, although the self continues to be completely dependent on external fabrication. Actually the misrecognized mirror self never really goes away, and its weaknesses are especially present when we are under stress. Nevertheless the oedipal self resembles that of the mirror in being still another identification with externalities.

The oedipal argument depends on the validity of the mirror argument, for the former assumes the inner emptiness that the latter has sealed in. If the oedipal child did have some inner structure, e.g. an early version of the dialogical self, it could not be as freely manipulated and positioned into the institutions. The mirror child's identification with something external implies that there is nothing internal. This inner vacuum, in turn, permits the drastic oedipal brainwashing of the child, including the all-at-once entry into gender.

My critique of the mirror argument, then, carries over into the oedipal argument, for the latter is built on the former. But the oedipal argument has its own weaknesses as well, not least that children usually learn language a year or two before they internalize the alleged capacity for language in the oedipal transition. In other words they usually learn language well before they have reached the Lacanian necessary conditions for this learning.

Lacan's interactionism resembles Wittgenstein's in being centered on an argument against the *sui generis* self. Let us say "effacement" is an argument against the self or one of its properties. In contrast "replacement" is the filling in of the space, created by the effacement, by some other level. Wittgenstein's effacement is aimed primarily at the first-person point of view, and Lacan's at internal reflexivity. But both effacements eliminate the level of the *sui generis* individual. Neither theorist is very explicit about the process of replacement. Instead their thought does this automatically, as air rushes into a vacuum. Wittgenstein replaces the first-person point of view with public language, which I am interpreting to mean not *langue* but *parole* (interaction). Lacan replaces internal reflexivity with outer identifications. The first is with the quasi-other of the mirror reflection. The second is with the shared culture of public language and law. Neither theorist is explicitly a reductionist, but in the implications of their thought they both are. In addition both interactionisms are highly influential in several disciplines, including psychiatry, philosophy, and literary criticism.

Social Organizational Reductions of the Self

Social organization and the closely related notion of social structure are conceptualized in a variety of ways in contemporary sociology. For me the former term refers to groups of substantial size, such as nations and the large organizations they contain. The latter refers to the patterns, designs, or meaning systems that define and regulate social organization. Social structure might be called the "form" of social organization. In discussing the social level, i.e. the one interposed between interaction and culture, I have usually referred to it as social organization, although sometimes also as social structure.

There is widespread disagreement concerning the make-up or composition of this level. For some it is primarily moral; for others relational, in a quasi-geometric sense; for others demographic; for others virtual and "deep;" and for still others primarily linguistic. Since social organization is quite comprehensive, it is possible to single out any of its components and make this the defining feature. I will not set out to clarify all the meanings of this level, for my task is merely to show the features that make it a level, and why it cannot be used to explain the level of the self.

It is important not to have an over-inclusive notion of social organization, or one's meta-theory will be too clumsy. Durkheim's notion, which is the classic statement in social theory, was too inclusive, for, as previously mentioned, it was a mixture of interaction, social organization proper, and culture. In addition he sometimes described it as purely relational, as in his discussion of social morphology, and sometimes as symbolically substantive, as in his conception of the collective consciousness. One reason why Durkheim's discussion of social facts, particularly in their exteriority and constraint, was so imprecise was that he was talking about all three social levels at once, each of which has a different kind of exteriority and constraint.

Given some kind of workable definition of social organization, one can then clarify social reductionism. Tables 7.1 and 7.2 show, analytically, what this reduction entails. It is the substitution of the social organizational semantic triad (collective agent–collective patient–organization) for the psychological one (I–you–me). Or, more specifically, it is the substitution of the social point of view, mode of reflexivity, solidarity, and materiality for the kind that pertain to the level of the self.

In the 19th century Hegel was the most noticeable social reductionist, although, like all theorists of this period, he did not distinguish the social from the cultural. Dewey and Mead were initially attracted to Hegel, partly as a counter-weight to Darwin's biological reduction. They gradually realized that neo-Hegelianism was an overreaction to Darwinism, making the same reductionist error, although at the opposite end of the levels spectrum. With the other pragmatists, they then established the *sui generis*, semiotic self, differentiating the psychological level from Darwinism below and Hegelianism above.

176

In addition to Hegel, there were a variety of other 19th-century European theorists, alluded to in table 6.1, whose thought had socially reductionist implications. The social reduction of the self has been around for a long time in social theory, and it can be treated more briefly than the one based on interaction.

I will use Durkheim as my major example, although there are many others, e.g. Althusser (1971), Mayhew (1981), Luhmann (1986), and the Marx of *Capital* (1867). Nancy DiTomaso (1982) included Parsons in her "Sociological Reductionism, from Parsons to Althusser," 1982, as a social reductionist, although he is also a cultural reductionist at times and at other times, as in his 1937 contribution to the classical template, a staunch anti-reductionist.

Before turning to Durkheim I will look briefly at the structural reductionism of Peter Muhlhäusler and Rom Harré (1990, pp. 87–105). Their linguistic reduction is an example of a current trend, though I am singling it out because of the specific way it contrasts with my position. These authors take the anti-Cartesian insight that the self is social and carry it so far that there is no more self. They call their position the theory of double location or double indexicality. Their first locational–indexical coordinate for defining the self is that of the body in time and space. This gives the person a "point of view." The second locational–indexical coordinate is the moral one of rights and duties, positioned in the field of human relationships.

Their dual indexicality contrasts with the kind I used in chapter 6 to explain the word "I." This word is psychologically indexical to the person saying it, and, in addition, physically indexical to the time–space position of the person's body. This nests the particularity of the person within the particularly of that person's body. The Muhlhäusler–Harré double indexicality never reaches the particularity of the person, or for that matter the *sui generis* level of the self. Their time–space indexicality is purely mechanical and physical. Its "point of view" lacks a viewer. And their moral or institutional indexicality – which is what makes them social reductionists – never reaches the individuality of the person either. The locus of rights and duties themselves is just another name for the rights and duties themselves, and it does not indicate a person. At best their moral location is a set of "identities," floating around without a self within which to inhere.

Turning to my major case, Durkheim might seem like a poor example, since he is well known for his assertion of an autonomous psychological level. In practice, however, his social structure was so powerful and autonomous that it absorbed the individual.

Another problem in using Durkheim is his running together of all the supra-individual levels. This means he was mixing elements of inter-actional and cultural, along with social organizational reductionism, although the last was the strongest.

The forked-tongue approach of Durkheim, which both (explicitly) denies and (implicitly) asserts reduction, is typical of reductionist literature. It is hard to find unambiguous reductions of the self, either downward or upward. Wittgenstein and Lacan were not pure cases either, for they both also asserted the reality of the human individual, although they did so in terms that had the effect of canceling this assertion. What John Searle says about downward (materialistic) reductions, could also be applied to upward:

> Before identifying some of these incredible views, I want to make an observation about presentational style. Authors who are about to say something silly very seldom come right out and say it. Usually a set of rhetorical or stylistic devices is employed to avoid having to say it in words of one syllable. The most obvious of these devices is to beat around the bush with a lot of evasive prose (Searle, 1992, p. 4).

When Durkheim describes how the social and individual levels are related, he does so in ways that, upon close examination, eliminate the autonomous self. He gives autonomy with one hand and takes it back with the other, and he does this in so many ways that his social level ends up dissolving the individual one. Durkheim is therefore in conflict with the classical template of American sociology.

An advantage of drawing on Durkheim is that he is the ancestor of recent French structuralism and post-structuralism, a point of view that includes several versions of upward reduction. All of the great intellectuals in this line of thought – Lévi-Strauss, Lacan, Barthes, Althusser, Foucault, and Derrida, among others – were decenterers or self-reductionists. They also all have genealogical connections to Durkheim, both directly and by way of Lévi-Strauss.

I will examine Durkheim's *de facto* reductionism from two points of view: semiotic power or solidarity; and semiotic content. I will also show how Durkheim's causal closure of the social realm, the "logical rule" that social facts can be caused only by other social facts, has reductionist implications.

Under the general umbrella of semiotic power or solidarity I am including bindingness or necessity, mana, and the sacred. Lacan's (misleadingly named) "phallus" also belongs with this set of concepts, but it is not directly relevant to the present discussion. Durkheim himself used only three of these terms: solidarity, the sacred, and mana. I have added semiotic power, bindingness–necessity, and Lacan's "phallus," in order to deepen the underlying concept. Durkheim consistently has these forces being created at the social level and then trickling down to that of the individual.

Take the sacred for example, which is the "locomotive" or causal agent of all Durkheim's semiotic power. In *The Elementary Forms of Religious Life* (1915/1965) the sacred exists primarily at the social level. Individuals have this quality only as derived from the society. Individual expressions of religion "are only the individualized forms of collective forces. Therefore, even when religion seems to be entirely within the individual conscience, it is still in society that it finds the living source from which it is nourished" (1915/1965, p. 472). Along with the sacred is "mana" and the various other terms that Durkheim (and assorted hunting and gathering societies) used to designate the sacred. I treat mana as separate from the sacred because mana is semiotic power, as Lévi-Strauss realized so clearly: he deepened and generalized it across the semiotic range. The sacred and its expression in mana originates only at the level of society. Society transmits these qualities to individuals, although without this transmission individuals would forever lack these qualities.

The force or power of all the forms of meaning, then, comes from society. Individuals have this power only because society gives it to them. Even in contemporary times, when many nations have granted inviolability and sacredness to their citizens, this sacredness, as Durkheim saw it, is still derived from society. The individuals of modern societies have no sacredness on their own; none that is intrinsic or self-generated. In the absence of internal sacredness, there is also the lack of mana, solidarity, bindingness–necessity, and semiotic power. All these things are borrowed from the society. Without these powers humans would no longer be humans. They would be back with the other primates again. Therefore if the seemingly distinct qualities of human nature are entirely created by and derived from society, human nature is reducible to society, and Durkheim is a social organizational reductionist.

Of course even though Durkheim makes society a necessary condition of the individual he also asserts that the individual is a necessary condition of society. In his mind neither can exist without the other. This may look like a virtuous (or hermeneutic) circle, which is how it looked to Durkheim. He did not see society reducing individuals or individuals reducing society, but rather two semi-autonomous, *sui generis* levels. But this makes no sense when his concepts are closely examined. Collective representations cannot come to be without pre-existing individual representations, which they synthesize at a higher level. And individual representations also cannot come to be without pre-existing collective representations, for the latter give semiotic power to the former. These two sentences contradict because for Durkheim individual representations already have full semiotic status. They do not lack meaning or mana. So they already have what they can supposedly get only from society.

When I turn to my second point of view, that of content, the same conclusion can be reached. The core of Durkheim's semantic or semiotic content was in his conceptual categories. This notion of fundamental or core concepts runs throughout the history of philosophy, although philosophers do not agree on exactly which concepts should have this status. Among those with distinct lists of categories are Aristotle, Kant, Hegel, and Peirce. Durkheim constructed a list of his own, along with a theory of how these concepts originated. Durkheim never states an official, definitive list of categories nor does he always use the same terms, but his list, as indicated in chapter 5, consists of more or less the following ten concepts: time; space; number; force or cause; group, kind, class, or genus-species; the universe, totality, or being; personality; substance; God; and left and right. This is a far cry from Aristotle's list of ten or Kant's twelve. It is also quite different from Peirce's early I–you–it and Lacan's infant–mother–father. But Durkheim's list is still an arguable batch of core concepts, and, even more so, his theory of their genesis is ingenious.

These categories are neither innate nor learned from reality. Instead they are based on and generalized from ordinary social relations. The local community is the concrete social group, from which all the categories emerged. For example, the abstract concept of group itself, along with its synonyms (kind, class, or genus-species) is merely an elaboration of the idea of the local community. The idea of the "personality" is an individualization of the group, insofar as the group is seen to have a corporate entity or "self." And "totality" or "being" is again the group and all it entails or possesses. Time and space are also group-based for they are merely extensions of the temporal and spatial patterns of the group.

Durkheim's categories are indispensable to any kind of meaning, consciousness, or, to use Husserl's equivalent term, "intentionality." All particular concepts are based on one or more of Durkheim's master categories. There are no concepts that are not built on and from the categories. This means that the level at which the categories originate is the decisive semiotic level. The Mead–Peirce approach regards all four semiotic levels as autonomous, i.e. each has independent access to the categories. Durkheim's scheme, in contrast, has the categories originating only at the group level, both morphologically and meaningfully.

The morphological origination is in the structure of the group, as previously mentioned. The make-up of the group originates the relationships that can be semioticized as the categories. These relationships are not, in their logistic origins, fully meaningful. The concepts of time and space, for example, are only implicitly present in the time–space routines of the community. Similarly the other categories are only latent in the concrete community. These concepts or categories are made meaningful when they enter the collective consciousness. Earlier I mentioned that for Durkheim social organization can be viewed morphologically, as a set of relationships, or semiotically, as a collective consciousness. This is the distinction I am now making between the logistic bases and the semantic content of the categories.

The important point, however, is that in both respects the categories originate at the group or social level. They become available at the individual level only as society distributes these resources to individuals. Just as the sacredness of the individual is a spillover effect from society, so are the elementary meanings of the conceptual categories. And since the crucial categories come from society, the more specific concepts, all of which are constructed from the underlying categories, also come, at least indirectly, from society.

To put this in slightly different, Durkheimian terms, the categories are primarily collective representations; only in a derived way are they individual representations. Durkheim is not always consistent in his distinction between these two kinds of representation or concept. In his essay "Individual and Collective Representations" (1898/1974) the distinction is sharp, and, moreover, the latter are *sui generis* emergents from ensembles of the former. In this paper the two levels of meaning, individual and social, are contrasted with their biological substratum, the human organism. But in his essay "The Dualism of Human Nature and its Social Conditions" (1914/1960) the two kinds of representation are collapsed into one, which he refers to as social. The "dualism" is between the body and the soul, self, or social aspect. This latter essay is about "homo duplex" but the former is about "homo triplex." This confusion and Durkheim's vacillating between whether he sees two levels of representation or one, reflect the ambiguous status of the categories in his theory. On the one hand, he seems to want the individual to have, in some way, autonomous access to meaning and the categories. This autonomy would permit the collective representations to emerge, in his technical sense of the word, from the individual, and human beings would, accordingly, be "triplex." On the other hand, given his theory of the social origin of the categories, the individual cannot really have autonomous access to them. They have to be borrowed from society, in which case humans are composites of the biological and the social, i.e. they are "duplex." The duplex–triplex confusion is another way of looking at his ambivalent reductionism.

181

Explicitly and officially he is an autonomist but implicitly and unofficially he is a reductionist.

Durkheim's notion of social closure is still another area in which one can find his *de facto* reductionist tendencies. He sees this closure in both efficient and final causes. He says:

> Hence we arrive at the following rule: *The determining cause of a social fact must be sought among antecedent social facts and not among the states of the individual consciousness.* Moreover, we can easily conceive that all that has been stated above applies to the determination of the function as well as the cause of a social fact. . . . Thus we can complement the preceding proposition by stating: *The function of a social fact must always be sought in the relationship that it bears to some social end* (1895/1982, p. 134).

This rule assumes that the individual level can never have any causal effect, efficient or final, on the social. The social always causes itself and is therefore sealed off from individual influences. There is no corresponding closure rule for the individual level. The social can affect the individual, as I have been pointing out throughout this section. It is not clear whether this rule also disallows the necessary conditional relation that, at times, he says the individual has to the social.

Since Durkheim is so over-inclusive in his notion of the social, it is difficult to interpret this rule about the causes of the social. Is he saying that interaction causes interaction, social organization causes social organization, and culture causes culture? Or can each of the three supra-psychological levels cause each other? This would mean, for example, that interaction could cause things to happen at the level of social organization, etc., but that the individual could never be part of this influence. Since I reject Durkheim's closure, it is not important in the context of this book to know exactly what he may have meant.

A good way of getting a sense of his closure rule is to look at the diametrically opposed rule that Thomas and Znaniecki stated. It should be remembered that these authors used "attitude" in an older sense to mean any and all elements of consciousness (e.g. emotional, cognitive, volitional, etc.), not just behavioral tendencies or pro–con leanings. They also used "value" in an older, inclusive sense to mean any symbolic or meaningful element of social organization or culture. They were not clear about the notion of interaction, although they seemed to include it implicitly in their notion of the social.

The fundamental methodological principle of both social psychology and sociology – the principle without which they can never reach scientific explanation – is therefore the following one:

The cause of a social or individual phenomenon is never another social or individual phenomenon alone, but always a combination of a social and an individual phenomenon.

Or, in more exact terms:

The cause of a value or of an attitude is never an attitude or value alone, but always a combination of an attitude and a value (vol. 1, p. 44).

Thomas and Znaneicki then add a clarifying footnote:

It may be objected that we have neglected to criticize the conception according to which the cause of a social phenomenon is to be sought, not in an individual, but exclusively in another social phenomenon (Durkheim). But a criticism of this conception is implied in the previous discussion of the data of social theory. As these data are both values and attitudes, a fact must include both, and a succession of values alone cannot constitute a fact. Of course much depends also on what we call a "social" phemononon (p. 44).

The Thomas and Znaniecki rule highlights the exclusion of psychological influences in Durkheim's rule. The social, for Durkheim, is clearly autonomous, *sui generis*, and unaffected by events from any other ontological level, particularly that of the self. Individuals, whether one at a time or in aggregate, do not affect social events. Only other social events affect social events. On the other hand Durkheim's social does affect his individual, both in the content and form of individual representations (Durkheim's name for Thomas's and Znaniecki's "attitudes," i.e. for all the elements of consciousness). The relation is asymmetrical for Durkheim, for the social affects the individual but the individual does not affect the social.

Thomas and Znaniecki make the influences symmetrical, for, not only does their social affect the individual, their individual also affects the social. The comparison I am drawing here distinguishes two disciplinary "foundings," the French one based on the social level and the American one, based jointly on the individual and social. It also shows how Thomas and Znaniecki affirmed the anti-reductionist template against Durkheim's upward reductionism.

Social closure reduces the individual to the social because causation is one-way, permitting the social to influence the individual but not the reverse. From causation follows dependency, and from these two follows reduction. Of course the specific way in which the individual depends on the social is, as previously explained, in the force (solidarity, sacredness, mana, etc.) and content (especially the categories) of the representations. Collective representations cause the individual kind but these do not cause the collective kind.

It might seem strange that American social theory, which tends to rest on an autonomous individual, has drawn so heavily on Durkheim in recent decades. Early American sociology, until the 1930s, was critical of Durkheim, precisely because of his reductionism and incompatibility with the template. But in the 1930s, particularly after Parsons's *Structure of Social Action* (1937), Durkheim was no longer interpreted as one who reduced individuals to the "group mind." This reinterpretation of Durkheim could be made only by ignoring the many reductionist implications in his thought. This is not difficult to do, since he too ignored them and spoke as though he were a consistent non-reductionist.

The major social reductionist of the late 20th century has been the post-structuralist Louis Althusser. Althusser's structural determinism intensifies, i.e. out-Durkheims Durkheim and, in addition, transforms him in a Marxist direction. Still, it retains Durkheim's circularity. Althusser also goes beyond Durkheim by arguing that there is no individual or self, except as constructed by (capitalist) society. Since capitalist society is supposed to do this by constructing a Lacanian mirror self, and since I have already discussed Lacan, it is unnecessary to go over the same ground again for Althusser. Returning to the effacement–replacement dialectic, while Wittgenstein effaced the first person and Lacan internal reflexivity, Durkheim in contrast effaced (internal) solidarity. He is frequently explicit about this alleged absence of intrinsic solidarity in the individual, particularly in his discussions of the sacred. This property is indigenous at the social level but only derivative at the individual. Since solidarity is missing in the individual, and all representations, both individual and collective, require solidarity for their mana, everything representational (in my terms symbolic or semiotic) about the individual is borrowed from and reducible to the social level.

In contrast to Wittgenstein and Lacan, it would have been difficult for Durkheim to replace the individual with the interactive level, because of what he effaced. *Parole* or interaction is close enough to the first person and to that person's reflexivity to finesse a replacement. If a vacuum is created by effacing those properties, interaction, in contrast to social organization and culture, is best fit to fill it. But if solidarity, in my sense of semiotic force or mana, is effaced, interaction is not the most efficient replacement. The level with the most dramatic and intense solidarity is social organization. And for Durkheim in particular, who virtually invented this concept, social solidarity had the most elective affinity with the (now effaced) individual. Thus the effacement–replacement implications of point of view and reflexivity lead to interactional reduction, but those of solidarity lead to the social organizational variety.

Finally it should be asked whether Durkheim's unawareness of his reductive implications makes him a poor example of social reduction. But there are no perfect examples. Nancy DiTomaso's cases of Althusser and Parsons, despite the ground-breaking insights of her paper (1982), are not usable for my purposes. Early Parsons was a crucial contributor to the anti-reductionist template, and Althusser was too dependent on Lacan to constitute a separate case. Durkheim's objective thought is reductionist, even though he did not realize it. In addition the fallacious character of social reduction is manifest in his several kinds of logical circularity. Each level, individual and social, is a necesssary condition of the other, and it is so "at the same time in the same way." This violates the principle of contradiction. Durkheim thought the two levels depended on each other in different ways, but he never showed what this difference was.

Cultural Reductions of the Self

The notion of culture as a semiotic level was gradually clarified by Franz Boas and his students in the early 20th century. As I mentioned in chapter 1, the semiotic social psychology of the American pragmatists was essential to this clarification. However the concept of culture always had a measure of imprecision, and this continues to the present day.

There were always two definitions: one wide and one narrow. The wide version comprises all of the supra-biological, i.e. everything in the entire symbolate or symbolic field(s). In this usage, all the symbolic levels are cultural: selves, interaction, social organization, and culture proper. The narrow definition restricts the term to the cultural level *sui generis*, omitting the cultural components of the lower, symbolic levels. Both definitions are useful for certain purposes, but my own analysis leans toward the narrow one.

During the decades when American anthropologists were attempting to clarify the concept of culture, they had trouble distinguishing the two meanings. As a discipline they stood to gain from both, and they seemed to want both. The wide-angled meaning made anthropology the all-inclusive social science, for all the social sciences are concerned with internalized and embedded culture. But more realistically the anthropologists also needed the narrow meaning to define the specificity of their field, to establish their epistemological niche (or paradigm space), and to legitimize their intellectual property against the claims of the other social sciences.

185

Even the defense of their specific niche was a problem, for the cultural level as such was claimed by other disciplines. Biology, psychology, and sociology all tended to annex, not only the wide but also the narrow conceptions of culture. To defend their niche, the anthropologists had to show that their space, that of culture, was above the biological, above the psychological, and also above the sociological. In making these arguments, however, they tended to use a different notion of culture for each binary confrontation. Against biology, they tended to define culture in the widest possible sense; against psychology they tended to merge the sociological and the cultural; and against sociology they were forced to retreat to the (now more or less established) narrow definition. It is little wonder that the concept of culture never quite became clarified.

At present there are several competing concepts of culture within anthropology: Geertz's semiotic, Goodenough's cognitive, Lévi-Strauss's structural, Harris's adaptationist, and the traditional symbolic conception, among others. There is also a coalition of anthropologists – critical, Marxist, and positivist – who, each for different reasons, are unhappy with the concept and want to see it dropped from the discipline.

Nevertheless, as the anthropologist Robert Winthrop put it, "the culture concept seems theoretically fragmented and philosophically vulnerable at precisely the time that its significance has come to be widely recognized outside the discipline" (Winthrop, 1990, p. 5). The concept has been migrating to literary criticism, philosophy, "cultural studies," semiotics, and sociology.

A major reason for this migration has been the steady rise of the linguistic analogy in the humanities and social sciences. Viewed as a set of forms or rules, language is part of culture, and hence the linguistic analogy is a cultural one. Richard Rorty (1967) distinguished two waves of the 20th-century linguistic turn, one positivist ("ideal" language) and the other interpretive ("ordinary" language), although the latter is currently more influential than the former. In philosophy, language now competes with logic as a theory of meaning.

But a third wave has come from French structuralism and post-structuralism. Lévi-Strauss introduced the linguistic analogy into anthropology itself, establishing the "structural" approach to that field. As his approach has come to be modified and developed by the French post-structuralists, the linguistic (and hence cultural) analogy is now deeply-rooted in both the social sciences and the humanities. In addition to challenging logic in the humanities, it challenges quantification and positivism in the social sciences.

The concept of culture is now doing very well in the academy. Anthropologists may be abandoning it, but virtually all other disciplines

186

are embracing it. Nevertheless this spread of the culture concept is creating its own intellectual difficulties. First, the distinction between the wide- and narrow-gauge definitions of the concept is again becoming blurred. Given that anthropology is the home of the narrow definition, and the other social sciences the home of the wide, this blurring follows from the migration. In addition the distinction among the social sciences on the one hand and between these sciences and philosophy on the other is also becoming blurred. The use of the linguistic analogy and the implied reversion to the "logic" of culture is tending to homogenize these disciplines. Third, and more relevant to the theme of this chapter, the spread of the concept of culture is giving credence to the cultural reduction of the self.

American anthropologists, particularly those following Leslie White's "culturology," made some minor gestures toward the cultural reduction of all the symbolic levels, including that of the self, but these gestures were never developed nor were they taken very seriously. Later, however, the anti-humanistic themes of French post-structuralism, expressed in such phrases as the death of man and the effacement of the subject, have constituted a much more effective cultural reduction of the self. Like the two reductions I have already considered, interactional and social organizational, this one replaces the semiotic self with an extra-personal semiotic system.

All of the post-structuralists have elements of cultural reduction in their writings, although the two that are best known for this position are Foucault and Derrida. Both thinkers hedge their positions at times (see Hekman, 1990, p. 69 for Foucault's hedges and p. 67 for Derrida's), and they therefore do not have completely unambiguous reductions, but they are nevertheless quite influential in the contemporary critique of the "subject." Derrida, in addition to outliving Foucault, has the more systematic reduction of the two, so I shall concentrate on him after a brief look at Foucault.

Foucault made the common misidentification of identity with self, as mentioned in the first chapter. Modern scientific and academic disciplines certainly did engage in a lot of talk (discursive practices) about the self, and there was always some political power and class interest interlarded in these discourses. Foucault is especially impressed by the identity-shaping power of criminology and medicine. He contrasts his discursive theory of the self, viewed as constructed by the discourse of social organizations and their spokespersons, with the overstructured Cartesian view (1966/1973, pp. 386–7). But this is to substitute one extreme position for another. He may have realized this in his later books on the history of sexuality, when he moved to the more moderate position of self-constitution.

Turning to Derrida, one way of identifying his reductionism is to ask what he effaceş in the individual. In contrast to the previous cases, where some aspect of the individual was singled out, Derrida systematically effaces all of these properties, for the very idea of the "subject" is a fallacy for him.

Derrida's idea of the subject, however, is questionable, for it is the privatized, asocial self of Edmund Husserl. Husserl isolated the self from others as a result of his phenomenological method. He softened Descartes' doubt of the ordinary certitudes by turning this doubt into a suspension or "bracketing." On the most important of these certitudes, the existence of the external world, Husserl took a neutral or agnostic position. In contrast to the later existentialists, Heidegger and Sartre, who would suspend essence to look at existence (being), Husserl suspended existence to look at essence. Rather than asserting that the world does or does not exist, he simply ignored the question and treated the world as a pure appearing (or "presence"). Since he included all other people in this world, these people too were placed into an existentially neutral category. His phenomenological philosophy then proceeded to explain the self without any reference to other people, i.e. as a purely privatized, isolated entity. Even though Husserl did depart from Descartes in significant ways, his idea of the self has a lot in common with Descartes'.

It should be mentioned, parenthetically, that the French post-structuralists presented an exaggerated interpretation of Sartre, as though he were a linear development of the Cartesian–Husserlian tradition. Lévi-Strauss and the post-structuralists were engaged in replacing Sartre's centrality in French intellectual life, so they were hardly in a position to appraise him accurately. But Sartre himself (1936–7/1957) was quite critical of Husserl's theory of the self. Not only did Sartre, following Heidegger, reverse the phenomenological strategy by bracketing essence to examine existence, he also decentered the Husserlian self in a way that foreshadowed and initiated the more extensive post-structuralist decentering. Sartre is not so much the opposite of post-structuralism as the initiation and clue to it.

The self or subject that Derrida abolishes, then, is not that of Sartre, but rather the unrealistically centered and privatized one of the Descartes–Husserl tradition. Indeed for several decades this non-social self has been something of a straw man in philosophy, ceremonially (and repeatedly) dismissed as the great error of the European Enlightenment. But instead of replacing this theory, as the pragmatists did, with a more social version, Derrida regarded the very existence of the individual or self as a fallacy and replaced it with language and culture.

Derrida (like Eco) was under the impression that he was following Peirce in his critique of the self. Peirce's casual comments that the human being is a "sign" or a "word" invited this misinterpretation. Nevertheless, as I

188

Finally Talcott Parsons, in a late version of the founding, followed
showed in chapter 2, the semiotic nature of human individuals does not
mean that they can be reduced to language, either in the interactional sense
of *parole* or the cultural sense of *langue*. Humans use language, both in the
sense that they speak to each other (*parole*) and follow linguistic rules
(*langue*). But they not only *use* language, they also *are* language. The word
or sign that they are is the I–me–you semiotic triad. Both Eco and Derrida
misinterpreted Peirce to be a linguistic reductionist because neither
understood the specialized sense in which humans are words.

Derrida also misunderstood Peirce's notion of the sign series, and how,
at least in principle, this series may be indefinitely open. Derrida says:

> Peirce goes very far in the direction that I have called the de-
> construction of the transcendental signified, which, at one time or
> another, would place a reassuring end to the reference from sign to
> sign. I have identified logocentrism and the metaphysics of presence
> as the exigent, powerful, systematic, and irrepressible desire for such
> a signified. Now Peirce considers the indefiniteness of reference as the
> criterion that allows us to recognize that we are dealing with a system
> of signs. *What broaches the movement of signification is what makes its
> interruption impossible. The thing itself is a sign* (1967/1976, p. 49).

The "thing itself" that I am most concerned with is the human individual,
and this individual certainly is a sign, but not in the sense that Derrida
thinks. This thing itself is a unique kind of word that makes and uses
words. In addition it is present to itself, not in the knife-edge "now" that
Derrida objects to, but in the I–you–me straddling of present, future, past.
Derrida's tendency to misinterpret Peirce as an early deconstructionist is
captured by Raymond Tallis, as follows:

> First, instead of seeing the endless chain of signs as the guarantor of
> the openness of consciousness, he interprets it to imply the closed-off-
> ness of language. Secondly, Peirce was talking about the relationship
> between one sign and another. Derrida misreads him as referring to
> the relationship between signifier and signified. The endlessness of
> the chain of signs is read as 'the absence of the transcendental
> signified' and consequently 'the destruction of ontotheology and
> the metaphysics of presence'. He confuses, in other words, the
> relationship between whole signs with the relationship between the
> signifier and the signified of an individual sign (1988, pp. 213–14).

Peirce did invite trouble when he used the word "sign," both for the whole semiotic triad and for one of its parts. When Peirce speaks of the (potentially) endless stream of (whole) signs, Derrida thinks he is talking about signs in the narrow sense of the word. In that sense they mean about the same as Derrida's signifier, which would put Peirce in agreement with Derrida's extra-subjective theory of meaning. Nevertheless this is an incautious reading of Peirce.

Derrida's linguistic hegemony also depends on his differential theory of meaning. Linguistic expressions get their meanings in two ways. One is by contrast, both with other, closely related words and with words in the linguistic context. A new color word, for example, is defined partly by the colors that it is not and partly by the sentences and paragraphs within which it is located. This mode of definition is based on differences. The second source of meaning, however, is in the reference of the word. Reference, in turn, has two meanings: it refers to the thing that the word stands for, i.e. its object – a new color word refers to things of that color; but it also refers to the meaning or conception that attaches to the word. Derrida accepts the differential theory of meaning but rejects the referential, in both senses.

In other words, for Derrida linguistic expressions get their meaning not from things or concepts but only from other words. Earlier in the 20th century Saussure had already reduced linguistics to the dyadicity of signifier and signified, the external world of objects being ignored. In Peircean terms this was the sign and interpretant without the object. Derrida went a step further and dropped the signified as well, or rather he made the signified or concept a derivative of the signifiers. In his differential theory of meaning, this derivation was produced by what he called the "play" of signifiers. In Peircean terms all Derrida had to work with was the sign (narrow sense of word) without either the object or the interpretant. When Peirce spoke of a possible endless stream of signs, producing a kind of "play" of meaning, he was referring to whole triadic signs. But when Derrida speaks of the play of meaning he is referring only to the signifiers or, in Peirce's terms, the (narrow sense) signs. The fact that Derrida misunderstood Peirce's stream of meaning does not change anything, for Derrida's theory of meaning would have the same weaknesses even if he had made no reference to Peirce.

A referential theory of meaning is not necessarily one that envisions clearly defined concepts or precisely delineated objects. Peirce regarded both referential relations as vague. The play of signs and the endless stream of interpretants is a theory built for vagueness. Derrida is objecting to overstructured theories of reference that claim intuitively self-evident concepts and unambiguous objects. This is the same thing the pragmatists were objecting to. But instead of throwing out the individual altogether, they decentered the individual in a semiotic manner. The differential theory of meaning, which ignores all referentiality, is a costly alternative to excessively intuitive theories. In addition to its logical problems, it violates common sense and creates problems for the theory of democracy. Pragmatism is another alternative to unrealistically intuitive theories, but it does the job more effectively: the individual is saved, common sense is left intact, and democracy is given a more solid foundation.

I have been calling Derrida's differential theory of meaning a cultural one, for it generates meanings by a system of pure signifiers or signs. But the signifiers, just as Peirce's (narrow sense of) signs, are dead. They are noises and visible markings but they have no inherent meanings, nor can they generate them by the play of differences. The differences are dead too. It is true that sometimes meaningful elements, such as Peirce's interpretants, become signifiers. When this happens a concept acts as though it were dead, and any life it has is smuggled in from its former life as an interpretant. If, as Derrida thinks, there were no Saussurean signifieds or Peircean interpretants, then the signifiers and signs would not have the aura of meaning that Derrida finds in them. They would not generate meanings and there would be no play of differences. Derrida thinks meaning comes after the play of signifiers, but it does so only because it also comes before that play.

Barthes has a helpful example of how a signified can act as a signifier, giving a diffuse meaning to an otherwise dead signifier.

> I am at the barber's, and a copy of *Paris-Match* is offered to me. On the cover, a young Negro in a French uniform is saluting, with his eyes uplifted, probably fixed on a fold of the tricolour. All this is the *meaning* of the picture. But, whether naively or not, I see very well what it signifies to me: that France is a great Empire, that all her sons, without any colour discrimination, faithfully serve under her flag, and that there is no better answer to the detractors of an alleged colonialism than the zeal shown by this Negro in serving his so-called oppressors. I am therefore again faced with a greater semiological system: there is a signifier, itself already formed with a previous system (*a black soldier is giving the French salute*); there is a signified (it is here a purposeful mixture of Frenchness and militariness); finally, there is a presence of the signified through the signifier (1957/1985, p. 116).

In this passage the saluting black has two semiotic roles. In one he functions as an entire semiological system (i.e. signifier and signified together), or, to put it in Peirce's language, as a whole semiotic triad. But at a higher level of meaning this saluting black is squeezed into the role of pure signifier (or, in

Peirce's narrow sense, sign). Now the salute signifies a clean bill for French colonialism. But why was the saluting black, when positioned in the signifier role, able to give meaning and generate a signified? As a pure signifier the photo was dead. But if meaning is smuggled into that signifier by virtue of its previous, more inclusive semiotic role, then there can be a meaningful play of difference and signifiers can generate signifieds.

If Derrida's signifiers did not have another life, the significance of which depends on referential meanings, their deadness would be more apparent. As signifiers they are always dead, but as signifieds-acting-as-signifiers, they can smuggle in meaning. Still, this source of meaning is ultimately referential and is therefore disallowed on Derrida's premises. There is a sense, then, in which Derrida is not cultural at all, in the way I am defining culture. Since he denies the independent sphere of meaning and conceptuality, making it a product of dead signifiers, he actually has no meaning or culture. This would make him a physicalist, and his upward reduction would be ultimately downward. But I am using Derrida as an example of cultural reduction, and it would be too far afield to talk about his relation to physicalism.

Derrida then represents the cultural reduction of the self from the standpoint of formal language (*langue*). He also has aspects of interactional (*parole*) reduction, just as Wittgenstein and Lacan have accepts of cultural (*langue*) reduction, but these are secondary implications. As examples of my types of upward reduction they serve reasonably well.

Conclusion and Summary

I described the three kinds of upward reduction, initially in abstract terms. I showed how these reductions shrink the definition of human beings by omitting the genus (the body); how they work with a "relation to the subject" that is too distant from the self; how they signify with semiotic triads that have the wrong three parts (table 7.1); and how they explain the self with semiotic properties that belong to the wrong triads (table 7.2). I also used examples from Wittgenstein, Lacan, Durkheim, and Derrida to concretize the abstract arguments and to specify in detail how these reductions work.

It is also useful to recall the distinction between self and identity discussed in chapter 1. Self is the I–you–me structure, itself universal and trans-historical. This structure is the organ of thought and abstract signs that evolved in our line of primates. Within this structure there is the whole range of semiotic processes. These processes are organized, not only by the overall structure but also by the systems of signs that I call identities. The various minority attributes and sub-cultures such as ethnicity, religion, gender, and sexual orientation are among the more politicized and controversial identities, although there are many that are less politicized as well. The three kinds of upward reduction all confuse identities with selves. The higher semiotic levels – interaction, social organization, and culture – all have a historically specific shaping effect on identities, but not on the trans-historical self-structures that house these identities.

I showed how Wittgenstein, Lacan, Durkheim, and Derrida all substitute higher semiotic properties for those that are proper to the level of the self. This list is quite Continental and, more specifically, French. British (materialistically tending) empiricism is the home of downward reduction and Continental (idealistically leaning) rationalism is the home of upward. Both reductions claim to be liberating, egalitarian positions, though neither has an individual in whom individual rights might inhere.

The upward reductions are all in the spirit of the social sciences, recognizing the interrelated and socially bonded qualities of human beings, but doing so to such a degree that these humans lose all autonomy. In the USA, however, the early sociologists made quite a point of preserving the autonomy of the individual, arguing against the reductions from above and below.

The upward reductionists also have a relatively inconstant and uncertain tone, seeming at times to contradict themselves. Wittgenstein seems to have given credence to subjective states and the "I" in some unpublished manuscripts and in conversation with his students. Lacan at times seems to believe in a decentered (or decenterable), but still autonomous self. Durkheim's official or reconstructed logic strongly commits him to the reality of the individual. And both Derrida and Foucault, the most flashy of the "death of man" theorists, sometimes say they are trying not to abolish but to "situate" the subject or self. Despite this backsliding, the overall impact of these positions is unquestionably reductionistic. In addition they constitute the newest and most influential positions in the theory of the self.

I have tried to show, with as much precision as possible, how each is in error. Each of these positions makes certain analytical mistakes, listed in the first paragraph of this conclusion. In addition they make more concrete mistakes, based on the materials appropriate to their favored semiotic level. For example, Lacan underrated the smartness of the human infant at the mirror, Wittgenstein did not seem to want to face his own pain, Durkheim engaged in wishful thinking about French solidarity, and Derrida thought that unjustly imposed identities made the very nature of the self an injustice.

The concerns of all these theorists and their reductionist positions can be handled more effectively, both intellectually and morally, by pragmatism's semiotic self. This theory decenters the self to an optimal extent, beyond which there is no more self. And it provides the political equality and freedom that the recent upward reductionisms have been seeking.

To give a comprehensive picture of reductionism it is also necessary to consider the major downward varieties. As this has already been done, from a position much like my own, by Alan Wolfe in his *Are Humans Different?* (1993), I will treat downward reductionism more briefly than I did the upward varieties. At the end of chapter 8 I will return to the relation between the two kinds of reduction.

8

Downward Reduction

The downward reductions were, until the 1960s, the major anti-humanist positions in social theory. They comprised the positivisms, which reduced humans to matter, and the biologisms, which reduced them to organic life. The upward reductions, emanating mainly from German idealism, were important forces in world ideology and politics but not in social theory. Thomas's and Znaniecki's *The Polish Peasant in Europe and America* (1918–20), for example, opposed both reductions, but was much more concerned with the former than the latter. This was also true of Mead's and Parsons's anti-reductionist writings.

This all changed in the 1970s when European theory made a surprising and unexpected comeback. After World War I European theory had declined and American theory gradually took over the field. The inter-war period, particularly the Nazi era, was a wasteland for Continental theory. And the years following World War II were actually semi-colonial, as American styles, both theoretical and empirical, became the dominant models. European theory was in an unnaturally backward state from 1914 onward. But during the 1970s Europe again began producing grand theory, and it was so novel and imaginative that it quickly seized or re-seized world leadership.

There were several new kinds of theory, including critical theory, hermeneutics, social phenomenology, neo-Marxism, and linguistic theories (ordinary language and Wittgensteinian), but the most influential variety was the kind coming from Paris. That wave had an undulating quality as it moved from structuralism to post-structuralism to post-modernism and deconstruction. Parisian thought first took over in literary criticism, language studies, and the humanities. Then it began gaining influence in

195

the social sciences. The new theories, led by the French cluster, tended to oppose the autonomous self in favor of the upward reductions. These could be interactional (e.g. Wittgenstein), structural (e.g. Foucault and Althusser), or cultural (e.g. Derrida).

In the 1970s the positivists had been all set to take over American, and presumably world, sociology. The Parsons–Merton functionalists had faded, the conflict theorists were disunited and the micro theorists, particularly the symbolic interactionists and ethnomethodologists, were busily fighting each other. Only the positivists were strong and unified. The computer had expanded their capabilities and quantification had surged in importance. This allowed the positivists to increase their share of university positions, research monies, and space in elite journals.

However, the take-over never quite happened, and one of the main reasons was that European theory got in the way. This is discussed in more detail in my essay on developments in sociological theory (1990), so here I will point out only how it upset the politics of reduction. The expected take-over was to have been, among other things, a downward reduction. The sociological positivists were not, explicitly and officially, logical positivists. In fact, many of them simply regarded themselves as empirical researchers, with no interest in or commitment to philosophy of any kind. But the logic, i.e. the implications, of their position pushed the positivists into alliance with physicalist epistemologies, including both (what was left of) logical positivism and the various softened positions into which it had evolved. The expected reduction, then, would have been to a vague agglomeration of physical matter, sensations, quantities and scientistic causal processes. That is quite an imprecise list, but the reality was equally imprecise, and there would have been plenty of time to worry about precision after the take-over.

Following the European comeback and the failure of the positivists to gain hegemony, the politics of reduction assumed new qualities. There were now two major kinds of reduction, upward as well as downward, the former having rapidly established itself throughout the humanities and social sciences. The two reductions were, despite minor similarities, in contradiction with each other. The anti-reductionist positions, which recognize the autonomy of the individual, were slow to notice the new reductionism, including its contradiction with the old. The positivists, having abandoned their alliance of approximately 1945–70 with the functionalists, began to ally themselves with a variety of reductionist positions in other disciplines, including behaviorist psychology, empiricism (the major successor of logical positivism) in philosophy, artificial intelligence, cybernetics, and various biologisms (neurophysiology, molecular biology, and sociobiology).

Downward reduction	Missing semiotic trait
Physicalist epistemology	Universality of meaning
Artificial intelligence	First-person point of view
Cybernetics	Meta reflexivity
Molecular biology	Teleology
Neurophysiology	Intentionality

Table 8.1 Form of downward reduction by missing semiotic trait

The new politics of reduction had become extremely complex. It was not always clear which positions were allied with which, or for that matter what ideas each held. Furthermore, several of the positions with which the positivists had allied themselves – particularly behaviorism and artificial intelligence in psychology, cybernetics in the social science, and empiricism in philosophy – were soon to decline in importance.

Because of this complexity my own discussion will be selective and limited. My main analytic device will be the semiotic triad. The downward reductions all reduce the human triad to dyadicity although each does it in a different way. I will not discuss all the downward reductions, although I will look at several leading versions. I will begin with the physicalist positions, including the materialistic epistemologies, artificial intelligence, and cybernetics. Then I will consider two biologisms: molecular biology and neurophysiology. These biologisms are also, ultimately, physicalist, although they originate in biology. I will give a brief description of each case, but my main point will be that they lack the human interpretant. Table 8.1 schematizes the argument, showing the various ways in which the interpretant may be missing. Human beings are multi-faceted, and if any trait or facet is reduced, the rest will go with it.

After I conclude the downward reductions I will return to the upward and again compare the two kinds. To a great extent the self is defined by the would-be reductions, although this is negative definition. To put it another way, I have spent a lot of time defining the self referentially, in relation to what it *is* (I–you–me, reflexivity, solidarity, freedom, etc.). But it is also illuminating to define the self differentially, by what it *is not*. And it is not any of the levels to which it is reduced. Looking at the two reductions together will facilitate this differential or negative insight.

Physicalist Epistemologies

Physicalist epistemologies reduce all things, including human beings, to the physical. They do not do this directly and ontologically but indirectly, by way of the theory of knowledge. These epistemologies explain meaning physically or materialistically: meaning must be traceable, one way or another, to physical sensations. By sheer epistemological fiat they confine reality to the physical-chemical level.

The best known of these positions are British empiricism, logical positivism, and operationism, although the positivism of social theory is another. The common denominator, with minor differences, is that knowledge is sensation. This maxim disallows cognitions that are abstract or universal, for these traits cannot be captured by sensations. It also disallows realities that cannot be so captured. This epistemological net defines the fish as those it can catch. Those that pass through or around are said not to exist.

Obviously the human person or self cannot be caught in this net. The body can, but its semiotic properties cannot. The net defines humans as bodies, and these are further reduced to their chemical elements. The semiotic self will pass right through the net, for it does not consist of sensations. There are sensational aspects, in diminishing order, from object to sign to interpretant, but these sensations are not in the semiotic realm. In Peirce's language they are dyadic rather than triadic.

The physicalist epistemologies constitute a set of premises that cannot be directly refuted. Still their critics have identified several logical problems with these approaches. The most aggressive recent physicalism, logical positivism, was virtually destroyed under a barrage of criticisms. Among these were: Wittgenstein's Indian rope trick (Janik and Toulmin, 1973, p. 189) or bridging problem; the impossibility of verifying the principle of (sensory) verifiability; Quine's observation that theory is underdetermined by facts; Gödel's proof that all logical systems must be either inconsistent or incomplete; the problem of dispositionals (counter-factuals); and Austin's "performatives." These criticisms did not hurt the more general spirit of positivism, which is certainly alive and well in social theory as well as in philosophy, but they did eliminate its most formal and extreme statement in logical positivism.

These epistemologies all, however, have the reflexive problem of meeting their own validity criteria. There is no operational definition of an operational definition. Logical positivism's verification principle cannot be verified. British empiricism's sensationalist criterion cannot be validated sensorily. And social theory's positivism does not rest on the objective, causal, and quantitative premises that it espouses. When the physicalist epistemologies are applied to themselves they all fail their own tests.

An advantage of pragmatism, including the Peirce–Mead synthesis, is that it can pass this test. As I pointed out in chapter 2, pragmatism's epistemological maxim has three features, all of which differentiate it from British empiricism: It has to do with consequences rather than antecedents; these consequences are defined not as sensations but as actions; and these definitions are not in formal, scientific language but in the ordinary language of culture. When you apply this maxim to itself you do not get physicalism's self-contradiction. Rather you get a coherent and non-contradictory self-description. The pragmatic maxim itself can be not only justified by its consequences, but viewed as actions and coded in everyday language.

The physicalist epistemologies, then, which reduce the human individual to the physical-chemical level, are unconvincing. The unique properties of human beings – their semiotic processes and behavioral autonomy – are lost, for they cannot be caught by the materialist epistemological net.

In addition the people who hold these positions must abandon them when they turn to their practical lives. I was told by someone who attended the memorial service of Rudolf Carnap (1891–1970), the leader of the logical positivists, that one of the senior philosophers there began to sob. Then he caught himself and said to the others, "I don't know what's getting into me. He was just atoms and molecules." But the tears said that Carnap was more than atoms and molecules, i.e. his humanity could not be captured by the principle of verifiability. They also said one could not live a life based on physicalist epistemology.

In contrast pragmatists have continuity between their philosophy and their practical lives. The characteristics of the epistemology – consequentialism, activity, and cultural embeddednes – apply in the same way, both to the philosophy and to everyday life.

Physicalist epistemologies, to return to table 8.1, are non-triadic because they cannot tolerate abstract or universal ideas. Semiotic symbols, however, are based on these ideas as their interpretants. Without them, these symbols are reduced to the dyadicity of signs and objects. If there are no abstract interpretants, humans cannot use them, and there can be no semiotic self.

Artificial Intelligence

The mechanical analogies of artificial intelligence and cybernetics are another avenue to physicalist reduction. These approaches take matter, shaped into artifacts, as their reductionist level. These artifacts have a variety of qualities that make them seem "higher" than ordinary matter, but all of these traits, imposed by the human creators, are actually the shadows of human nature.

Nevertheless it is evidently tempting to say that humans are machines and that some machines are human. Scholars are especially prone to make this claim when the machines involve electricity. This natural force seems to have an aura of magic: it is invisible, powerful, seemingly instantaneous, active at a distance, deadly to humans, etc. In some respects it resembles Durkheim's social solidarity or mana, which has a similar set of traits. In fact Durkheim often used electrical analogies to describe this semiotic force (Takla and Pope, 1985). When the claim is made that humans are the same as cybernetic machines or computers, the electrical analogy is pressed to the point of reduction.

In the 1960s and 1970s, during the early successes of artificial intelligence, its spokespersons asserted that computers could (or soon would) do anything humans could do. A related claim was that humans were merely complicated computers. This claim was sometimes fused with neurophysiology to argue that the brain was a computer. Perhaps the most extreme aggrandizement of the computer was the claim of Gary Drescher, then a graduate student, that computers have rights, and that "killing one is a new form of murder" (Turkle, 1984, p. 261).

By the 1990s, however, it had become increasingly clear that the computer was a specialized tool and could never equal human intelligence. Accordingly artificial intelligence began to deflate its claims. Neither common-sense problem-solving nor the expert variety could be reproduced with the computer, and Hubert Dreyfus, the best-known critic of artificial intelligence, began to refer to it as a "degenerating research program" (1992, p. ix). The computer was never able to achieve the informal reasoning power of humans, who can juggle an indefinite number of factors in an implicit manner.

I think the major difference between the computer and the self can be captured by the contrast in their points of view. The human is in the first person and the computer is, in two respects, in the third. Obviously it is in the third person when we refer to it as "it." If we say "the computer" or "it" can perform this or that operation, or that "it" knows this or that, we are referring to it as something external to a dyadic interaction. "I" (the first person) speak to "you" (the second person, singular or plural) about some person, persons, or things. The object of this "aboutness" is outside the conversation and is therefore external to its meaning system. Being outside the two-part system, it is "third." This is the usual meaning of "third person."

But the computer is third in another, more subtle way as well. From within, natural persons are in the first person. Internally they have a first-person viewpoint. But "from within" computers are in the third person, not the first. This means when they observe what they know, it is as though some outside or third person (e.g. the programmer) had the knowledge. I think this is implied in a point made by Searle (1984) that computers lack a grasp of meaning or "intentionality," although this limitation is expressed in another way. This is mechanical knowledge, for, like a clock or a thermometer, the computer knows what it knows only via its maker. In itself, as physical-chemical matter, it knows nothing. It is as though it were looking through another's mind and knowing things from another's point of view.

The category I am trying to describe seems to be present, to use a loose analogy, in some schizophrenics, particularly during hallucinatory experience. The schizophrenic may "hear" voices as though some outside person were doing the talking. Hallucinatory information is not perceived in the first person, even though other people, such as psychotherapists, might urge the disturbed person to perceive it in that way. Cognitively, the computer is a little like the psychotic in perceiving information as coming from without.

The computer's third-person point of view seems to be why it cannot reason in the same informal, implicit, contextual way that humans can. Humans have what Dreyfus calls "global sensitivity" (1992, p. xliv). This means they can simultaneously pay attention to an indefinite number of factors. Some may be at the center of attention and (many) others may be over to the side, as though seen with peripheral vision. But they can all be cognized simultaneously. This is the power of the first-person point of view, for this viewpoint is comprehensively sensitive to all that it can see. The centralized position of the first person allows this kind of cognition.

In contrast the third-person point of view lacks global sensitivity. It is aware of limited amounts of information, and it has to process that information consecutively and serially. No matter how fast it can do this, it is not simultaneous and global.

There are many other reasons why computers are, in principle, different from humans, and the literature is full of these lists of limitations, but I think the difference in point of view is a major and inadequately understood factor.

The problem I have been talking about is especially true of traditional AI. The connectionist or parallel processing approach, which has received increasing attention in recent years, also has this point of view problem, but less severely. This is because connectionism uses trial and error rather than deduction from programmed rules. Like its predecessors, connectionism is incapable of doing what humans can do, but its spokespersons, who have abandoned reductive claims, are admitting this. As the sociologist Alan Wolfe says, "The lesson learned in artificial intelligence experiments, in short, is that it makes more sense to model machines on humans than to try and design humans based on machines" (1992, p. 1733).

In semiotic terms, the AI model lacks an indispensable trait of the human interpretant, the first-person point of view. Without this, the knowledge, being from without, is mechanical and physicalist.

Cybernetics

In the 1940s and 1950s there was a race between artificial intelligence and cybernetics for the best mechanical theory of human nature. AI seems to have won, at least for the time being, although several versions of cybernetics still exist and some are influential in the social sciences. At present it is not completely clear, however, what is and what is not cybernetics, or how many varieties there are. This is because the field has been changing in a way that has produced new self-definitions, divisions, coalitions, and so on (Richardson, 1991). The version that seems most closely related to social theory at present is autopoeisis.

Autopoeisis, which was originally a biological concept, means self-creation. Maturana and Varela (1972/1980), who originated this approach, were not merely referring to self-repair or self-maintenance (in the common biological sense of homeostasis or equilibrium) but went further to say that the organism creates itself in the first place. This resembles Fichte's notion of the self reflexively creating itself.

Niklas Luhmann (1982) extended this biological idea to what he calls the human psychological system as well as to social systems at various levels. Now the most influential cybernetics theorist, Luhmann began his sociological training with Parsonian functionalism, but he shifted functionalism in a mechanistic direction. He evidently wanted to avoid Parsons's tendency toward value consensus and the resulting inability to explain conflict, although, as I will show later, he created parallel problems of his own.

Luhmann recognizes six levels, although only the last four are of concern to his theory: mechanical, organic, psychological, interactional, organizational, and societal. All of these systems self-create, and in that sense they are all based on reflexivity. They are also all closed off from each other, i.e. lower levels do not in any way bring about or constitute the higher levels. Instead each level is a completely new kind of reality, sealed off from the others.

The strengths of Luhmann's sociology are those of any mechanical theory. He has no problem explaining the ambiguities and complexities of human beings because there are no human beings in his theory. The closest he comes to humanity is in his psychological system, although he is quite explicit in excluding the concept of the self or subject (1986, p. 320). He also has no problems with dissent, conflict, or change, all of which can be defined out of machines.

Luhmann uses a strong computer or AI analogy, which contributes both to his mechanistic framework and to his rejection of the concept of self. This gives him such conceptual tools as AI reflexivity, input–output logic, binary coding and the notion of programming.

There are several weaknesses with Luhmann's theory, however, despite its originality and comprehensiveness. His reflexivity is at best mechanical or organic, and, as I will show later, it cannot explain the power of human self-reference. Also his computer analogy is getting weaker as the kind of AI he had in mind is becoming increasingly modest in its claims, at least as a standard against which to model human beings.

In addition Luhmann has a weakness much like the value consensus problem of Parsons. To avoid values and the underlying notion of the self Luhmann went in a narrowly cognitive direction, modelling his systems levels after computers. But the assumption of cognitive consensus is at least as much trouble as Parsons's value consensus. Not only does society have lots of value dissensus, it also has plenty of cognitive dissensus – in fact the latter often causes the former.

Therefore Luhmann needs something to patch up his unrealistically consensual assumptions. I think he tacitly uses the computer analogy for this purpose, by assuming that all information can be forced into binaries (acceptable and unacceptable, so to speak). In this way cognitive dissensus (e.g. social protest of any kind) automatically gets labeled as the bad, unacceptable binary. The notion of the program stands behind and reinforces the power of the binaries, although the equilibrating function of the program is just as unrealistic as Parsons's common values.

Luhmann's anomaolies are continuing to deteriorate, for the theory is tied to an obsolete notion of AI, to an earlier period in Germany's political situation, and to a time when the defense of capitalism from communism was almost as important as maintaining democracy. Luhmann has a particular problem with democracy, for his social level, including that of the democratic state, is closed to all outside influences, including those of the individual citizen or voter.

Luhmann's major limitation, however, is in his concept of reflexivity, for he uses a weak, sub-human variety to explain the much stronger, human kind. This has to do with the capacity of humans to be meta to themselves.

In general, reflexivity includes all relations a thing can have to itself, or, in the case of humans, all forms of self-reference. Among these, as mentioned earlier, are the cognitive, moral, emotional, and agentic (Rosenberg, 1990), i.e. we may talk to or know ourselves, judge ourselves, have feelings toward ourselves, or act to maintain or change ourselves. There can also be reflexivity in organisms and artifacts, but in a way that is less powerful than in humans.

The reflexivity of artifacts, such as thermostats, warning lights and computers, is never, as in humans, a "complete" reflexivity. The incompleteness arises from the fact that the artifact has to be divided into two parts, the reflecting and the reflected, and the part that does the reflecting can never reflect on itself. In other words the monitoring device cannot monitor itself, or if so, the problem is merely shuffled to another monitoring device (Johnstone, 1970, pp. 1–14).

The reflexivity of artifacts, like the point of view of the computer, has the quality of being imposed from without. It is not a property of the material particles themselves but of the organization humans give to them.

The reflexivity of organisms has some resemblance to that of artifacts, for it too has a physically based blind spot. Animals can sense (see, touch, hear, etc.) themselves, but the organ that does the sensing cannot sense itself, e.g. the eye cannot see the eye. On the other hand, animals' reflexivity, unlike that of artifacts, is internal and from within. It derives from the natural make-up of the organisms, without there being any need for humans to impose it.

In contrast the human can reflect totally on his or her self. There need be no incompleteness or partial reflexivity. Instead what the self does is to duplicate itself at the meta level, this meta self or "I" being the reflecting organ. It is true that the meta self cannot reflect on itself, the "I" cannot see the "I." But at the first order the entire self can be the object of reflexivity.

In the case of physical and biological reflexivities, the blind spot is at the first order, i.e. part of the object is invisible to itself because that part is the viewing or reflecting device. The entity splits into two parts, and therefore it can see only part of itself.

The self-reflecting human also splits into two, but it does so not by dividing but by doubling itself. The reflecting person creates a kind of clone or duplicate of itself, doing so at the second or meta level. The blind spot is now outside the object entirely. The self-reflecting artifact or organism can perceive only part of itself, its blind spot being within. The self-reflecting person can see all of itself, its blind spot being without, i.e. at the meta perch from which it views itself.

All reflexivity (except that of the Christian Trinity or Hegel's self-reflecting God) entails a blind spot, for the reflecting element cannot reflect on itself. But the content of this blind spot, and its implications for the completeness of reflexivity, varies by level. Luhmann is wrong in thinking the reflexivity of the human can be accounted for by that of the animal or physical artifact, including the computer. The former has reflexive powers that completely exceed those of the latter two.

The notion of "feedback," which often arises in discussions of cybernetics, is equivalent to reflexivity. Accordingly the feedback of machines or animals is always "incomplete," and that of humans is or can be complete. For that reason all theories of cybernetics that equate human reflexivity with sub-human feedback have the same inadequacy as Luhmann does in his attempt to reduce human reflexivity to the mechanical kind.

In semiotic terms human reflexivity is another aspect of the human interpretant. Artificial and animal reflexivity (or feedback) is not fully semiotic for it is two-part or dyadic. Once the human goes meta and creates an "I" the reflexivity is complete and triadic. Any attempt to explain human reflexivity with the dyadic, sub-human kind is a fallacious, downward reduction.

Biologist Reduction

Biological reductions, which declined in the 1920s, have made a strong comeback in recent years (Deglar, 1991). Perhaps the discovery of DNA provided the major impetus, although several other developments contributed as well. There is a large literature, pro and con, concerning the determinist and reductive character of biology. Much of this literature is in the philosophy of science, a discipline long dominated by physics but now turning to biology (Ruse, 1988).

I will begin with a brief historical review. This will show that the biologisms have long been a factor in social theory and how, despite their periodic demise, they keep returning in new ways. Then I will consider two current reductions, molecular biology and neurophysiology.

History of Biological Reductions

Lamarckian biology, which preceded and for a while paralleled Darwinism, was partly reductionist, although it could be interpreted in either a liberal or conservative political direction. For Lamarckians, acquired characteristics became part of the organism and were transmitted in reproduction. The father might learn to play the violin, but the child would tend to come by it as an inborn trait. Lamarckianism was gradually replaced by Darwinism. This had the effect of turning biology, at least in its popular impact, in a more conservative direction.

Late 19th-century evolutionary theory, as originated by Darwin, reduced the human species to non-Lamarckian evolutionary processes. The social Darwinists and eugenicists, who politicized Darwinism, went still further. They interpreted the biological survival of the fittest as the legitimation of class hierarchies, both within and among nations. These conservative positions were opposed by many social scientists, especially in sociology, but they were nevertheless quite influential, both in academia and public affairs.

One variant of turn-of-the-century evolution was the instinct theory of American psychology (Cravens, 1978, pp. 191–223). In the USA psychology began with introspectionism, then turned to instincts, then to behaviorism, and finally to cognitive theory. Instincts were vaguely defined as traits that caused specific behaviors, such as those that allegedly characterized ethnic groups. Much of what later came to be attributed to culture was said to be – via instincts – biologically determined. It was this theory in particular that stimulated early American sociology to put together the anti-reductionist template. Although now defunct for several decades, instinct theory was quite powerful and distinctly anti-democratic during its time (e.g. in McDougall, 1921).

The most recent of the now-gone biological reductionisms is psychological behaviorism, the paradigm that psychology adopted after discarding instincts. As I pointed out in chapter 1, John Watson's early behaviorism was sharply critical of instinct theory's biological determinism. Instead of an organic determinism at birth, behaviorism explained human nature by ordinary learning processes.

The organism was born in a flexible condition, without much biological direction or imprinting. Instead traits were taken on by way of learning through reward and/or punishment. Pleasure (called reinforcements or rewards) determined behavior, and it did so not by ordinary causal processes but by a feedback loop.

Ironically behaviorism turned out to be a biological determinism of its own. Unlike the other varieties, it did not explain behavior on the basis of traits present at birth and inherited from parents. Instead the hedonistic, i.e. pain-pleasure, environment in which the organism lived subsequent to birth would, by purely biological forces, determine behavior. These biological forces are the living organism's tendency to be drawn toward pleasure and away from pain. In this way the human organism is the same as, and therefore reduced to, all other animals, for they all learn by virtue of the same reinforcement processes.

Accordingly consciousness was unnecessary and therefore ignored in the behaviorist paradigm. Meanings, e.g. in language, were reduced to hedonistic responses. Words and sentences were spoken, not to communicate meanings – a category which had no place in behaviorism – but to get pleasure (see Chomsky, 1959, for the classic critique of this position).

Gradually this paradigm accumulated too many anomalies, too many experimental data that contradicted its premises. Consciousness and meaning seemed important after all, both as a means of being oriented to and motivated toward the world. Behaviorism gradually fell of its own (anomalous) weight, cognitive theory becoming the replacement. It did not take many years for cognitive theory to also build up too many anomalies (Taylor, 1985, p. 127) and begin to fall, partly because it leaned heavily on AI, which is also declining.

The obsolete reductions are useful for what they tell us about the present, for all reductions share certain philosophical and social implications. They deny that humans are a *sui generis* species. They imply that humans cannot make free choices. They reduce moral equality to biological inequality. And they weaken the arguments for voting and civil liberties in democracy. In looking at two current reductions I will not be so much interested in their technical arguments as in their implications for the politics of reduction.

Molecular Biology

In biology there has been a paradigm struggle between organic and molecular approaches for several decades. The molecular biologists hold that vital or living phenomena can be explained chemically and that organic concepts and methods should be abandoned. They deny the existence of a biological level, qualitatively distinct from the physical-chemical. In their view biology is a branch of chemistry. The organic biologists in response concede that it may be possible to explain vital phenomena biochemically in the long run, but at present chemistry is nowhere near having this kind of explanatory power. Instead they think far more can be explained with

207

organic concepts, with the idea of a biological level and, in particular, with a carefully qualified concept of teleology.

This teleology or directionality is the main bone of contention between those adhering to the two paradigms. For the organicists there are three kinds: the conscious purposivity of human beings; the non-conscious goal-directedness of organisms; and the constructed directionality of artifacts (Ayala, 1977, pp. 497–504; Mayr, 1988, pp. 38–66; Ruse, 1988, pp. 43–49; Jacobs, 1986). Material things as such, i.e. viewed not as artifacts but as physical-chemical matter, have no teleology at all, even though they were once thought to have God-given purposes.

Entities at the supra-human levels, such as face-to-face groups, organizations, and cultures also have teleological features at times, though the clarity and degree of this feature is often quite slight. It is common for sub-groups to have opposed goals, subordinating the force of teleology to that of conflict. Examples are labor-management conflict in business corporations and ethnic conflict in nations. In the social theory of the 1950s and 1960s the functionalism of Talcott Parsons assumed relatively clear and unified social teleologies, the organic analogy being the carrier of this implication. But since the decline of functionalism (Wiley, 1990, pp. 394–6) sociologists have been wary of this idea.

The three teleologies are quite different from each other. The artificial kind is neither internal nor conscious, having been imposed by the artisan. The organic kind is internal but not conscious. And the human kind, in addition to being organic, is internal and conscious. Downward reductions either substitute a lower teleology for a higher, or they reduce teleological phenomena to non-teleological matter. Humans are not artifacts, such as computers, and their teleology cannot be represented as extrinsic. Nor do they have an internal but non-conscious teleology like the other animals. Theirs is uniquely conscious. And they are certainly not merely physical-chemical particles, completely lacking in teleology. Therefore they have to be represented with the appropriate internal and conscious teleology.

The upward reductionist position attempts to discredit teleology as a roundabout and misleading version of ordinary, non-teleological causation. The argument is that teleology has no explanatory power beyond ordinary causal logic. This position was stated by Ernest Nagel (1951), before the DNA discovery gave molecular biology its present prestige, and it is now being argued with increasing forcefulness.

But teleology has unique explanatory contributions in biology. It is a source of hypotheses concerning the means-end chain, both within individual organisms and in their populations. These hypotheses often lead to the discovery of properties that can be explained only on teleological premises. If, at the present time, biology were to discard everything that cannot be proved biochemically, very little would be left.

The end which a behavior or structure moves toward is different from an ordinary cause. As Aristotle said, it is a final rather than an efficient cause. This means it is a different kind of cause, the knowledge of which gives its own kind of explanation. I want to emphasize, however, that organic biologists are not using the concept of teleology in the metaphysically freighted way in which Aristotle and the Scholastics used it. They confine it to conditions that have a measurable effect on survival, ranging from subsystems to the whole organism, including its reproduction. They have transformed this idea from a semi-theological into an empirical concept.

Given this demystified conceptualization of teleology, it can be better understood if it is compared with its two weak imitators: the behavior of physical objects and that of socio-cultural entities. Neither of these behaviors moves toward a goal. Physical things were once thought to have been designed by God to serve human ends, but teleology now refers only to the ends of objects themselves or to those of their human makers, not to those of divine producers or human users. Socio-cultural processes, in turn, are weak examples of teleology because they usually move toward multiple and often contradictory ends, their outcome being the resultant of opposed forces. In contrast, authentic teleologies are directed toward self-serving ends and have enough unity to exhibit clear goal-directedness.

Both molecular and organic biologies have useful insights, but each needs the other. This means that ideally the two would not compete for hegemony. Instead, in the phrase of Niels Bohr and Max Delbert (Kaye, 1986, p. 64), they would act as "complementary."

In fact, however, molecular biology is beginning to dominate the field, and organic biology may be headed toward becoming a minor specialty. To a great extent this is a result of the Human Genome Project, a well-funded, internationally collaborative attempt to map and sequence the human genetic system. This is a laudable goal, but it is proceeding with very little public oversight or criticism. In particular too much is being made of its possible practical value and too little of its possible threat to civil liberties.

Not only is there the obvious problem of explaining how clumps of material particles should or can have rights in a democracy. In addition genetic engineering is especially vulnerable to abuse during the kind of "bad economy" the industrial world has been suffering since the early 1970s. For one thing venture capitalism will be tempted to do any kind of genetic engineering that can make a profit, regardless of its threat to human freedoms, and it will be difficult to contain this tendency with legal regulations. In addition, however, during this downwardly-mobile time, there has been an increasing tendency for threatened groups to engage in racial and biological scapegoating. A big victory for molecular biology will create an atmosphere in which scapegoating can be more easily legitimized and might become more widespread.

Molecular biology is central to the politics of reduction. Obviously if living organisms can be reduced to chemicals, human beings can too. Humans, of course, have bodies and therefore they have all the teleological features of their primate organisms. Beyond that, however, I am singling out their semiotic teleology because this property is another facet of the human interpretant. Mead and Peirce thought of purposivity as the driving force behind the human semiotic process. The self, in addition to being characterized by abstraction, the first-person point of view, and (complete) reflexivity, is propelled by teleology. This teleology is, moreover, twofold: not only is it the seeking of goals but also their creation. The interpretive process is, within limits, open and free, and this permits the semiotic self to define, in a cultural manner, the nature of the world. That power in turn allows humans to create as well as to pursue goals. The reduction of this sophisticated teleology to blind chemistry both falsifies human experience and erases the semiotic self.

Neurophysiology

Brain science in itself is not necessarily reductive, but in contemporary philosophy the idea that everything distinctively human can be reduced to the brain has become widely accepted. These philosophers also assume that the brain works like an artificial intelligence machine. This position is in the same family as molecular biology, although the latter reduces humans to chemicals and the former to a computer. Of course a computer's components include chemicals, but its mechanical design is more important than its physical constituents. Attempts have been made to integrate molecular biology, neurophysiology and AI into a general theory of information and cognition, but these have not gotten beyond the stage of metaphor.

The brain reductionists make a point of ridiculing consciousness, both in its content and form, as a kind of prejudice or "folk psychology." They compare the idea that humans have consciousness to the notions that the sun rotates around the earth or that the earth is flat, i.e. as scientifically obsolete ideas (see Greenwood, 1991 for relevant essays). It is true that, in the more advanced areas of science, folk or common-sense knowledge is inferior knowledge. But these technical branches of science are among the "special realities," and they have a subordinate position in the overall universe of experience. They are located within, subordinate to, and contextualized by ordinary common sense. This contextual reality is

210

inherently an everyday or "folk" (or democratic) experience. Ordinary consciousness is the medium within which the "main reality" is apprehended and lived. To call this fundamental reality "folk" in the pejorative sense is tantamount to opting out of human life itself, including the semiotic, interactional, and cultural forms in which we experience it.

In other words "folk" knowledge has two distinct meanings. In the specialized or scientific areas of experience it refers to imprecise or untrained knowledge, and it is accordingly inferior to non-folk or trained knowledge. But in the everyday or main areas of experience it refers to the knowledge that ordinary, i.e. non-psychotic, people have. In this sense "folk" is the preferred knowledge, central in Durkheim's terms to the collective consciousness. In this medium, "non-folk" means abnormal, cognitively deviant, or delusive. The brain reductionists, then, are basing their argument on a verbal sleight of hand, in which "folk" in the untrained sense is quietly substituted for "folk" in the sense of the collective consciousness.

This position has all the weaknesses of logical positivism, such as being unable to explain itself and having to live a contradiction in the transition from philosophy to practical life, without its saving graces. At least logical positivism did have consciousness, albeit reduced to sensation. This position regards all of consciousness as a hoax. One has to believe rather strongly in the computer and artificial intelligence to pronounce consciousness invalid, particularly when the pronouncement is itself located in consciousness. AI was the strength of this position, allowing its followers to ignore the absurdity of ridiculing consciousness. Now that AI is weakening, the obvious validity and inescapability of consciousness is reasserting itself. Accordingly brain reduction, along with AI, is becoming less influential.

Brain reduction disallows the semiotic self in all respects, but I have been emphasizing the semantic content or intentionality of consciousness. All normal humans work within some kind of shared categories of experience, even though these vary from culture to culture. These categories constitute the semiotic form, collective consciousness, folk knowledge, or culture of any given society. Brain reductionists declare this shared knowledge to be delusive and superstructural to some more basic, if non-conscious, kind of knowledge. They do so at the cost of all social institutions, including democracy, as well as the notion of normal, non-psychotic consciousness.

The Two Reductions Compared

I compared the two reductions in chapter 6, and I will now return to the comparison to make it more systematic. Earlier I looked at Parsons's comprehensive anti-reductionist argument. According to him both reductions omit defining elements of the "structure of social action," and both kinds close off important logical–methodological avenues. I agreed with Parsons, although I translated his functionalism into semiotics.

I also pointed out that both kinds of reductionists regard their positions as morally superior to the *sui generis* self. Downward reductionists view the idea of the self as a barrier to science, blocking rational explanation and preventing human liberation. They see the idea of the self as obscurantist, traditional, authoritarian, and, in principle, opposed to (or rather afraid of) science.

Upward reductionists, in turn, view the *sui generis* self as the Enlightenment error, unrealistically private and excessively centered. In addition they view the self as "owned" by the elite or ruling class, in other words they think that the elite, as opposed to the non-elite, can lay the strongest claims on the self. *They* have one and others do not (or barely do). Elites can also flesh out the definition of the self with the identities that appeal to them, thereby strengthening their claim. This sounds like faculty psychology again with its built-in set of unequal capacities. It also suggests how little attention has been given to pragmatism's semiotic self, which replaced faculty psychology a long time ago.

Both reductionists take the high moral ground, but they do so only by caricaturing the idea of the self. The pragmatic approach does not have the mystified obscurantism that the downward reductionists object to. Its concepts are clearly defined, and its proof, i.e. its empirical ground, is available to ordinary experience. It is true that physical science has been religiously blocked at various times and places. This has made some scientists see their work as a quasi-religious attempt to replace oppressive kinds of religion. But the pragmatic theory of the self is not an oppressive religion. It is a rational attempt to explain the distinctive qualities of human beings, and it has just as much claim to scientificity as anything else.

Nor does the semiotic self have an elitist tilt, as the upward reductionists often assume. This self is not white, male, heterosexual, Protestant, rich, or anything else that is historically specific or socially restrictive. It is not an identity or set of identities. Those are determinations that give specification or individuation to selves. First there must be (generic) selves before a particular kind of self can develop. I would say that the semiotic self, rather than being a socially oppressive idea, is just the opposite. This theory explains how everyone is the same, i.e. equal, and it thereby shows how everyone has equal rights.

Both reductions misunderstand the *sui generis* self because both, being dyadic, are based on faulty semiotics. In the pragmatic scheme there are three semiotic elements that can be missing: the sign, interpretant, or object. Accordingly there are three dyadic ways of representing, or rather misrepresenting, the self. Two of these are the reductions and the third is that great straw man, the Cartesian self.

If the interpretant is missing, leaving only the sign and object, this is the positivistic approach, both to the sign and to the self. Peirce usually referred to this as nominalism, but it can also be called materialism. With this dyadicism the self is reduced from below, and it is claimed to exist, as I have been pointing out, at the physical-chemical or biological level. Without an interpretant there is no "interpreter," i.e. no human being, person, or self. There is only the animal or physical machine.

If the object is missing the dyad is one of sign and interpretant. This position is idealistic in the philosophical sense, and the resulting reduction is from above. The cultural–linguistic, social, and interactional reductions are of this nature. Both the upward and downward forms of reduction are fallacious because they both lack the complete semiotic triad. They attempt to represent signs and the sign-user, i.e. the self, dyadically. This produces an incomplete and distorted picture of the self.

The third dyad, which lacks the sign, consists only of the interpretant and the object. This is the Cartesian fallacy, which Peirce examined in detail. For Descartes, ideas were not the interpretation of signs. They were direct intuitions into their objects. Similarly the Cartesian self was a dyad of interpretant (the soul) and the object (the body). Lacking the mediation of signs, the Cartesian body and soul lived in different, uncommunicating worlds.

The problem with the two reductions, in addition to their being semantically dyadic, is that they are busily reducing various forms of the Cartesian self, which is a fake self. The Cartesian self may seem to be an unreduced, *sui generis* self, subsisting at its own level, but it is actually an unstable combination of materialism and idealism. In other words it is a combination of the two reduced selves. Descartes' body is a machine, belonging to a level below the human being. His soul is a purely ideational structure, belonging to a level above the human being. When Descartes combined this downwardly reduced body with this upwardly reduced soul or self, he appeared to be putting together a construct that belonged at the human or psychological level. Actually his self is reduced, although it is reduced in both directions at once.

What the two reductions share then is a thinned-out picture of the *sui generis* self. Downward reduction ignores the Cartesian soul and focuses on the body. Upward reduction ignores the Cartesian body and focuses on the soul. Both reductions are, in effect, attacking each other, for if each can refute the opposite half of the Cartesian self they are left, free and clear, with their own half.

But a non-Cartesian pragmatic self, which has the complete semiotic triad, cannot be so reduced. On the contrary, this self shows the mistakes of the reductions, as I have been describing in this and the previous chapter.

Summary and Conclusion

I went through several physical and biological reductions to show how each one subtracts something from the semiotic self. The ontological levels below the psychological are all dyadic, in the sense that they operate solely according to cause and effect or, in semiotic terms, sign and object. Humans are triadic, for they both *are* interpretants and *use* interpretants. Non-human animals deal with their environments by causal trial and error, e.g. by grasping, moving around, putting things in their mouths, etc. Humans can do all these things too, but they can also shine a semiotic light on their surroundings. This means of coping is not dyadic and causal but triadic and meaningful.

The upward reductions all lack some essential feature of the semiotic capacity. Table 8.1 showed which reductions lack which features. Actually all reductions lack all features, for the semiotic properties come in a bundle, and if one is lacking all are lacking. But different reductions go about their work in different pathways, and the easiest way to see the inadequacies of each is to start with the semiotic property that is most obviously missing.

This chapter parallels the discussion of the upward reductions in chapter 7. Together they constitute the anti-reductionist argument of the semiotic self. They also reveal the similarities and shared weaknesses of the two reductions. Both reductions attack concepts of the self that are versions of the Cartesian fallacy. In semiotic terms they are attacking a dyadic, non-semiotic self. This concept of the self is historically obsolete and therefore an irrelevant, if easy, target. The pragmatist semiotic self has replaced Cartesianism. Accordingly it is social, decentered, non-elitist, democratic, and invulnerable to both reductions.

9

Conclusion

In a sense my conclusions are already in the text: the political in chapter 1, and the theoretical throughout. But it will be useful to examine these in a different order. First I will review the theoretical conclusions, and then applying theory to practice, the political.

Theoretical Conclusions

Instead of proceeding from chapter to chapter, I will draw the threads closer together by concentrating on three clusters of ideas: that humans are the juncture of three triads; that the two internal dialogues constitute a trialogue; and that the *sui generis* self disallows the two reductions. As the third point has just been elaborately analyzed in chapters 5, 7, and 8, I will treat it more briefly than the other two.

The Three Triads

Humans combine the temporal, semiotic, and dialogical triads. There are many theories that draw on one or more of these dimensions, and it is widely accepted that humans are inherently related to all three. But the connections among them have not been adequately captured. The Peirce–Mead theory argues that the three are not only closely related but that they imply each other. Humans are a triad of triads, and, in addition, the three triads merge into one. As merged I usually refer to them, in dialogical short-hand, as the I, you, and me, though the more precise names are I–present–sign, you–future–interpretant, and me–past–object. Human

215

beings are not any one of the three (or nine). They are the three together, including both the elements and the relations among these elements. Humans consist of present, future, and past; sign, interpretant, and ct; I, you, and me; and all the overlap, and connectedness, and solidarity among these elements.

The definitions of humans as temporal, semiotic and dialogical are each full of difficulties. One reason they have not been merged before is that, taken one by one, they are so problematic. If there are three incomplete theories the wise course would normally seem, not to merge them, but to first work on each separately. In this case, however, the solution to each emerges from their synthesis, this theoretical whole being greater than the sum of its parts. Let me illustrate by looking at each dimension separately and then by looking at them together.

Humans as Temporal   Humans are sprawled across time in several ways, some of which I discussed in chapter 3: they can remember the past and anticipate the future; they can expand the present, in a psychological or "felt" manner, to include an indefinite amount of the past and future; they can abstract or generalize so that the spatial here and temporal now is transcended. Unlike the first two capacities, which permit humans to inhabit much or all of time, the third one permits them to go beyond time.

These three time-binding abilities allow humans a great deal of control over temporality. In addition the complexity and connectedness of these abilities suggest why time is such an elusive, ineffable experience.

The triad of triads, however, adds a fourth way in which humans are the masters of time. They exist not only in the present, but, by their very structure, in the past and future as well. The previous three capacities are positioned in the present, and from that base humans remember and anticipate, stretch, and abstract. In each case they expand from the present to some more comprehensive location in time.

But in the triadic relation they simultaneously exist in all three realms – present, past, and future – without having to expand into the latter two. They are, so to speak, "three-legged," with one leg in the present, a second in the future and a third in the past. This notion makes sense only if it is combined with the semiotic and dialogical views of the self.

Humans as Semiotic   Turning to the semiotic triad, I must begin with Peirce's claim that humans are nothing more than "words," "word signs," "signs," and so on. This claim can easily be interpreted to mean that humans are nothing more than language, whether *parole*, *langue*, or both.

This is a version of upward reduction, but it is nevertheless an arguable way of interpreting the semiotic self. The idea that humans are only language and culture is widespread today. Not only is it central to French structuralism, post-structuralism, post-modernism, and deconstructionism, it is also in the interactional or *parole*-based versions of the argument, such as those of Wittgenstein, Lacan, Habermas, Benveniste and Muhlhäusler and Harré. Peirce himself, though disagreeing with the upward reductions, never explained how the self could be both semiotic and autonomous. Umberto Eco's interpretation of Peirce as a linguistic reductionist is, in fact, suggested by some of the things Peirce said.

I approached this problem by distinguishing two meanings of sign: structural and processual. This is the same as the distinction between the user of signs and the signs that the user uses. Humans are signs that use signs, semiotic structures that function semiotically. This distinction was explained in chapter 2.

The closest Peirce came to making this distinction was in his theory of the self's discovery of itself. This process was initiated by the encounter with ignorance and error. The child who impulsively touched the stove and burned a hand discovered that the parents were right after all. The stove was hot and it was not to be touched. According to Peirce, the child not only discovered his or her own ignorance and error but that there must be a self within which this ignorance and error inhered. The child's arrogant and self-centered behavior functioned smoothly for a while. Eventually, however, a serious mistake was made and the impact of the mistake led back to the discovery of the self that had made it. Of course the child simultaneously realized not only that the semiotic mistake inhered in the self, but also that all semiotic activity – valid as well as invalid – inhered in the self. I used this idea in chapter 6 to give a Peircean criticism of Wittgenstein's theory of pain and Lacan's theory of the mirror self. Now I am using it against Eco's theory of the linguistic self.

The idea that the self is semiotically triadic in its structure as well as in its activities explains how the self can be both semiotic and autonomous. For Eco the self is a sign in the same way that ordinary words are signs. But obviously we are not signs in the same way that the words in this sentence are signs. Otherwise these words, or others like them, would also be humans. All signs are semiotic triads, consisting of "sign," interpretant, and object, but humans are triads in a unique way. They are the signs behind the signs, or to put it another way, they are bi-leveled signs.

The triadic semiotic structure of the self is the same as the triadic relation the self has to time. Sign, interpretant, and object are also present, future, and past. This means that for humans time is not just a line or continuum, nor even an experiential or "felt" flow. It is these things to be sure, but in addition it is a reflexive circuit of meaning (Giddens, 1991, pp. 1–9). It is a "history" in the sense of a narrative or story. The present constantly projects and re-projects the meaning of the past onto the future (Jacobs, 1984, pp. 30–44). Time is an inherently meaning-generating process. Or, to put it another way, it is a semiotic flow within which one segment (the present) shapes another (the future) in response to a third (the past). The three temporal legs are, at the same time, the three semiotic elements. For humans, the structure of time and that of the self-as-sign are the same. Not only are they both triadic, they are the same triad, looked at in different ways.

Humans as Dialogical   Earlier I pointed out that in my theory "dialogical" actually means "trialogical," for there are three conversational poles or quasi-persons. It is true that Mead had only two (I and me) and Peirce two (I and you), but I have shown how each missed one of the poles. Moreover, each had the one the other missed, so if you combine the two theories you have the I–you–me trialogue.

The particular way in which the internal conversation proceeds is exceedingly complex. I tried to give an ethnography or "map" of it in chapter 3, but the reality is far more subtle than my web of concepts could capture. Nevertheless the triadic, I–you–me approach does show how this conversation relates to the semiotic and temporal features of the self. To say that the I is actually the I–present–sign; the you, the you–future–interpretant; and the me, the me–past–object is more than just stringing words together. These expressions designate the functional interplay of time, semiotic, and the internal conversation. This is more obvious if the two component dialogues are looked at separately. The direct conversation between the I and the you is also the interaction between sign and interpretant and between present and future. The indirect conversation between I and me is also the interaction between sign and object and between present and past.

It should also be noted that Mead's key concept of reflexivity is a subordinate and embedded constituent of the semiotic triad. This feature is the I's relation to the me, expressed conversationally as indirect discourse. Before I realized how to combine Peirce and Mead, I was centering on the latter theorist, with Peirce as a secondary figure. My key concept was reflexivity and I planned to call this book *The Reflexive Self*. Then, when I figured out how to integrate Peirce and Mead around the three triads, my choice of key theorist shifted from Mead to Peirce, my main concept from reflexivity to semiotic and my book title from the one listed above to the one I have actually used. Mead lacked Peirce's idea of how the I and you converse interpretively, but Peirce lacked Mead's idea of how the I and the me converse reflexively. In combination these two produce the conversational trialogue, with interpretation and reflexivity each being one of the constituent dialogues.

Each definition of the self, then, taken in isolation, has a weak spot. Regarding temporality, it is difficult to see how humans, confined to the present, can flow so freely into the past and future. As St Augustine said, we experience time but we cannot understand it. But to define humans as simultaneously present, future, and past (the "three-legged" temporality) makes it easier to see how they can pervade all the realms of time. If anything it is an effort and unnatural for humans to confine themselves to the present, particularly the mechanistic or "clock" present.

Regarding semiotic, it is quite cryptic to say that humans are "signs," for this seems to make them no more than little bubbles of culture. This characterization is incompatible with human agency, autonomy, freedom, and, for that matter, moral equality. On this view humans become whatever the culture says they are. Certainly humans, in their historically specific identities, are culturally shaped to some extent. This is the kernel of truth in the upward reductions. But the humans that are being shaped by culture have natures of their own, independently of culture. This nature or structure is the semiotic self, viewed, not as a process, but as the structure that engages in the process.

Regarding dialogue, it is difficult to explain all features of thought, not to mention other mental processes, in dialogical terms. This is probably why this potentially fruitful line of research has remained so underdeveloped. Neither Peirce's nor Mead's model can take one very far, and the scholars in these two traditions have not done much to extend them. The most likely person to have done this would have been Herbert Blumer, who championed Mead's ideas in sociology from the 1930s to the 1980s (Blumer, 1969). Yet Blumer abandoned Mead's I–me scheme for the much looser and less precise concepts of "communication with oneself," "self-interaction," and (in his specialized sense) "interpretation" (Blumer, 1969, p. 5, Athens, 1993, p. 186 and n. 8). There do not seem to have been any Peircean scholars who attempted to develop Peirce's dialogical views until the probes by Thomas Kent (1989), Vincent Colapietro (1989), and Eugene Rochberg-Halton (1986).

When empirical psychologists turned to the study of what they call "private experience" (Singer and Killigian, Jr., 1987), they found virtually no usable theory, nor did they seem to feel the need for any. This is why their results have remained relatively devoid of generalization.

But the Peirce–Mead merger gives a much more comprehensive theory of inner life than either can give alone. Not only does this synthesis offer a useful scheme for organizing empirical research, including the kind now done by empirical psychologists, it also develops and completes the pragmatist theory of the self.

By themselves, then, each of the three theories has problems, but in combination the problems disappear. The self is a triad of triadic media: temporal, semiotic, and dialogical. Thus far, in discussing the nature of this higher-level triad, I have had little to say. I think one can certainly say that these are three ways of looking at the same concrete entity, the self, but this does not go very far. I have also shown the interlocking character of the three triads and this indicates their functional interplay. But the further question arises whether this second-order triad is itself still another semiotic triad. Peirce was skilled at identifying the semiotic aspects of triads, his examples ranging from the physical processes of nature to the triune God. In that spirit it could probably be argued that: the I–you–me triad is the sign; the sign–interpretation–object triad is the interpretant; and the present–future–past triad is the object. I think that argument too tidy, so I will stop short of that assertion. Instead, let me simply conclude that the self is the integration of three triads and that the exact unity of these three is a matter of interpretation.

The Internal Conversation

In addition to viewing the internal conversation as one of the three triads, I examined it, in detail, as the workplace of the self. The merging of the I–me and I–you dialogues permitted a nuanced description of the thought process. Mead has usually been considered the main theorist of the internal conversation, his concept of "reflexivity" being the central analytic tool. But he used the I–me distinction in other ways as well. His I was the source of creativity, and his me of conformity. His I was freedom, and his me determinism. His I was the individual, and his me the community or "generalized other." Unfortunately he did not distinguish these uses with enough precision, and as a result the dialogical scheme was not sufficiently clarified. Does the me respond verbally to the I, for example, or just listen? If the former, is it confined to yes–no answers or can it speak more fully? And when the I (or me) speaks, does it do so in the same kind of gestural triads that Mead sees in interpersonal conversation, or is there some other semantic currency? He is also less than clear about power, for the me seems to command the I, but the I nevertheless can do whatever it wants.

In contrast to Mead's I–me, Peirce's I–you (or "tuism") has not been used much for the description of inner dialogue, although it too has insufficiencies. Within the discipline of sociology, the "symbolic interactionists," who are the ones most interested in this topic, have stayed close to Mead and tended to ignore Peirce (but see Perinbanayagam, 1991 and Rochberg-Halton, 1986). The Peirceans, who are primarily philosophers rather than social scientists or psychologists, have also paid little attention to Peirce's I–you scheme. In particular they have not connected it very closely to his semiotics (Colapietro, 1989, is an exception).

Taken in isolation from each other, there are problems with each scheme. But if Mead and Peirce are merged, many of the problems disappear, for the theories complement each other. The most obvious advantage, pointed out in the previous section, is that triadicity is now achieved conversationally as well as semiotically and temporally. As I see it, Mead's I–me scheme is non-triadic in three ways: it lacks the future, it lacks the interpretant, and it lacks the "you" pole of the internal conversation. To see how these three elements are missing, all you have to do, particularly if you are an English-speaker, is to listen to your own internal conversation. You will often hear the word "you" applied to yourself, you will sense that you are sometimes addressing yourself in the future, and you will see the flow of interpretants.

In contrast Peirce is non-triadic in lacking the Meadean elements: the past, the object, and the me. Again, a little eavesdropping on your own internal trialogue will show the presence of these three. It may seem odd to say that Peirce, who is known as "Mister Triad," is excessively dyadic in his picture of the self. To clarify this let me recall the distinction between the self as structure and process or between the user of signs and the signs being used. Peirce and Mead are certainly triadic in the latter sense, concerning the signs themselves, but their picture of the user or structure was, in some respects, non-triadic. This differs, as I showed in chapter 8, from theories that picture the signs themselves as dyadic, i.e. as lacking one of the three semiotic elements.

Once triadicity is clarified, lesser problems can be cleared up more easily. Mead's me, for example, does not actually speak, at least not in the role of me. Instead it does so only if it in some way enters the role of the I, a process which I discussed in chapter 3. Peirce's you also gets to talk only when it plays the role of the I, though it does so in a completely different way than is the case with the me. Both Mead's me and Peirce's you have aspects of social conformity, though, again, in different ways.

Another advantage of the synthesis is that the concepts of reflexivity and interpretation are more clearly distinguished from each other. In addition, the idea of internal solidarity emerges from this distinction.

Mead defined the self, in effect, as reflexivity. "The self has the characteristic that it is an object to itself, and that characteristic distinguishes it from other objects and from the body" (1934, p. 135). This was Mead's key concept, both for intra- and interpersonal communication. The latter was defined in relation to "role-taking," but this was a detoured or indirect version of reflexivity. Mead appears to have read little or nothing of Peirce, and perhaps this why he lacked Peirce's "interpretation" as a formal concept.

Reflexivity and interpretation, however, are simultaneous but distinct aspects of communication. Internally the I speaks interpretively to the you and reflexively to the me (i.e. to itself). The self, then, is not just the reflexive, but the reflexive–interpretive animal, and it is this trait that distinguishes it "from other objects and from the body." Both processes are necessary to define the self, for they are both distinctive of the human being. We could not be internally reflexive without being interpretive, and vice versa.

The self can speak to itself, simultaneously, in these two ways because it has internal solidarity, which is my name for its inner field of meaning. Like most things about the self, this solidarity is triadic, for it envelops and unites the three communicative poles. Or to say the same thing, it allows the coordinated use of the two blades, interpretation and reflexivity. The concept of internal solidarity highlights the way society's meaning system, its social solidarity, articulates with the self. In addition it shows how Durkheim, the macro theorist, can be integrated with Peirce and Mead, the micro theorists. Durkheim's "mana" or semiotic power is what gives solidarity to the community. In internalized form, however, it also gives semiotic power to the intra-personal process.

The role of internal solidarity is especially noticeable when it is defective or absent. Social theory is full of terms like self-deceit, bad faith, alienation, and the divided self, not to mention such clinical ones as depression, schizophrenia, delusion, and hallucination. All of these faulty self-conditions entail some discrepancy or dysolidarity between interpretation and reflexivity. In dysolidarity these two processes work against each other, the self fighting itself.

In addition I showed that the concept of solidarity can throw light on a variety of problems in self theory. It explains the self-feeling tradition. It clarifies Hegel's concept of recognition. It shows what truth, goodness, and beauty have in common and how they bind. It helps understand the self-maintaining function of the internal conversation. It shows what Garfinkel's ethnomethodology adds to the semiotic self. It offers hypotheses about the difference between male and female styles. And it suggests some interesting ideas concerning the origin of the self in the early primates.

The Sui Generis Self and the Reductions

The *sui generis* self and the arguments against the reductions fit together. The classical American sociologists made this point repeatedly, as I explained in chapter 6. What I called the classical template combined the symbolically defined self with a comprehensive anti-reductionism. In this book I am re-visiting the template, my purpose being to restore, update, and strengthen its arguments.

The key to this is in theorizing the self. The anti-reductions follow automatically from a well-theorized self. The pragmatists had a certain way of explaining autonomous human beings. From this autonomy followed the clarification of the psychological level and its differentiation from all other levels. As a neo-pragmatist I am continuing this line of argument. It is my position that the reductions both give incorrect descriptions of human nature. They picture it on the wrong level and, for that reason, cannot capture its semiotic triadicity. But an accurately described triadic self cannot be placed on the wrong level, unless someone proceeds to squeeze it out of shape (i.e. dyadicize it). A semiotically triadic self, then, resists all reductions.

Political Conclusions

In the first chapter I discussed the role of the semiotic self, both in American intellectual history and in the contemporary politics of identity. I took the position that the classical pragmatists had replaced the founding fathers' theory of the self. The faculty psychology of the nation-building period had provided a weak basis for democracy, particularly in respect to equality and freedom, and by the Populist–Progressive period it had become obsolete. There was then a three-way fight for the philosophical succession among the upwardly reductionist neo-Hegelians, the downwardly reductionist social Darwinists, and the anti-reductionist pragmatists. The pragmatists' theory of the self had the best fit with democracy, and its proponents also had the most intellectual ammunition. These philosophers allied with the anthropologists and sociologists to form the new theory of human nature and the self. This theory won the fight and replaced the ideas of the founding fathers in what might be called a "second founding" of the Republic.

The contemporary period has placed new stresses on democratic institutions, and there is again discussion of the person or self. Pragmatism is now represented by several versions of neo-pragmatism, including the one in this book. In addition there is another three-way fight emerging, remarkably similar to the one at the turn of the century.

I will not again describe the three positions, for I have repeatedly contrasted the Peirce–Mead synthesis with the two reductions. Instead I will argue that this synthesis has the strongest elective affinity with the times and is the best choice for the contemporary American situation. This argument will have three parts: that democracy works best if it has a theory of the self; that this theory should explain equality, freedom, and the inviolability of the self; and that the Peirce–Mead synthesis is especially useful at this particular time in American history.

Democracy and the Theory of the Self

Richard Rorty (1988/1991) raised the question whether democracy needs a theory of the self at all, or whether it might not be better off without one. John Rawls's influential political philosophy (1971 and 1993) seems to be in at least partial agreement with Rorty. Rorty draws an analogy with religion, arguing that self theory too should be kept outside the public sphere. This way the nation avoids an unnecessary problem and gets along, efficiently, with a minimum of philosophical beliefs. Rorty's view is an organizational version of Occam's razor, implying that a potentially divisive idea should be kept out of the political sphere if possible. I think this is a faulty analogy, for government can operate without reference to religion, but it cannot operate without reference to human beings (selves). I will now discuss in more detail the democratic advantages of a self theory.

The Reality of Democratic Selves   Apart from any specific features of the self, such as equality and freedom, democracy assumes the simple existence or reality of selves. If there were only the forms and rules of society, without human beings, the notion of democracy (rule of the "demos" or "people") would make no sense. It would be *langue* without *parole* or, in Durkheim's terms, a collective consciousness without anything to collect.

This means that, to begin with, democracy assumes an anti-reductionist theory of the self, quite apart from any further features such a theory might have. The upward reductions of communal and cultural absorption and the downward reductions of physicalism and biologism disallow the autonomous self. This disallowance makes democratic institutions incoherent and contradictory.

Let me give some examples. If there were no autonomous and free voters, the institution of voting would be pointless, for there would be no one doing the voting. If the self is regarded as reduced, effaced, or "dead" (all of which mean non-existent), voting is meaningless. Similarly if the ordinary consciousness, on the basis of which people form their votes, is a cognitively invalid "folk psychology" (Greenwood, 1991) then the votes are also invalid.

If there were no people to hold office, to give another example, there would be no one to vote for. Offices could not be filled and elections would lack both voters and candidates.

In addition if there were no individuals or selves, within which rights could inhere, the bill of rights and other legal powers would have no "place" or locus within which they existed. There would also be no persons to whom these rights and powers applied. Persons, by their natures, have inherent rights, and institutions can (and, under democracy, do) recognize these rights with appropriate laws. The rights reside in selves much as Peirce's "ignorance and error" reside in selves.

The classical template of early American sociology represented the sort of minimal self theory I am now talking about. It was a bit fuzzy, but it opposed the two reductionisms and affirmed the autonomous self. In that respect it filled the democratic functions I just described in the examples. Moreover it did so to strengthen democracy against theories (and social movements) that denied the autonomy of human beings. Parsons's *Structure of Social Action* (1937), which is the most recent statement of the template, is a systematic defense of the autonomous (in Parsons's terms, "voluntaristic") self. He pitted this self against the downward reductions of positivism and the upward reductions of German idealism by defining the self as the unreduced human agent.

An initial difficulty, then, of Rorty's keeping social psychology out of democratic theory is that democracy presupposes the reality of human beings or citizens. Further it assumes not only that they have physical bodies but that, in addition, they are conscious and can engage in free political and moral actions. In other words the currently influential reductionist positions on the self, both upward and downward, are logically incompatible with the presuppositions of democracy. Therefore the theory of the self has to be included inside the theory of democracy, at least to the extent of affirming the reality or existence of the unreduced, autonomous self.

History and Culture of Democracy The USA has always worked with a relatively explicit theory of human nature or the self, both in the political and legal institutions. I explained the characteristics of this theory in the nation-building period and described its historical passage up to the present.

In the founding era this theory was more explicit in the Declaration of Independence than in the Constitution, although the *Federalist Papers*

225

clarified the presuppositions of the latter. Both founding documents drew on the same pool of European ideas, although the former had a distinctly more egalitarian theory of human nature than did the latter. As Gary Wills (1992) pointed out, Lincoln's Gettysburg Address placed the national emphasis back on the Declaration, thereby positioning this document (and its ideals) *inside* the Constitution. I do not think Lincoln's redefinition of the Constitution was as important as the pragmatist's own, much more systematic and extensive, redefinition of human nature, so I have transferred Wills's "second founding" idea from Lincoln to the pragmatists. Nevertheless Wills convincingly shows how important the changing theory of the self is in the history of American democracy.

The notion of the human being or self as central to democracy is also part of the political culture, by which I mean the way ordinary people define politics. The American people think of democracy as a form of government in which they, as individuals, are sovereign. This means it is a "free country" (for them, as individuals), and that it is "government of the people, by the people, and for the people." This bottom-up view of the American government is, from one point of view, constituent of that government, for if a population defines its institutions in a certain way, these definitions become part of the institutions. Put another way, the "natural attitude" of the American people places the human self at the center of democracy. If an attempt is made to define democracy as a closed institutional system, independent of the selves or citizens who make up the population, this view will be inconsistent with the embedded, political beliefs of the people.

Both the historical self-definitions of democracy and the popular culture of the citizenry, then, include human beings or selves within this form of government. To exclude them, even if only within the philosophical realm, seems an over-zealous use of Occam's razor.

Equality and Freedom   In addition to whether there are selves at all – the minimal, anti-reductionist theory – there is the further question of what attributes these selves might have. Democracy assumes that the citizens are free and equal. Its whole point is that humans all have the same moral worth, that they should direct their government in a bottom-up fashion and that they have the capacities, cognitive and volitional, to do this. If the theory of the self is declared "outside" democracy, then the freedom and equality of institutions will not be anchored in human beings. Instead these qualities will have to be justified in some self-legitimizing manner, which would make them both logically circular and unconnected to the citizens.

If instead the theory of the self is available to explain why the citizens are morally equal, it justifies their political and legal equality in the institutions. In addition if the theory locates autonomy in some reasoned explanation of how freedom works, the freedom of institutions will not just be hanging in the air. It will express and draw on an attribute of selves.

These three arguments show that democracy makes the most sense when it is based on a theory of the self. It is true that this theory should be kept as generic as possible, otherwise it could become divisive and even get caught up in religious differences. Theories of human nature that ascribe motives or affective tendencies to the self are unnecessarily specific, for people differ a great deal in what they think the key motives are. An innocent Rousseauian or, at the other extreme, a depraved Calvinistic self might be too particularized for democratic theory today, but a more cognitively leaning one, unspecified in moral or emotional tendencies, side-steps this problem. The semiotic self is quite generic in motivation and therefore elastic enough to represent a population of diverse values.

Equality, Freedom and Inviolability

Not all theories of the self entail equality, freedom, or inviolability. Historically the reductions often did not. The German idealisms, as Mead (1929/1964) and somewhat heavy handedly, Dewey (1915) pointed out, were justifications of monarchy, aristocracy, serfdom, and the corresponding inequalities. Also all dictatorships tend to justify themselves with theories that absorb the individual into the party or state. These are versions of upward reduction.

In the Populist–Progressive period the downward reductions of social Darwinism were also opposed to equality. Biological nature was not a democracy but a matter of tooth and claw. Translated socially this meant might makes right and the survival of the fittest. These ideas were used to attack the citizenship of blacks and other ethnic minorities. When the Ku Klux Klan controlled the politics of about a dozen states in the early 1920s they based their policies on biologically reductionist ideas. And when the Nazis took over Germany in the early 1930s they also opposed political equality with pseudo-biology.

I think that at the very least one can say there is a tendency for the reductions to drive out notions of moral, legal, and political equality. At the present time in the United States, however, I do not think one could say the people who represent the reductionist positions, upward or downward, *personally* oppose equality or any other aspect of democracy. On the contrary the partisans of these positions present themselves as politically progressive, opposed to the alleged rigidities of foundationalism and committed to the liberalizing effects of science. The natural sciences are supposed to liberate with downward reduction, and (some of) the cultural sciences are also supposed to liberate with upward. Unlike the reductions that the pragmatists and the classical template opposed, the current reductions present themselves as benign and more pro-humanity than the humanistic positions.

Nevertheless there are two problems with the current reductions. First, they draw an inaccurate picture of the self theory they want to reduce. The downward reductions of the natural sciences picture it as anti-scientific and sponsored by oligarchic organizations, such as the Catholic church. The upward reductions of (some of) the cultural sciences picture self theory in narrowly Cartesian terms, as though this were the only kind. But the Peirce–Mead model avoids the weaknesses of Cartesianism and still offers an autonomous, unreduced self.

The other weakness of the current, benign-looking reductions is that they cannot explain the value of the person. What happens to the intrinsic inviolability of the human being, let alone freedom and equality, if humans are denied their *sui generis* status? These qualities are totally lacking at the sub-human levels and culturally relative at the supra-human.

In the Peirce–Mead model equality is based on the semiotic structure of humans as such. Right from the very first primate-cum-human they are all triads of triads. This implies that moral equality is not just something peculiar to certain times and places but universal, regardless of whether or not it is recognized by social institutions. All people are equal because they all consist of an I, a you, and a me, i.e. they are all semiotic signs.

They are all internally free because the semiotic process is, to some extent, autonomous. The object does not determine the sign or interpretant, as it does in positivistic dyadicism. Signs and interpretants are selected from many possibilities, and the selection process is free.

Mead had trouble with free will when he read the Calvinist theologian Jonathan Edwards (Cook, 1993, p. 5). Edwards criticized the narrowly volitional idea of freedom as a contradiction in terms. But later, Mead shifted to the cognitive theory of freedom, which avoids this critique. This theory bases freedom on the internal conversation, which is both controlled by the person and, to some extent, controlling of (our definitions of) reality. These definitions may, more or less, determine conduct, but we determine the definitions. Peirce too, much more effortlessly than Mead, adhered to the semiotic theory of freedom. In fact he elaborated his theory of human freedom, in his terms "autonomy," in a highly developed manner (Colapietro, 1989, pp. 99–118).

In addition to equality and freedom, though, there is another important property of the self that the Peirce–Mead model can explain. This is the quality of being inherently valuable. More so than all the other things in nature, both at lower and higher ontological levels, humans are valuable in themselves. Kant referred to this as inviolability and spoke of humans as a "kingdom of ends." Durkheim regarded the modern self (though I would change this to all selves) as sacred. Weber saw the human being as the charismatic foundation of substantive rationality. The corresponding concept in the Peirce–Mead model is internal solidarity. This is the force that gives semiotic power and bindingness to the values: truth, beauty, and goodness. It is the quality that underlies Kant's categorical imperative, Durkheim's religion of humanity, and Weber's charisma. Since internal solidarity is an emergent of human triadicity it is a normal constituent of the semiotic self. In other words the Peirce–Mead model has a powerful explanation of human value. This quality, along with equality and freedom, is an indispensable feature of the democratic self.

The Peirce–Mead Model Today

To apply the model to the present requires a split consciousness, retaining abstractness but surrounding it with historical concreteness. In other words it is necessary to hold on to the consciousness of theory but also to add that of temporally embedded practice. This requires reference to specific events at particular times.

During the years since the oil crisis of 1973 the American political economy has been overloaded in two ways, both of which can be best approached by the theory of the semiotic self. For one, there has been continuous recession, with minor fluctuations, up to the present. The longest previous downturn in American history was from 1866 to 1897, but that was an *agricultural* depression. The most intense downturn was, of course, the Great Depression, but that only lasted from 1929 until the beginning of World War II. The current slump is the longest general or across-the-board recession in American history. This has brought about a loss of well-paying jobs to other countries, the reduction of income for average Americans, a decline in tax revenues for government, and a general sense of downward mobility. At the same time wealthy Americans have managed to increase their share of both property and income with the result that the rich are getting richer, the poor are getting poorer, and the middle class is getting smaller. The long recession with its bleak material consequences is overload number one.

During this time there has certainly been an abundance of economic issues on the political agenda. But the strange thing is that there have been so many life-style – also called status, moral, cultural, and evaluative – issues as well. Max Weber (1922/1946) was the one who distinguished class (or life chances) from status (or life-style) stratification, along with their politicial expression. Cultural issues have been so intense that recent presidential elections have centered as much on them as on economic matters. In the first chapter I discussed the identity issues of race, ethnicity, gender, and sexual orientation, all of which divide into more specific cultural issues. In addition, however, there are abortion, street drugs, pornography, schools and hate crimes. The appearance of these moral issues is counter-intuitive, for during hard times people normally concentrate on material interests and postpone value concerns for later. This mixture of issues, which is unusual in American history, is overload number two.

The result is the worst of both worlds. The economy is stuck in recession, to the material detriment of the population and the institutions. In addition Americans are fighting, not just over their life chances, but over their values and life styles.

In the first chapter I pointed out that turn-of-the-century pragmatism was useful for absorbing the Catholics and Jews. Its theory of the semiotic self explained cultural variation in a democratic manner, saving the day for American institutions. The USA had recruited its industrial labor force largely from Catholic and Jewish populations. This meant that class and status politics would be intermixed. These peoples were America's Marxian proletariat and it was inevitable that they would bring an abundance of material issues to politics, as well as to the private battles of the workplace. The fact that they differed from the native population in religion, language, and national origins, however, meant that there would be an abundance of status issues as well. Politics in the Populist–Progressive period, particularly after the new immigration began in the early 1880s, was a complicated mixture of class and status conflict. In addition, not only were there real issues in both spheres, the elites did their best to manipulate ethnic hostilities, hoping thereby to further divide the proletariat.

It should be remembered that the faculty psychology of the founding period was primarily built for material and class, rather than status, politics. The Declaration and the Constitution were both conceptualized within the shadow of revolution, the former to justify it and the latter to prevent it. The checks and balances of the latter were intended largely to block the masses from revolutionary acts. After some two centuries it certainly must be acknowledged that the Constitution, along with other important factors, has achieved its anti-revolutionary purpose.

But the ethnic diversity of the proletariat, although a barrier to class politics, had the previously mentioned effect of intensifying status conflict. Even if faculty psychology had not already faded, it would have been a poor tool for guiding this form of politics through the institutions. Faculty psychology was over-adapted to class and lacked the culturally sensitive categories of status. Indeed its adaptation to slavery showed how easy it could collapse into undemocratic classifications of the population.

During the three-way fight for the succession the social Darwinisms, like faculty psychology, were also over-adapted to class politics. The Darwinisms were constructed to legitimize economic elites and class stratification, doing so with quasi-biological categories. For status politics they were quite ill-adapted, for they tended to turn each status or ethnic group into a different biological sub-species, thereby undermining the equality requirement of democracy.

In contrast the neo-Hegelian option, much like the cultural-linguistic reductions of today, was over-adapted to status politics. Cultural differences could easily be explained non-biologically, for humans were nothing more than culture. What the neo-Hegelians could not explain was class conflict itself, for this went on in the hard material world and not at some higher cultural level.

Pragmatism won the turn-of-the-century philosophical battle because, in addition to having the most conceptual affinity with democracy, it was not over-adapted to one kind of issue. The highly elastic model of the semiotic self was the only theory that could explain both class and status politics (democratically).

We are now back where we were at the century's turn. There is a complex mixture of class and status politics, which, given the uncertainty of the world political economy, may persist for a long time. There is also a three-way fight for the theory of the self, with the downward reductionists too adapted to material issues, the upward reductionists too adapted to cultural issues, and the neo-pragmatists optimally adapted to both.

It may be that any of these three models, or even Rorty's exclusion of them, could work for the USA in the years ahead. Ideas are not all important, and institutions can have an inner toughness of their own. But all the indications are that the USA, along the rest of the world, is in for some rough sailing, and it will need every resource it can get. Therefore my political conclusion is that, not only does democracy need some theory of the autonomous self, the Peirce–Mead model is the best option for the job. It comes out of America's distinctive pragmatic tradition, its structure is closest to democratic institutions, and it has the most flexibility for meeting the contemporary range of issues.

Bibliography

Where two dates are given, the first is that of the original publication, the second that of a later edition or translation.

Aboulafia, Mitchell. 1986. *The Mediating Self: Mead, Sartre and Self-Determination*. New Haven: Yale University Press.

Alexander, Richard D. 1989. "Evolution of the Human Psyche," pp. 454–513 in Mellars, Paul and Chris Stringer (eds), *The Human Revolution: Behavioural and Biological Perspectives on the Origins of Modern Humans*. Edinburgh: Edinburgh University Press.

Alpert, Harry. 1939/1961. *Emile Durkheim and his Sociology*. New York: Russell & Russell.

Alston, William. 1956. "Pragmatism and the Theory of Signs in Peirce," *Philosophy and Phenomenological Research*, 17:79–88.

Althusser, Louis. 1968/1971. *Lenin and Philosophy and other Essays*. New York: Monthly Review Press.

Anderson, James R. 1984. "The Development of Self-Recognition: A Review," *Developmental Psychobiology*, 17:35–49.

Aristotle. 384–322 BC/1984a. *Physics*, pp. 315–446 in *The Complete Works of Aristotle*, vol. 1. Princeton: Princeton University Press.

———. 384–322 BC/1984b. *Metaphysics*, pp. 1552–1728 in *The Complete Works of Aristotle*, vol. 2. Princeton: Princeton University Press.

Arkin, Arthur M. 1981. *Sleep-Talking: Psychology and Psychophysiology*. Hillsdale, New Jersey: Lawrence Erlbaum Associates.

Ashmore, Malcolm. 1989. *The Reflexive Thesis*. Chicago: University of Chicago Press.

Athens, Lonnie. 1993. "Blumer's Advanced Course in Social Psychology," *Studies in Symbolic Interaction*, 14:163–93.

Ayala, Francisco J. 1977. "Philosophical Issues," pp. 474–516 in Theodosius

BIBLIOGRAPHY

Dobzhansky, Francisco J. Ayala, G. Ledyard Stebbins, and James W. Valentine, *Evolution*. San Francisco: W. H. Freeman & Company.

Bakhtin, M. M. 1975/1981. *The Dialogical Imagination*. Austin: University of Texas Press.

Baldwin, James Mark. 1899/1973. *Social and Ethical Interpretations of Mental Development*. New York: Arno Press.

Banfield, Ann. 1982. *Unspeakable Sentences*. Boston: Routledge & Kegan Paul.

Barthes, Roland. 1957/1985. *Mythologies*. New York: Hill & Wang.

Bartlett, Steven J. (ed.). 1992. *Reflexivity: A Source-Book in Self-Reference*. Amsterdam: North Holland.

Bartlett, Steven J. and Peter Suber (eds). 1987. *Self-Reference: Reflections on Reflexivity*. Dordrecht, Holland: Martinus Nijhoff.

Bellah, Robert N. 1970. *Beyond Belief*. New York: Harper & Row.

Benveniste, Emile. 1966/1971. *Problems in General Linguistics*. Coral Gables: University of Miami Press.

Bickerton, Derek, 1990. *Language and Species*. Chicago: University of Chicago Press.

Blumer, Herbert. 1969. *Symbolic Interaction*. Englewood Cliffs, New Jersey: Prentice-Hall, Inc.

Boas, Franz. 1901. "The Mind of Primitive Man," *The Journal of American Folk-Lore*, 14:1–11.

——. 1911/1938. *The Mind of Primitive Man*. New York: Macmillan Company.

Boorstin, Daniel J. 1948. *The Lost World of Thomas Jefferson*. New York: Henry Holt & Company.

Bourdieu, Pierre. 1972/1977. *Outline of a Theory of Practice*. Cambridge: Cambridge University Press.

Brent, Joseph. 1993. *Charles Sanders Peirce: A Life*. Bloomington: Indiana University Press.

Brint, Michael and William Weaver (eds). 1991. *Pragmatism in Law and Society*. Boulder: Westview Press.

Butler, Judith. 1987. *Subjects of Desire: Hegelian Reflections in Twentieth-Century France*. New York: Columbia University Press.

Caird, Edward. 1889/1968. *The Critical Philosophy of Immanuel Kant*, vol. 1. New York: Kraus Reprint Co.

Canfield, John V. 1990. *The Looking-Glass Self*. New York: Praeger.

Caughey, John L. 1984. *Imaginary Social Worlds: A Cultural Approach*. Lincoln: University of Nebraska Press.

Chodorow, Nancy. 1978. *The Reproduction of Mothering*. Berkeley: University of California Press.

Chomsky, Noam. 1959. Review of B. F. Skinner's *Verbal Behavior*, *Linguistics*, 35:26–58.

Cladis, Mark S. 1992. *A Communitarian Defense of Liberalism: Emile Durkheim and Contemporary Social Theory*. Stanford: Stanford University Press.

Cohen, Morris R. and Ernest Nagel. 1934. *An Introduction to Logic and Scientific Method*. New York: Harcourt, Brace & World, Inc.

Cohen-Solal, Annie. 1985/1987. *Sartre: A Life*. London: Heinemann.

Cohn, Dorrit. 1978. *Transparent Minds*. Princeton: Princeton University Press.

Colapietro, Vincent M. 1989. *Peirce's Approach to the Self*. Albany: State University of New York Press.

——. 1990. "The Vanishing Subject of Contemporary Discourse: A Pragmatic Response," *The Journal of Philosophy*, 87:644–55.

Collins, Randall. 1982. *Sociological Insight*. New York: Oxford University Press.

——. 1989. "Toward a Neo-Meadian Sociology of Mind," *Symbolic Interaction*, 12:1–32.

Cook, Gary A. 1993. *George Herbert Mead*. Urbana: University of Illinois Press.

Cooley, Charles Horton. 1922/1964. *Human Nature and the Social Order*. Revised Edition. New York: Shocken Books. [Original version published in 1902].

Cornell, Drucilla. 1993. "Pragmatism, Recollective Imagination, and Transformative Legal Interpretation," pp. 23–44 in Drucilla Cornell, *Transformations: Recollective Imagination and Sexual Difference*. New York: Routledge.

Corrington, Robert S. 1993. *An Introduction to C. S. Peirce*. Lanham, MD: Rowman & Littlefield Publishers, Inc.

Coser, Lewis. 1988. "Primitive Classification Revisited," *Sociological Theory*, 6:85–90.

Cravens, Hamilton. 1978. *The Triumph of Evolution*. Philadelphia: University of Pennsylvania Press.

Curti, Merle. 1980. *Human Nature in American Thought*. Madison: University of Wisconsin Press.

Deese, James. 1985. *American Freedom and the Social Sciences*. New York: Columbia University Press.

Deglar, Carl N. 1991. *In Search of Human Nature*. New York: Oxford University Press.

Denzin, Norman K. 1984. *On Understanding Emotion*. San Francisco: Jossey-Bass Publishers.

Derrida, Jacques. 1962/1989. *Edmund Husserl's Origin of Geometry: An Introduction*. Lincoln: University of Nebraska Press.

——. 1967/1973. *Speech and Phenomena*. Evanston: Northwestern University Press.

——. 1967/1976. *Of Grammatology*. Baltimore: Johns Hopkins University Press.

——. 1967/1978. *Writing and Difference*. Chicago: University of Chicago Press.

Dewey, John. 1890/1969. *John Dewey: The Early Works*, vol. 3. Carbondale: Southern Illinois University Press.

——. 1915. *German Philosophy and Politics*. New York: H. Holt & Co.

Dews, Peter. 1987. *Logics of Disintegration*. London: Verso.

Diggins, John P. 1979. "The Socialization of Authority and the Dilemmas of American Liberalism," *Social Research*, 46:454–86.

——. 1984. *The Lost Soul of American Politics*. New York: Basic Books Inc.

DiTomaso, Nancy. 1982. " 'Sociological Reductionism' from Parsons to Althusser:

Linking Action and Structure in Social Theory," *American Sociological Review*, 47:14–28.

Domhoff, G. William. 1993. "The Repetition of Dreams and Dream Elements: A Possible Clue to a Function of Dreams," pp. 293–320 in Alan Moffitt, Milton Kramer, and Robert Hoffmann (eds), *The Functions of Dreaming*. Albany: State University of New York Press.

Dreyfus, Hubert L. 1992. *What Computers Still Can't Do*. Cambridge: MIT Press.

Durkheim, Emile 1893/1964. *The Division of Labor in Society*. New York: The Free Press.

——. 1895/1982. *The Rules of Sociological Method*. New York: The Free Press.

——. 1897/1951. *Suicide*. New York: The Free Press.

——. 1898/1974. "Individual and Collective Representations," pp. 1–34 in *Emile Durkheim: Sociology and Philosophy*. New York: The Free Press.

——. 1913–14/1983. *Pragmatism and Sociology*. Cambridge: Cambridge University Press.

——. 1914/1960. "The Dualism of Human Nature and its Social Conditions," pp. 325–40 in Emile Durkheim et al., *Essays on Sociology & Philosophy*. New York: Harper & Row.

——. 1912/1965. *The Elementary Forms of the Religious Life*. New York: The Free Press.

Eco, Umberto. 1976. *A Theory of Semiotics*. Bloomington: Indiana University Press.

Emerson, Caryl. 1983. "The Outer World and Inner Speech: Bakhtin, Vygotsky, and the Internalization of Language," *Critical Inquiry*, 10:245–64.

Epstein, David F. 1984. "A Study of Federalist 10," pp. 59–110 in David F. Epstein, *The Political Theory of the Federalist*. Chicago: University of Chicago Press.

Feffer, Andrew. 1993. *The Chicago Pragmatists and American Progressivism*. Ithaca: Cornell University Press.

Fisch, Max H. 1982. "Introduction." pp. xv–xxxv in *Writings of Charles S. Peirce*, vol. 1. Bloomington: Indiana University Press.

——. 1986. *Peirce, Semeiotic, and Pragmatism: Essays by Max H. Fisch*. Bloomington: Indiana University Press.

Flower, Elizabeth and Murray G. Murphey. 1977. *A History of Philosophy in America*. 2 vols. New York: G. P. Putnam's Sons.

Foucault, Michel. 1966/1973. *The Order of Things*. New York: Vintage Books.

Fraiberg, Selma H. 1959. *The Magic Years*. New York: Charles Scribner's Sons.

Frankfurt, Harry G. 1971. "Freedom of the Will and the Concept of a Person," *Journal of Philosophy*, 88:5–20.

Furner, Mary O. 1975. *Advocacy and Objectivity*. Lexington: University of Kentucky Press.

Gackenbach, Jayne and Stephen LaBerge. 1988. *Conscious Mind, Sleeping Brain*. New York: Plenum Press.

Garfinkel, Harold. 1963. "A Conception of, and Experiments with, 'Trust' as a

Condition of Stable Concerted Actions," pp. 187–238 in O.J. Harvey (ed.), *Motivation and Social Interaction*. New York: Ronald Press.

———. 1967. *Studies in Ethnomethodology*. Englewood Cliffs: Prentice-Hall, Inc., Cambridge, Polity Press.

Gasche, Rodolphe, 1986. *The Tain of the Mirror: Derrida and the Philosophy of Reflection*. Cambridge: Harvard University Press.

Geertz, Clifford. 1973. *The Interpretation of Cultures*. New York: Basic Books, Inc.

Giddens, Anthony. 1979. *Central Problems in Social Theory*. Berkeley: University of California Press.

———. 1991. *Modernity and Self-Identity*. Stanford: Stanford University Press; Cambridge, Polity Press.

Gleason, Phillip. 1983/1992. "Identifying Identity: A Semantic History," pp. 123–49 in Phillip Gleason, *Speaking of Diversity*. Baltimore: Johns Hopkins University Press.

Gödel, Kurt. 1931/1962. *Kurt Gödel on Formally Undecidable Propositions of Principia Mathematica and Related Systems*. New York: Basic Books.

Goethe, Johann Wolfgang von. 1811–32/1974. *The Autobiography of Johann Wolfgang Von Goethe*, vol. 2. Chicago: University of Chicago Press.

Goffman, Erving. 1967. *Interaction Ritual*. Garden City: Doubleday & Co.

Goodenough, Ward H. 1990. "Evolution of the Human Capacity for Beliefs," *American Anthropologist*, 92:597–612.

Gouldner, Alvin W. 1970. *The Coming Crisis of Western Sociology*. New York: Avon Books.

Greenberg, Jay R. and Stephen A. Mitchell. 1983. *Object Relations in Psychoanalytic Theory*. Cambridge: Harvard University Press.

Greenwood, John D. (ed.). 1991. *The Future of Folk Psychology*. Cambridge: Cambridge University Press.

Gunn, Giles. 1992. *Thinking across the American Grain: Ideology, Intellect and the New Pragmatism*. Chicago: University of Chicago Press.

Gurvitch, Georges. 1964. *The Spectrum of Social Time*. Dordrecht: D. Reidel.

Habermas, Jürgen. 1981/1984. *The Theory of Communicative Action*, vol. 1. Boston: Beacon Press; Cambridge, Polity Press.

———. 1981/1987. *The Theory of Communicative Action*, vol. 2. Boston: Beacon Press; Cambridge, Polity Press.

Hamilton, Gary G. and John R. Sutton. 1989. "The Problem of Control in the Weak State." *Theory and Society*, 18:1–46.

Harding, Sandra (ed.). 1987. *Feminism and Methodology*. Bloomington: Indiana University Press.

Harding, Sandra and Merrill B. Hintikka (eds). 1983. *Discovering Reality: Feminist Perspectives on Epistemology, Metaphysics, Methodology and Philosophy of Science*. Dordrecht: D. Reidel.

Harris, H. S. 1983. *Hegel's Development*. Oxford: Clarendon Press.

Hayward, J. E. S. 1959. "Solidarity: The Social History of an Idea in Nineteenth Century France," *International Review of Social History*, 4:261–84.

236

BIBLIOGRAPHY

Hegel, G. W. F. 1807/1979. *Phenomenology of Spirit.* Oxford: Oxford University Press.

Hekman, Susan J. 1990. *Gender and Knowledge: Elements of a Postmodern Feminism.* Boston: Northeastern University Press; Cambridge, Polity Press.

Henrich, Dieter. 1982. "Fichte's Original Insight," pp. 15–53 in Darrel E. Christensen, et al. (eds), *Contemporary German Philosophy*, vol. 1. University Park: Pennsylvania State University Press.

Hilbert, Richard A. 1992. *The Classical Roots of Ethnomethodology: Durkheim, Weber, and Garfinkel.* Chapel Hill: University of North Carolina Press.

Hirschman, Albert O. 1977. *The Passions and the Interests.* Princeton: Princeton University Press.

Hogan, David. 1990. "The Novel and the Internal Conversation." Unpublished seminar paper. University of Illinois at Urbana.

Hollinger, David A. 1980. "The Problem of Pragmatism in American History," *The Journal of American History*, 67:88–107.

Horwitz, Morton J. 1992. *The Transformation of American Law: 1870–1960.* New York: Oxford University Press.

Howe, Daniel Walker. 1982. "European Sources of Political Ideas in Jeffersonian America," *Reviews in American History*, 10:28–44.

———. 1987. "The Political Psychology of *The Federalist*," *William and Mary Quarterly*, 46:485–509.

Hurlburt, Russell T. 1990. *Sampling Normal and Schizophrenic Inner Experience.* New York: Plenum Press.

Husserl, Edmund. 1891/1970. *Philosophie der Arithmetik.* The Hague: Martinus Nijhoff.

———. 1913/1970. *Logical Investigations.* vol. 1. London: Routledge & Kegan Paul.

Jacobs, Jonathan. 1984. "The Idea of a Personal History," *International Philosophical Quarterly*, 24:179–87.

———. 1986. "Teleology and Reduction in Biology," *Biology and Philosophy*, 1:389–99.

James, William. 1890/1950. *The Principles of Psychology.* 2 vols. New York: Dover Publications.

Janik, Allan and Stephen Toulmin. 1973. *Wittgenstein's Vienna.* Cambridge: Harvard University Press.

Johnson, Barbara. 1993. "Introduction," pp. 1–16 in Barbara Johnson (ed.), *Freedom and Interpretation: The Oxford Amnesty Lectures.* New York: Basic Books.

Johnstone, Henry W., Jr. 1970. *The Problem of the Self.* University Park: Pennsylvania State University Press.

Kant, Immanuel. 1787/1965. *Critique of Pure Reason.* New York: St. Martin's Press.

———. 1804/1983. *What Real Progress Has Metaphysics Made in Germany since the Time of Leibniz and Wolff?* New York: Abaris Books Inc.

Kaplan, Abraham. 1964. *The Conduct of Inquiry.* San Francisco: Chandler Publishing Company.

Kaye, Howard L. 1986. *The Social Meaning of Modern Biology*. New Haven: Yale University Press.

Kehr, Marguerite Witmer. 1916. "The Doctrine of the Self in St Augustine and in Descartes," *Philosophical Review*, 25:587–615.

Kent, Thomas. 1989. "Dialogic Semiotics," *The American Journal of Semiotics*, 6:221–37.

Kierkegaard, Søren. 1846/1941. *Concluding Unscientific Postscript*. Princeton: Princeton University Press.

Kline, Morris. 1980. *Mathematics: The Loss of Certainty*. New York: Oxford University Press.

Kloppenberg, James T. 1986. *Uncertain Victory: Social Democracy and Progressivism in European and American Thought, 1870–1920*. New York: Oxford University Press.

Knorr-Cetina, Karin D. 1981. "The Micro-Sociological Challenge of Macro-Sociology," pp. 1–47 in K. D. Knorr-Cetina and A. V. Cicourel. *Advances in Social Theory and Methodology: Toward an Integration of Micro- and Macro-Sociologies*. Boston: Routledge & Kegan Paul.

Kohut, Heinz. 1959. "Introspection, Empathy and Psychoanalysis," *Journal of the American Psychoanalytical Association*, 7:459–83.

——. 1971. *The Analysis of the Self*. New York: International Universities Press, Inc.

Kroeber, A. L. 1948. *Anthropology*. New York: Harcourt, Brace and Co.

——. 1952. *The Nature of Culture*. Chicago: University of Chicago Press.

Kroeber, A. L. and Talcott Parsons. 1958. "The Concepts of Culture and of Social System," *American Sociological Review*, 23:582–3.

Kuhn, Thomas S. 1962/1970. *The Structure of Scientific Revolutions*. Second Edition, Enlarged. Chicago: University of Chicago Press.

Lacan, Jacques. 1966/1977. *Ecrits*. New York: W. W. Norton.

Laing, R. D. 1959/1965. *The Divided Self*. London: Tavistock Publications; Harmondsworth and Baltimore: Penguin Books.

Lavine, Thelma Z. 1984. "Pragmatism and the Constitution in the Culture of Modernism," *Transactions of the Charles S. Peirce Society*, 20:1–10.

Lawson, Hilary. 1985. *Reflexivity*. La Salle: Open Court.

Lever, Janet. 1978. "Sex Differences in the Complexity of Children's Play and Games," *American Sociological Review*, 43:471–83.

Levine, Donald N. 1989. "Parsons' *Structure* (and Simmel) Revisited," *Sociological Theory*, 7:110–17.

Levine, Donald N., E. B. Carter, and E. M. Gorman. 1976. "Simmel's Influence on American Sociology, I and II," *American Journal of Sociology*, 81:813–45, 1112–30.

Lévi-Strauss, Claude. 1950/1987. *Introduction to the Work of Marcel Mauss*. London: Routledge & Kegan Paul.

Lewis, David. 1972. "Peirce, Mead, and the Objectivity of Meaning," *The Kansas Journal of Sociology*, 8:111–22.

Lewis, David and Richard L. Smith. 1980. *American Sociology and Pragmatism: Mead, Chicago Sociology, and Symbolic Interaction*. Chicago: University of Chicago Press.

Liberman, Kenneth. 1985. *Understanding Interaction in Central Australia: An Ethnomethodological Study of Australian Aboriginal People*. London: Routledge & Kegan Paul.

Locke, John. 1689/1975. *An Essay Concerning Human Understanding*. Oxford: Oxford University Press.

Lorraine, Tamsin. 1990. *Gender, Identity and the Production of Meaning*. Boulder: Westview Press.

Lovejoy, Arthur O. 1936. *The Great Chain of Being*. Cambridge: Harvard University Press.

Luhmann, Niklas. 1975. "Interaktion, Organisation, Gesellschaft," pp. 9–20 in Niklas Luhmann, *Sociologische Aufklärung 2*. Opladen: Westdeutscher Verlag.

———. 1982. *The Differentiation of Society*. New York: Columbia University Press.

———. 1986. "The Individuality of the Individual," pp. 313–25 in Thomas C. Heller, Morton Sosna, and David E. Wellbery (eds), *Reconstructing Individualism*. Stanford: Stanford University Press.

Lukes, Steven. 1973/1985. *Emile Durkheim*. Stanford: Stanford University Press.

Macey, David. 1988. *Lacan in Contexts*. London: Verso.

Macpherson, C.B. 1962. *The Political Theory of Possessive Individualism: Hobbes to Locke*. Oxford: Clarendon Press.

Madison, James. 1787/1961. "Federalist 10," pp. 129–36 in Alexander Hamilton, James Madison, and John Jay, *The Federalist*. Cambridge: Harvard University Press.

Malachowski, Alan (ed.). 1990. *Reading Rorty*. Cambridge: Basil Blackwell Inc.; Oxford: Blackwell.

Markova, Ivana. 1982. *Paradigms, Thought, and Language*. New York: John Wiley & Sons.

Marks, Elaine and Isabelle de Courtivron (eds). 1981. *New French Feminisms*. New York: Schocken Books.

Matthews, Fred. 1990. "The Attack on 'Historicism': Allan Bloom's Indictment of Contemporary American Historical Scholarship," *American Historical Review*, 95:429–47.

Maturana, Humberto R. and Francisco J. Varela. 1972/1980. *Autopoeisis and Cognition*. Dordrecht: D. Reidel.

Mayhew, Bruce. 1981. "Structuralism versus Individualism: Part I," *Social Forces*, 59:335–75.

Mayr, Ernst. 1988. *Toward a New Philosophy of Biology*. Cambridge: The Belknap Press of Harvard University Press.

McDougall, William. 1921. *Is America Safe for Democracy?*. New York: Charles Scribner's Sons.

McPherson, James M. 1990. *Abraham Lincoln and the Second American Revolution*. New York: Oxford University Press.

Mead, George Herbert. 1913/1964 "The Social Self," pp. 142–9 in George Herbert Mead, *Selected Writings*. Indianapolis: Bobbs-Merrill.

———. 1922/1964. "A Behavioristic Account of the Significant Symbol," pp. 240–47 in George Herbert Mead, *Selected Writings*, Indianapolis: Bobbs-Merrill.

———. 1929/1964. "The Philosophies of Royce, James and Dewey in their American Setting," pp. 371–91 in George Herbert Mead, *Selected Writings*. Indianapolis: Bobbs Merrill.

———. 1930. "Cooley's Contribution to American Social Thought," *American Journal of Sociology*, 35:693–706.

———. 1934. *Mind, Self, and Society*. Chicago: University of Chicago Press.

———. 1938. *The Philosophy of the Act*. Chicago: University of Chicago Press.

Mehlman, Jeffrey. 1972. "The 'Floating Signifier': From Lévi-Strauss to Lacan," *Yale French Studies*, 48:10–37.

Miller, David L. 1973. "Mead's Theory of Universals," pp. 89–106 in Walter Robert Corti (ed.), *The Philosophy of George Herbert Mead*. Winterthur, Switzerland: Archiv für genetische Philosophie.

Mitchell, W. J. T. (ed.). 1985. *Against Theory: Literary Studies and the New Pragmatism*. Chicago: University of Chicago Press.

Moi, Toril (ed.). 1987. *French Feminist Thought: A Reader*. Oxford: Blackwell.

Monk, Ray. 1990. *Ludwig Wittgenstein*. New York: The Free Press; London, Cape.

Morris, Charles W. 1938. "Peirce, Mead and Pragmatism." *The Philosophical Review*, 47:109–27.

Mouzelis, Nicos P. 1991. "Reductionism: Neglecting Hierarchical Levels," pp. 137–65 in Nicos P. Mouzelis, *Back to Sociological Theory*. London: Macmillan.

Muhlhäusler, Peter and Rom Harré. 1990. *Pronouns and People: The Linguistic Construction of Social and Personal Identity*. Oxford: Blackwell.

Mukarovsky, Jan. 1977. *The World and Verbal Art*. New Haven: Yale University Press.

Murphey, Murray G. 1968. "Kant's Children: The Cambridge Pragmatists." *Transactions of the Charles S. Peirce Society*, 4:3–33.

Nagel, Ernest. 1951. "Mechanistic Explanation and Organismic Biology." *Philosophy and Phenomenological Research*, 11:327–38.

———. 1961. "The Reduction of Theories," pp. 336–97 in Ernest Nagel, *The Structure of Science*. New York: Harcourt, Brace & World, Inc.

Natanson, Maurice. 1955. "The Concept of the Given in Peirce and Mead," *The Modern Schoolman*, 32:143–57.

Neely, Wright. 1974. "Freedom and Desire," *Philosophical Review*, 83:32–54.

Neuhouser, Frederick. 1990. *Fichte's Theory of Subjectivity*. Cambridge: Cambridge University Press.

Nozick, Robert. 1981. *Philosophical Explanations*. Cambridge: The Belknap Press of Harvard University Press.

O'Callaghan, Louis T. 1948. *The Function of Reflection in the Psychology of Saint Thomas Aquinas*. Unpublished Ph.D. Dissertation. New York: Fordham University.

Organ, Troy Wilson. 1987. *Philosophy and the Self: East and West*. Selinsgrove: Susquehanna University Press; London: Associated University Presses.

Ornstein, Paul H. 1978. "Introduction: The Evolution of Heinz Kohut's Psychoanalytic Psychology of the Self," pp. 1–106 in Paul H. Ornstein (ed.), *The Search for the Self: Selected Writings of Heinz Kohut: 1950–1978*, vol. 1. New York: International Universities Press, Inc.

Palaci, Jacques. 1980. "Psychoanalysis of the Self and Psychotherapy," pp. 317–335 in Arnold Goldberg (ed.), *Advances in Self Psychology*. New York: International Universities Press, Inc.

Park, Robert E. 1931. "The Sociological Methods of William Graham Sumner and of William I. Thomas and Florian Znaniecki," pp. 154–75 in Stuart A. Rice (ed.), *Methods in Social Science*. Chicago: University of Chicago Press.

Park, Robert E. and Ernest W. Burgess. 1921. *Introduction to the Science of Sociology*. Chicago: University of Chicago Press. [2nd edn, 1924].

Parsons, Talcott. 1937. *The Structure of Social Action*. New York: McGraw Hill.

——. 1951. *The Social System*. Glencoe: The Free Press.

Pellerey, Roberto. 1989. "Thomas Aquinas: Natural Semiotics and the Epistemological Process." In Umberto Eco and Costantino Marmo (eds), *On the Medieval Theory of Signs*. Philadelphia: John Benjamins Publishing Company.

Percy, Walker. 1989. "The Divided Creature," *The Wilson Quarterly*, 13:77–87.

Perinbanayagam, R. S. 1991. *Discursive Acts*. New York: Aldine de Gruyter.

Pippin, Robert B. 1989. *Hegel's Idealism: The Satisfactions of Self-Consciousness*. Cambridge: Cambridge University Press.

Plato. 368 BC/1961. "The Theaetetus," pp. 845–919 in Plato, *The Collected Dialogues of Plato*. Princeton: Princeton University Press.

Quine, W. V. 1981. "The Pragmatists' Place in Empiricism," pp. 21–39 in Robert J. Mulvaney and Philip M. Zeltner (eds), *Pragmatism: Its Sources and Prospects*. Columbia: University of South Carolina.

Ragland-Sullivan, Ellie. 1986. *Jacques Lacan and the Philosophy of Psychoanalysis*. Urbana: University of Illinois Press.

Rawls, Anne Warfield. 1987. "The Interaction Order Sui Generis: Goffman's Contribution to Social Theory," *Sociological Theory*, 5:136–49.

Rawls, John. 1971. *A Theory of Justice*. Cambridge: The Belknap Press of Harvard University Press.

——. 1993. *Political Liberalism*. New York: Columbia University Press.

Richardson, George P. 1991. *Feedback Thought in Social Science and Systems Theory*. Philadelphia: University of Pennsylvania Press.

Ritzer, George. 1991. *Metatheorizing in Sociology*. Lexington: D. C. Heath.

Rochberg-Halton, Eugene. 1986. *Meaning and Modernity*. Chicago: University of Chicago Press.

Rorty, Richard (ed.). 1967. *The Linguistic Turn*. Chicago: University of Chicago Press.

——. 1988/1991. "Solidarity or Objectivity?," pp. 21–34 in Richard Rorty, *Objectivity, Relativism, and Truth*. Cambridge: Cambridge University Press.

——. 1991. "The Priority of Democracy to Philosophy," pp. 175–96 in Richard

241

Rorty, *Objectivity, Relativism, and Truth*. Cambridge: Cambridge University Press.

Rosenau, Pauline Marie. 1992. *Post-Modernism and the Social Sciences*. Princeton: Princeton University Press.

Rosenberg, Morris. 1979. *Conceiving the Self*. New York: Basic Books, Inc.

———. 1990. "Reflexivity and Emotions," *Social Psychology Quarterly*, 53:3–12.

Rosenblatt, Paul C., Cynthia J. Meyer, and Terri A. Karis. 1991. "Internal Interaction with God or Therapist," *Imagination, Cognition and Personality*, 11:85–97.

Rosenthal, Sandra B. 1969. "Peirce, Mead and the Logic of Concepts," *Transactions of the Charles S. Peirce Society*, 5:173–87.

Royce, Josiah. 1918/1968. *The Problem of Christianity*. Chicago: University of Chicago Press.

Ruse, Michael. 1988. *Philosophy of Biology Today*. Albany: State University of New York Press.

Russell, Bertrand. 1945. *A History of Western Philosophy*. New York: Clarion; 1946. London: George Allen & Unwin.

———. 1912/1959. *The Problems of Philosophy*. Oxford: Oxford University Press.

Sartre, Jean-Paul. 1936–7/1957. *The Transcendence of the Ego*. New York: Farrar, Straus and Giroux.

———. 1938/1964. *Nausea*. New York: New Directions.

———. 1943/1956. *Being and Nothingness*. New York: Philosophical Library.

Schmidt, Robert W. 1966. *The Domain of Logic According to Saint Thomas Aquinas*. The Hague: Martinus Nijhoff.

Schmitt, Richard. 1967. Entry on Husserl, pp. 96–9 in Paul Edwards (ed.), *The Encyclopedia of Philosophy*, vol. 3–4. New York: Collier Macmillan Publishers.

Schutz, Alfred. 1932/1967. *The Phenomenology of the Social World*. Evanston: Northwestern University Press.

———. 1973. *Collected Papers*, vol. 1. The Hague: Martinus Nijhoff.

Schwartz, Barry. 1987. *George Washington: The Making of an American Symbol*. New York: The Free Press.

Searle, John. 1969. *Speech Acts*. Cambridge: Cambridge University Press.

———. 1975/1986. "The Logical Status of Fictional Discourse," pp. 58–75 in John Searle, *Expression and Meaning*. Cambridge: Cambridge University Press.

———. 1984. "Can Computers Think?," pp. 28–41 in John Searle, *Minds, Brains and Science*. Cambridge: Harvard University Press.

———. 1992. *The Rediscovery of Mind*. Cambridge: MIT Press.

Sebeok, Thomas. 1991. *A Sign is Just a Sign*. Bloomington, Indiana: Indiana University Press.

Sheriff, John K. 1989. *The Fate of Meaning: Charles Peirce, Structuralism, and Literature*. Princeton: Princeton University Press.

Shrauger, J. Sidney and Thomas J. Schoeneman. 1979. "Symbolic Interactionist View of Self-Concept: Through the Looking Glass Darkly," *Psychological Bulletin*, 86:549–73.

Singer, Jerome L. and John Kolligian, Jr. 1987. "Personality: Developments in the Study of Private Experience," *Annual Review of Psychology*, 38:533–74.

Singer, Milton. 1984. *Man's Glassy Essence*. Bloomington: Indiana University Press.

Smith, Adam. 1759/1982. *The Theory of Moral Sentiments*. Indianapolis: Liberty Classics.

Smith, John E. 1968. "Introduction," pp. 1–36 in Josiah Royce, *The Problem of Christianity*. Chicago: University of Chicago Press.

Sorokin, Pitirim A. 1962. *Society, Culture, and Personality*. New York: Cooper Square Publishers, Inc.

Spencer, Jonathan. 1989. "Anthropology as a Kind of Writing," *Man*, 24:145–64.

Sprengnether, Madelon. 1990. *The Spectral Mother: Freud, Feminism and Psychoanalysis*. Ithaca: Cornell University Press.

Stone, Gregory P. and Harvey A. Farberman. 1967. "On the Edge of Rapprochement: Was Durkheim Moving towards the Perspective of Symbolic Interaction?," *Sociological Quarterly*, 8:149–64.

Sumner, William Graham. 1906. *Folkways*. Boston: Ginn Publishers.

Takla Tendzin N. and Whitney Pope. 1985. "The Force Imagery in Durkheim," *Sociological Theory*, 3:74–88.

Tallis, Raymond. 1988. *Not Saussure: A Critique of Post-Saussurean Literary Theory*. London: Macmillan.

Taylor, Charles. 1985. *Human Agency and Language*. Cambridge: Cambridge University Press.

———. 1991. *The Malaise of Modernity*. Concord, Ontario: House of Anansi Press Limited. *ref* p 9,

Tejera, V. 1988. *Semiotics from Peirce to Barthes*. Leiden: E. J. Brill.

Thayer, H. S. 1968/1981. *Meaning and Action: A Critical History of Pragmatism*. Indianapolis: Hackett Publishing Company.

Thomas, William I. and Florian Znaniecki. 1918–20. *The Polish Peasant in Europe and America*, 5 vols. Boston: Richard G. Badger.

Tibbets, Paul. 1975. "Peirce and Mead on Perceptual Immediacy and Human Action," *Philosophy and Phenomenological Research*, 34:222–32.

Tompkins, Jane P. (ed.). 1980. *Reader–Response Criticism*. Baltimore: Johns Hopkins University Press.

Toulmin, Stephen E. 1978. "Self-Knowledge and Knowledge of the 'Self'," pp. 291–317 in Theodore Mischel (ed.), *The Self: Psychological and Philosophical Issues*. Oxford: Oxford University Press.

Tugendhat, Ernst. 1979/1986. *Self-Consciousness and Self-Determination*. Cambridge: MIT Press.

Turkle, Sherry. 1984. *The Second Self: Computers and the Human Spirit*. New York: Simon & Schuster, Inc.

Turner, Jonathan H. 1988. *A Theory of Social Interaction*. Stanford: Stanford University Press; Cambridge, Polity Press.

Volosinov, V. M. 1973. *Marxism and the Philosophy of Language*. Cambridge: Harvard University Press.

Vygotsky, Lev. 1934/1962. *Thought and Language*. Cambridge: MIT Press.

Wall, Kevin. 1973. "Hegel: The Theological Roots of his Dialectic," *The Thomist*, 37:734–42.

Weber, Marianne. 1926/1975. *Max Weber: A Biography*. New York: John Wiley & Sons.

Weber, Max. 1922/1946. "Class, Status, Party," pp. 180–95 in H. H. Gerth and C. Wright Mills (eds), *From Max Weber*. New York: Oxford University Press.

Wertsch, James V. 1985. *Vygotsky and the Social Formation of Mind*, Cambridge: Harvard University Press.

West, Cornel. 1989. *The American Evasion of Philosophy*. Madison: University of Wisconsin Press.

Westby, David L. 1991. *The Growth of Sociological Theory*. Englewood Cliffs, New Jersey: Prentice-Hall, Inc.

White, Leslie. 1959/1987. "The Concept of Culture," pp. 173–97 in Beth Dillingham and Robert L. Carneiro (eds), *Leslie A. White: Ethnological Essays*. Albuquerque: University of New Mexico Press.

White, Morton. 1978. *The Philosophy of the American Revolution*. New York: Oxford University Press.

——. 1987. *Philosophy: The Federalist and the Constitution*. New York: Oxford University Press.

Whitehead, Alfred North. 1938/1966. *Modes of Thought*. New York: The Free Press.

Wiley, Norbert. 1967. "America's Unique Class Politics," *American Sociological Review*, 32:529–41.

——. 1979. "The Rise and Fall of Dominating Theories in American Sociology," pp. 47–79 in William E. Snizek, Ellsworth F. Fuhrman, and Michael K. Miller (eds), *Contemporary Issues in Theory and Research: A Metasociological Perspective*. Westport, Connecticut: Greenwood Press.

——. 1983. "The Congruence of Weber and Keynes," *Sociological Theory*, 1:30–57.

——. 1985. "The Current Interregnum in American Sociology," *Social Research*, 52:179–207.

——. 1986. "Early American Sociology and the *Polish Peasant*," *Sociological Theory*, 4:21–40.

——. 1989. "The Complementarity of Durkheim and Mead," *Symbolic Interaction*, 12:77–9.

——. 1990. "The History and Politics of Recent Sociological Theory," pp. 392–415 in George Ritzer (ed.), *Frontiers of Social Theory*. New York: Columbia.

——. 1992. Review of Vincent M. Colapietro's *Peirce's Approach to the Self*, *Symbolic Interaction*, 15:383–7.

Wills, Gary. 1978. *Inventing America*. Garden City: Doubleday & Company.

——. 1981. *Explaining America*. Garden City: Doubleday & Company.

——. 1992. *Lincoln at Gettysburg: The Words that Remade America*. New York: Simon & Schuster.

Wimsatt, William C. 1981. "Robustness, Reliability, and Overdetermination," pp. 124–63 in Marilynn B. Brewer and Barry E. Collins (eds), *Scientific Inquiry and the Social Sciences*. San Francisco: Jossey-Bass Publishers.

Winnicott, D. W. 1960/1965. "Ego Distortion in Terms of True and False Self," pp. 140–52 in *The Maturational Process and the Facilitating Environment*. London: The Hogarth Press.

Winthrop, Robert H. 1990. "Introduction," pp. 1–13 in Robert H. Winthrop (ed.), *Culture and the Anthropological Tradition*. Lanham: University Press of America.

Wittgenstein, Ludwig. 1921/1922. *Tractatus Logico-Philosophicus*. London: Routledge & Kegan Paul.

———. 1953. *Philosophical Investigations*. New York: The Macmillan Company.

Wolfe, Alan. 1992. "Sociological Theory in the Absence of People: The Limits of Luhmann's Systems Theory," *Cardozo Law Review*, 13:1729–43.

———. 1993. *Are Humans Different?*. Berkeley: University of California Press.

Wolfe, Don M. 1957/1970. *The Image of Man in America*. Second Edition. New York: Thomas Y. Crowell Company.

Wood, David. 1990. *Philosophy at the Limit*. London: Unwin Hyman.

Woolgar, Steve (ed.). 1988. *Knowledge and Reflexivity*. London: Sage Publications.

Yinger, J. Milton. 1965. "Levels of Analysis," pp. 18–37 in J. Milton Yinger, *Toward a Field Theory of Behavior: Personality and Social Structure*. New York: McGraw-Hill.

Index